# SEVEN SEAS ENTERTAINMENT PRESENTS

## The High School
# FUDAN

story and art by ATAMI MICHIN

TRANSLATION
**Ryan Peterson**

ADAPTATION
**Lianne Sentar**

LETTERING AND RETOUCH
**Ray Steeves**

COVER DESIGN
**KC Fabellon**

PROOFREADER
**Dayna Abel**
**Danielle King**

EDITOR
**Jenn Grunigen**

PRODUCTION MANAGER
**Lissa Pattillo**

MANAGING EDITOR
**Julie Davis**

EDITOR-IN-CHIEF
**Adam Arnold**

PUBLISHER
**Jason DeAngelis**

THE HIGH SCHOOL LIFE OF A FUDANSHI VOL. 5
© Atami Michinoku 2018
First published in Japan in 2018 by ICHIJINSHA Inc., Tokyo.
English translation rights arranged with ICHIJINSHA Inc., Tokyo, Japan.

Seven Seas press and purchase enquiries can be sent to Marketing Manager Lianne Sentar at press@gomanga.com. Information regarding the distribution and purchase of digital editions is available from Digital Manager CK Russell at digital@gomanga.com.

ISBN: 978-1-64275-692-0

Printed in Canada

First Printing: September 2019

10 9 8 7 6 5 4 3 2 1

**FOLLOW US ONLINE: www.sevenseasentertainment.com**

# READING DIRECTIONS

This book reads from *right to left*, Japanese style. If this is your first time reading manga, you start reading from the top right panel on each page and take it from there. If you get lost, just follow the numbered diagram here. It may seem backwards at first, but you'll get the hang of it! Have fun!!

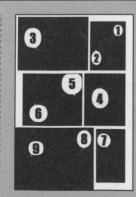

# CHAPTER 35
## Happy Birthday to You

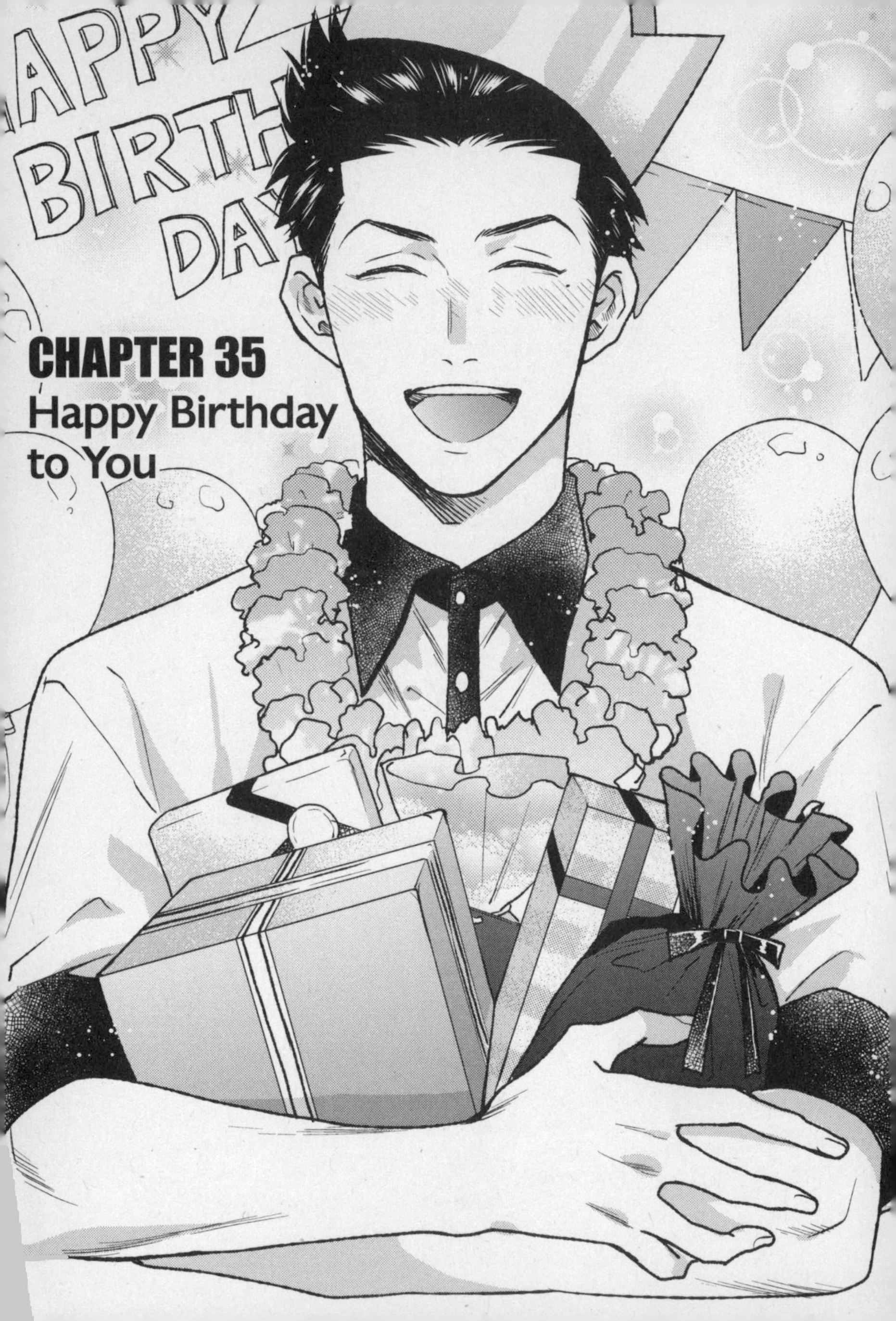
APPY
BIRTH
DA

# BIRTH OF ME

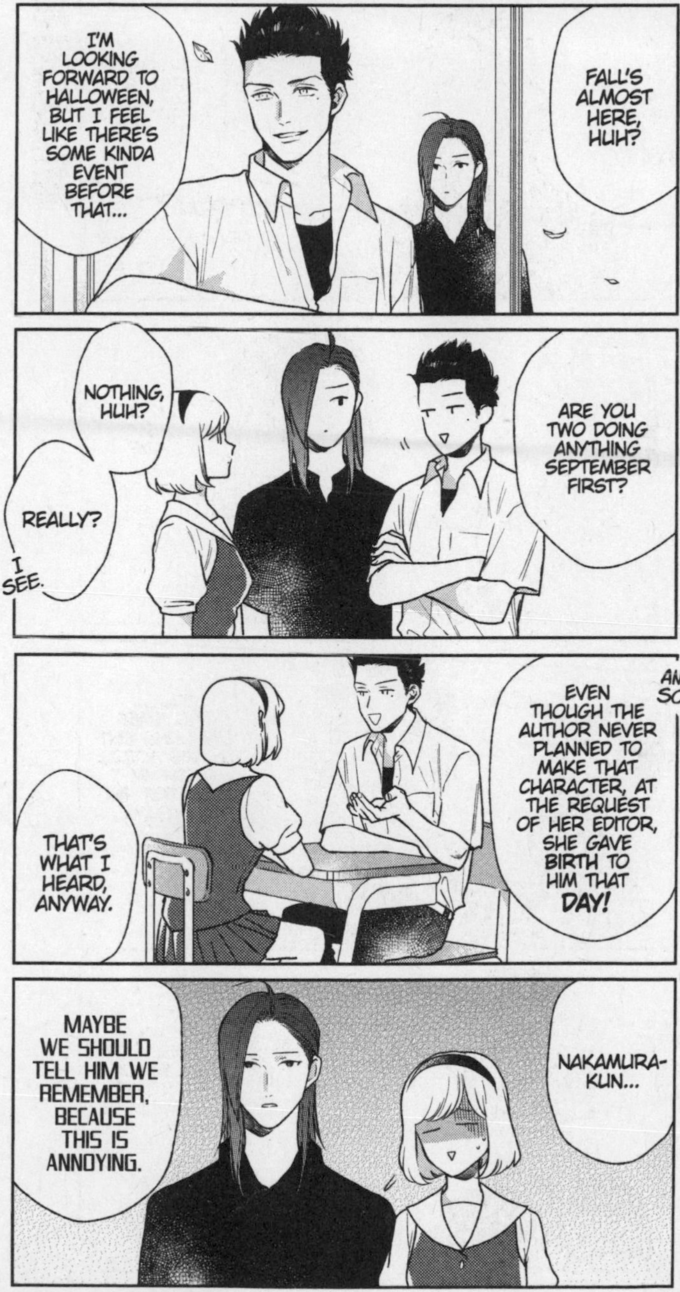
FALL'S ALMOST HERE, HUH?
I'M LOOKING FORWARD TO HALLOWEEN, BUT I FEEL LIKE THERE'S SOME KINDA EVENT BEFORE THAT...
ARE YOU TWO DOING ANYTHING SEPTEMBER FIRST?
NOTHING, HUH?
REALLY?
I SEE.
AND SO...
EVEN THOUGH THE AUTHOR NEVER PLANNED TO MAKE THAT CHARACTER, AT THE REQUEST OF HER EDITOR, SHE GAVE BIRTH TO HIM THAT DAY!
THAT'S WHAT I HEARD, ANYWAY.
NAKAMURA-KUN...
MAYBE WE SHOULD TELL HIM WE REMEMBER, BECAUSE THIS IS ANNOYING.

# DELUSIONAL

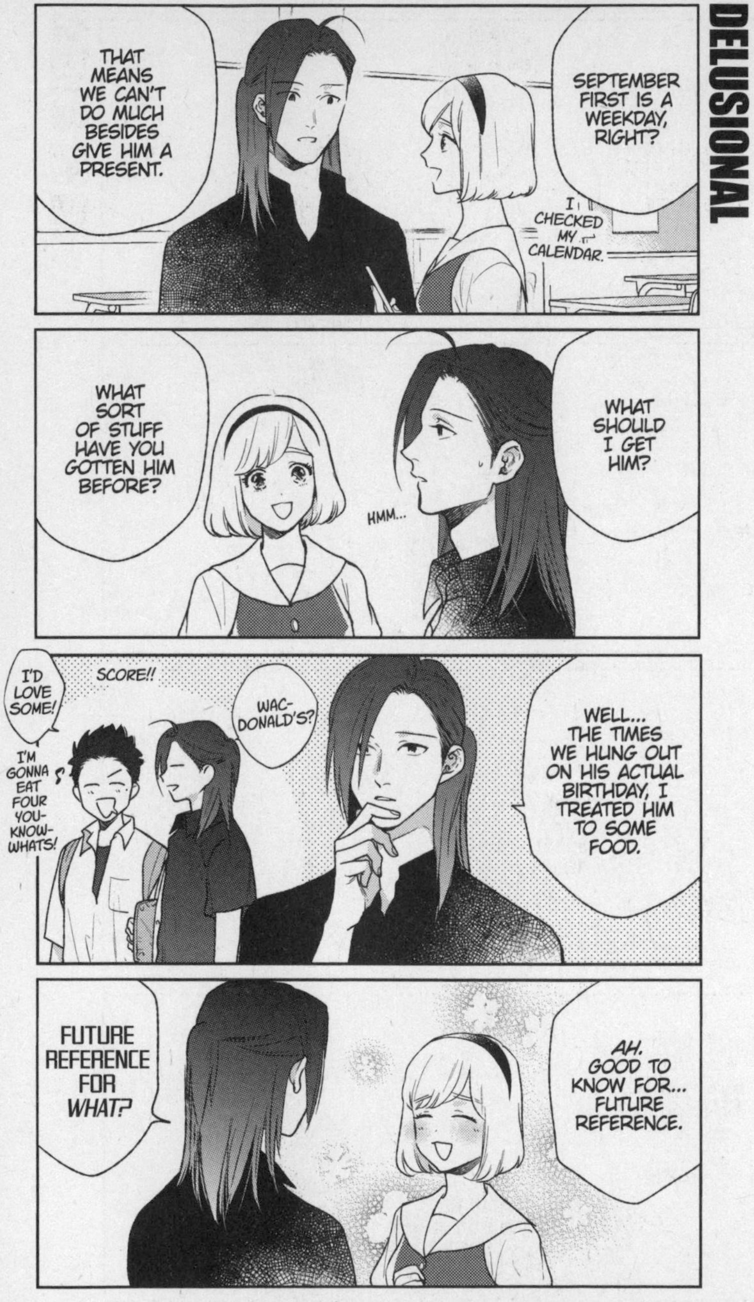
SEPTEMBER FIRST IS A WEEKDAY, RIGHT?
I CHECKED MY CALENDAR.
THAT MEANS WE CAN'T DO MUCH BESIDES GIVE HIM A PRESENT.
WHAT SHOULD I GET HIM?
HMM...
WHAT SORT OF STUFF HAVE YOU GOTTEN HIM BEFORE?
WELL... THE TIMES WE HUNG OUT ON HIS ACTUAL BIRTHDAY, I TREATED HIM TO SOME FOOD.
WAC-DONALD'S?
SCORE!!
I'D LOVE SOME!
I'M GONNA EAT FOUR YOU-KNOW-WHATS!
AH. GOOD TO KNOW FOR... FUTURE REFERENCE.
FUTURE REFERENCE FOR WHAT?

# SOURCE OF STRESS

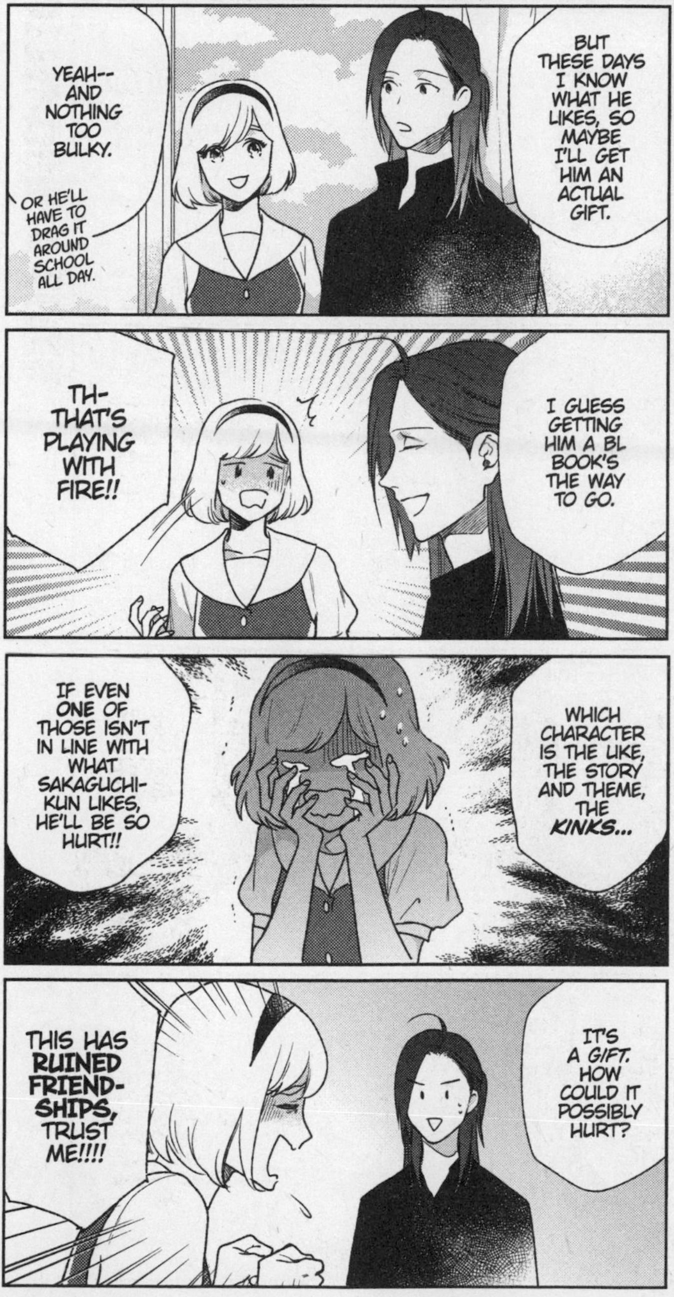
BUT THESE DAYS I KNOW WHAT HE LIKES, SO MAYBE I'LL GET HIM AN ACTUAL GIFT.
YEAH-- AND NOTHING TOO BULKY.
OR HE'LL HAVE TO DRAG IT AROUND SCHOOL ALL DAY.
I GUESS GETTING HIM A BL BOOK'S THE WAY TO GO.
TH- THAT'S PLAYING WITH FIRE!!
WHICH CHARACTER IS THE UKE, THE STORY AND THEME, THE *KINKS...*
IF EVEN ONE OF THOSE ISN'T IN LINE WITH WHAT SAKAGUCHI-KUN LIKES, HE'LL BE SO HURT!!
IT'S A *GIFT.* HOW COULD IT POSSIBLY HURT?
THIS HAS **RUINED FRIEND-SHIPS,** TRUST ME!!!!

## ATTENTION TO DETAIL

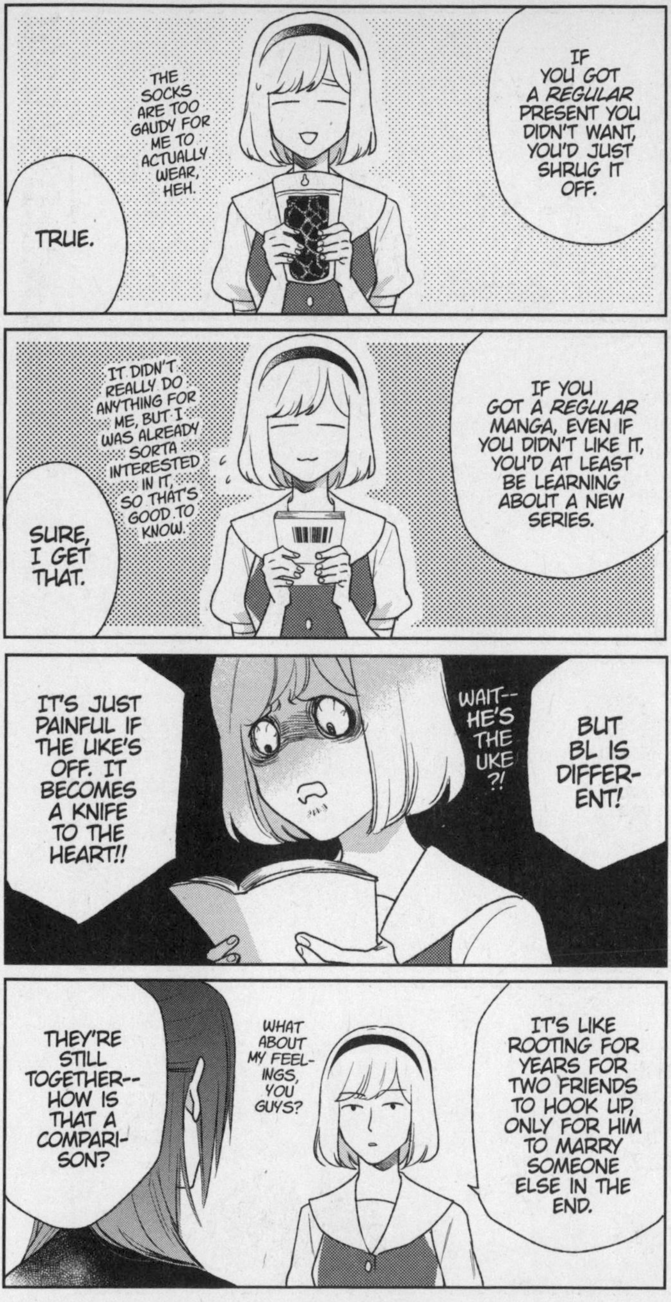
IF YOU GOT A *REGULAR* PRESENT YOU DIDN'T WANT, YOU'D JUST SHRUG IT OFF.
THE SOCKS ARE TOO GAUDY FOR ME TO ACTUALLY WEAR, HEH.
TRUE.
IF YOU GOT A *REGULAR* MANGA, EVEN IF YOU DIDN'T LIKE IT, YOU'D AT LEAST BE LEARNING ABOUT A NEW SERIES.
IT DIDN'T REALLY DO ANYTHING FOR ME, BUT I WAS ALREADY SORTA INTERESTED IN IT, SO THAT'S GOOD TO KNOW.
SURE, I GET THAT.
BUT BL IS DIFFER-ENT!
WAIT-- HE'S THE UKE ?!
IT'S JUST PAINFUL IF THE UKE'S OFF. IT BECOMES A KNIFE TO THE HEART!!
IT'S LIKE ROOTING FOR YEARS FOR TWO FRIENDS TO HOOK UP, ONLY FOR HIM TO MARRY SOMEONE ELSE IN THE END.
WHAT ABOUT MY FEEL-INGS, YOU GUYS?
THEY'RE STILL TOGETHER-- HOW IS THAT A COMPARI-SON?

# THE PAIN OF THE INFLEXIBLE FANGIRL

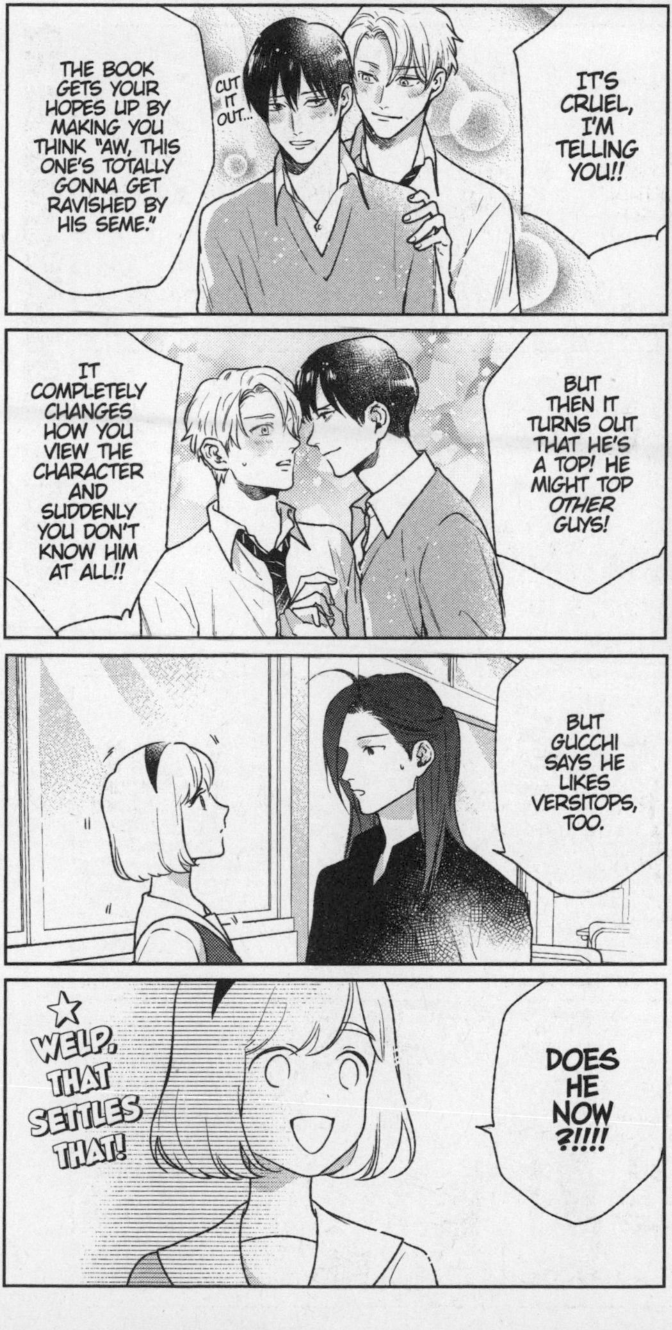
IT'S CRUEL, I'M TELLING YOU!!
CUT IT OUT...
THE BOOK GETS YOUR HOPES UP BY MAKING YOU THINK "AW, THIS ONE'S TOTALLY GONNA GET RAVISHED BY HIS SEME."
BUT THEN IT TURNS OUT THAT HE'S A TOP! HE MIGHT TOP *OTHER* GUYS!
IT COMPLETELY CHANGES HOW YOU VIEW THE CHARACTER AND SUDDENLY YOU DON'T KNOW HIM AT ALL!!
BUT GUCCHI SAYS HE LIKES VERSITOPS, TOO.
DOES HE NOW?!!!!
☆ WELP. THAT SETTLES THAT!

# AN EXTRAVAGANT CELEBRATION

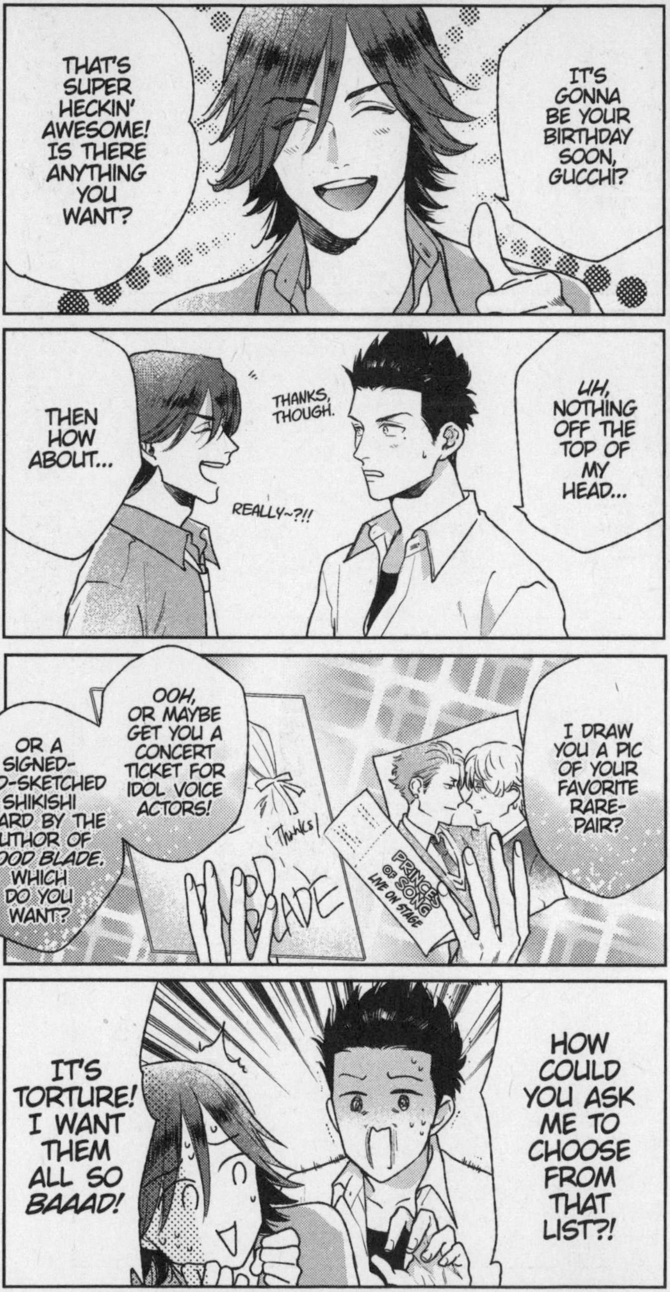
IT'S GONNA BE YOUR BIRTHDAY SOON, GUCCHI?
THAT'S SUPER HECKIN' AWESOME! IS THERE ANYTHING YOU WANT?
UH, NOTHING OFF THE TOP OF MY HEAD...
THANKS, THOUGH.
REALLY~?!!
THEN HOW ABOUT...
I DRAW YOU A PIC OF YOUR FAVORITE RARE-PAIR?
PRINCE OF SONG LIVE ON STAGE
OOH, OR MAYBE GET YOU A CONCERT TICKET FOR IDOL VOICE ACTORS!
Thanks!
OR A SIGNED-AND-SKETCHED SHIKISHI BOARD BY THE AUTHOR OF *BLOOD BLADE*. WHICH DO YOU WANT?
HOW COULD YOU ASK ME TO CHOOSE FROM THAT LIST?!
IT'S TORTURE! I WANT THEM ALL SO *BAAAD!*

# PREFERENCES

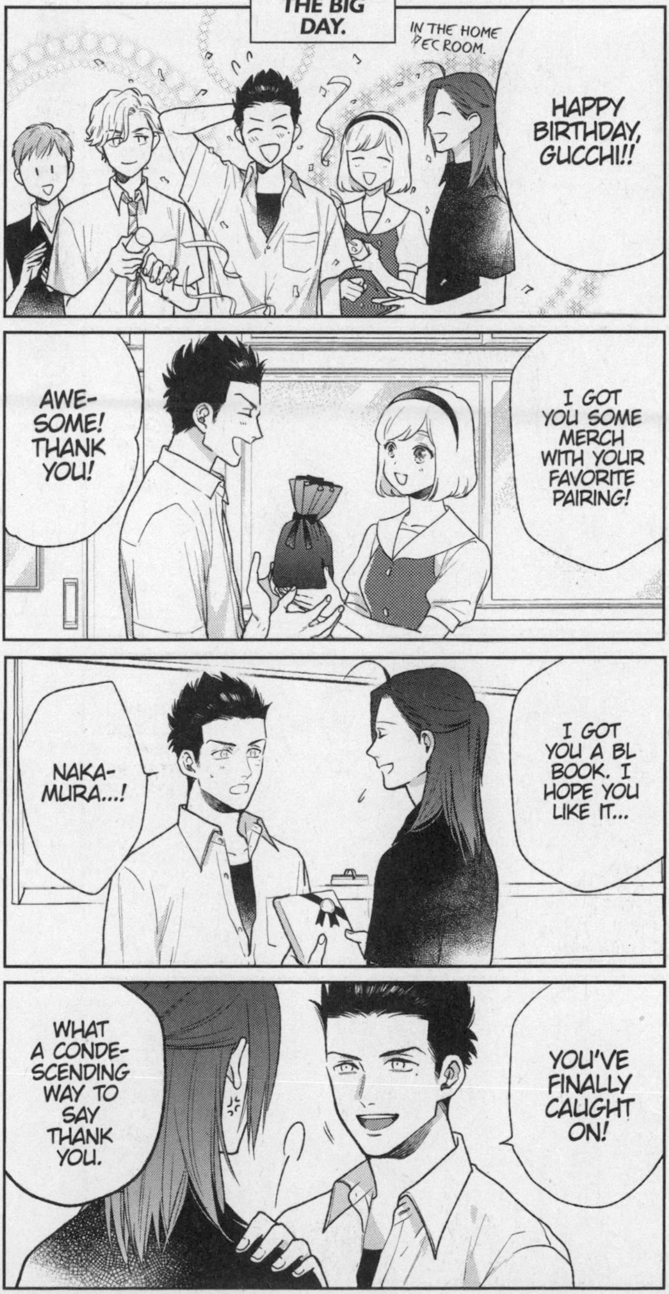
THE BIG DAY.
IN THE HOME EC ROOM.
HAPPY BIRTHDAY, GUCCHI!!
I GOT YOU SOME MERCH WITH YOUR FAVORITE PAIRING!
AWE-SOME! THANK YOU!
I GOT YOU A BL BOOK. I HOPE YOU LIKE IT...
NAKA-MURA...!
YOU'VE FINALLY CAUGHT ON!
WHAT A CONDE-SCENDING WAY TO SAY THANK YOU.

# VALUABLE TO ME

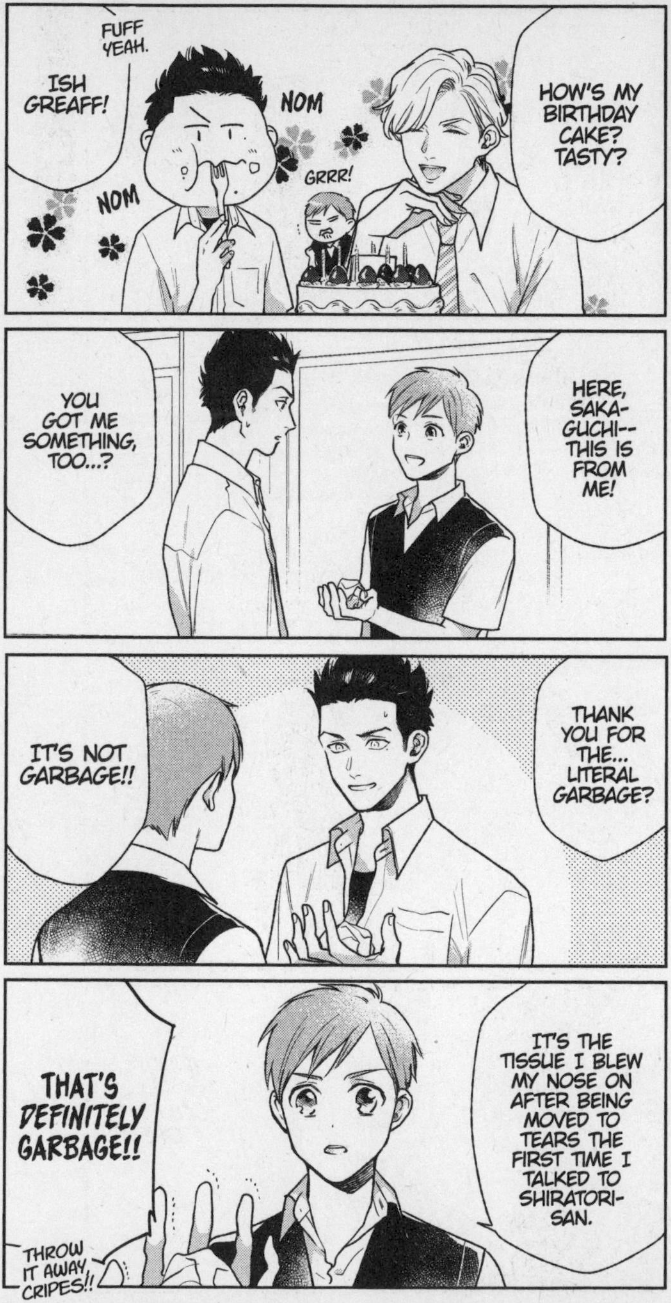
HOW'S MY BIRTHDAY CAKE? TASTY?
NOM
FUFF YEAH.
ISH GREAFF!
GRRR!
NOM
HERE, SAKA-GUCHI-- THIS IS FROM ME!
YOU GOT ME SOMETHING, TOO...?
THANK YOU FOR THE... LITERAL GARBAGE?
IT'S NOT GARBAGE!!
IT'S THE TISSUE I BLEW MY NOSE ON AFTER BEING MOVED TO TEARS THE FIRST TIME I TALKED TO SHIRATORI-SAN.
THAT'S DEFINITELY GARBAGE!!
THROW IT AWAY, CRIPES!!

# BEFORE YOU BUY

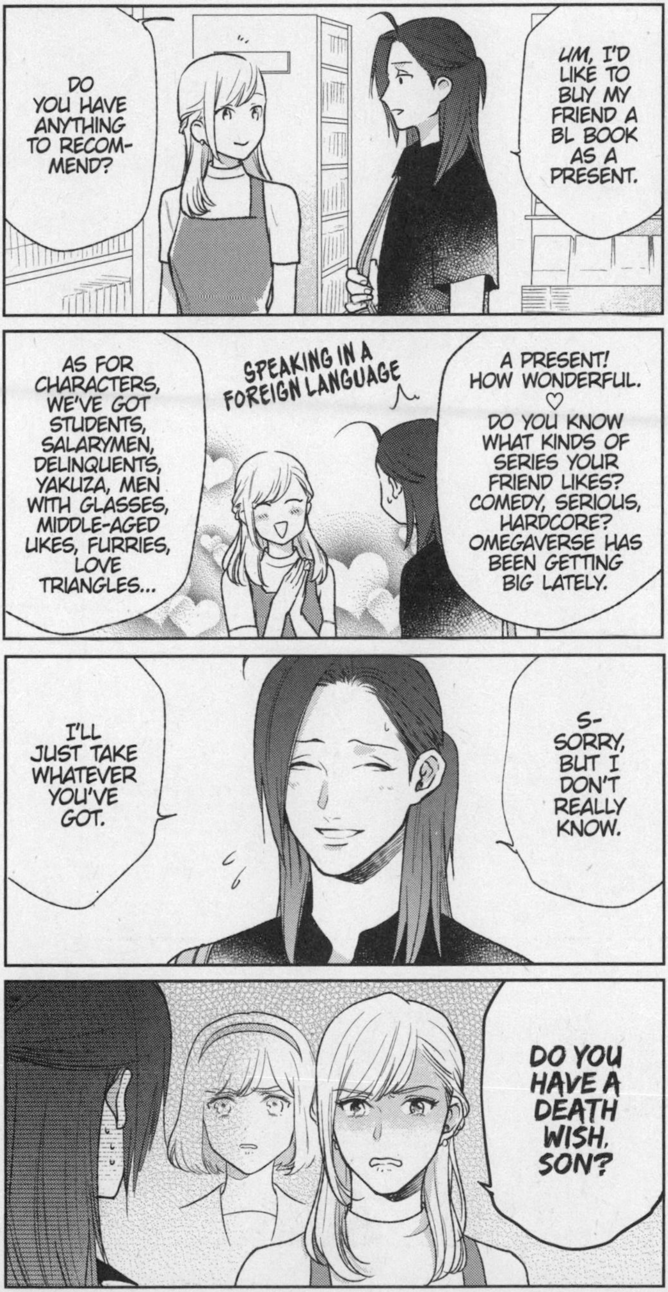
UM, I'D LIKE TO BUY MY FRIEND A BL BOOK AS A PRESENT.
DO YOU HAVE ANYTHING TO RECOM-MEND?
A PRESENT! HOW WONDERFUL. ♡ DO YOU KNOW WHAT KINDS OF SERIES YOUR FRIEND LIKES? COMEDY, SERIOUS, HARDCORE? OMEGAVERSE HAS BEEN GETTING BIG LATELY.
SPEAKING IN A FOREIGN LANGUAGE
AS FOR CHARACTERS, WE'VE GOT STUDENTS, SALARYMEN, DELINQUENTS, YAKUZA, MEN WITH GLASSES, MIDDLE-AGED UKES, FURRIES, LOVE TRIANGLES...
S- SORRY, BUT I DON'T REALLY KNOW.
I'LL JUST TAKE WHATEVER YOU'VE GOT.
DO YOU HAVE A DEATH WISH, SON?

IT'S THE TISSUE I BLEW MY NOSE ON AFTER BEING MOVED TO TEARS THE FIRST TIME I TALKED TO SHIRATORI-SAN.
THAT'S DEFINITELY GARBAGE!!
THROW IT AWAY, CRIPES!!

KFS

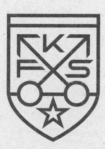

# CHAPTER 36
## Different Ways of Celebrating the Lord's Birth

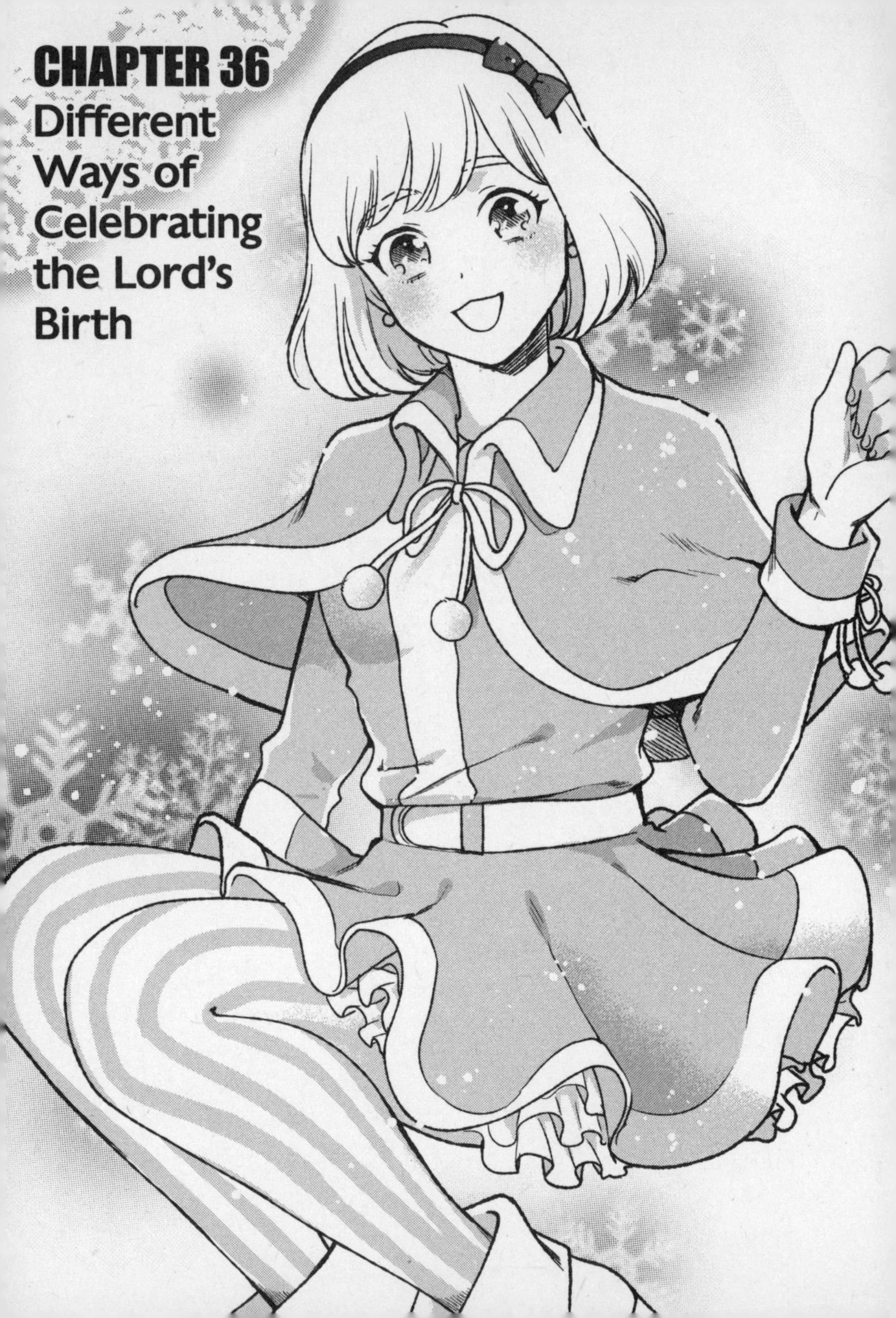

# BY THE SKIN OF HIS TEETH

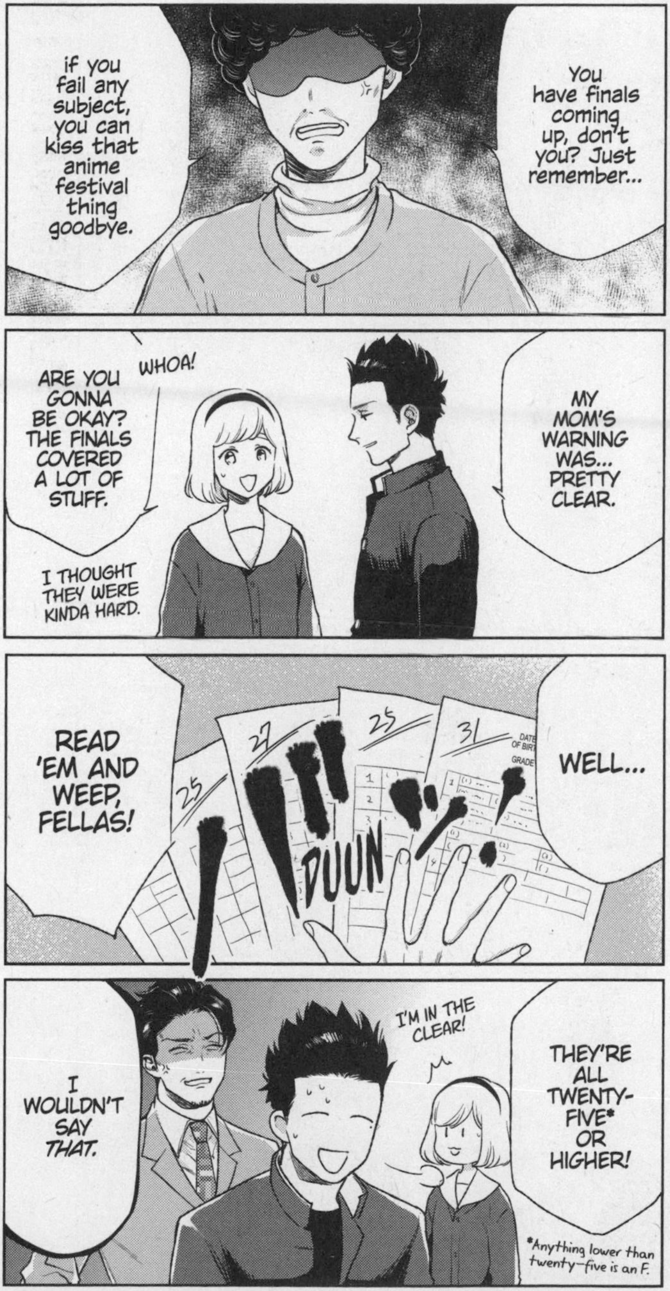
You have finals coming up, don't you? Just remember...
if you fail any subject, you can kiss that anime festival thing goodbye.
MY MOM'S WARNING WAS... PRETTY CLEAR.
WHOA!
ARE YOU GONNA BE OKAY? THE FINALS COVERED A LOT OF STUFF.
I THOUGHT THEY WERE KINDA HARD.
WELL...
31
25
27
25
READ 'EM AND WEEP, FELLAS!
DUUN
THEY'RE ALL TWENTY-FIVE* OR HIGHER!
I'M IN THE CLEAR!
I WOULDN'T SAY *THAT.*
*Anything lower than twenty-five is an F.

# IF I HAD THINGS MY WAY

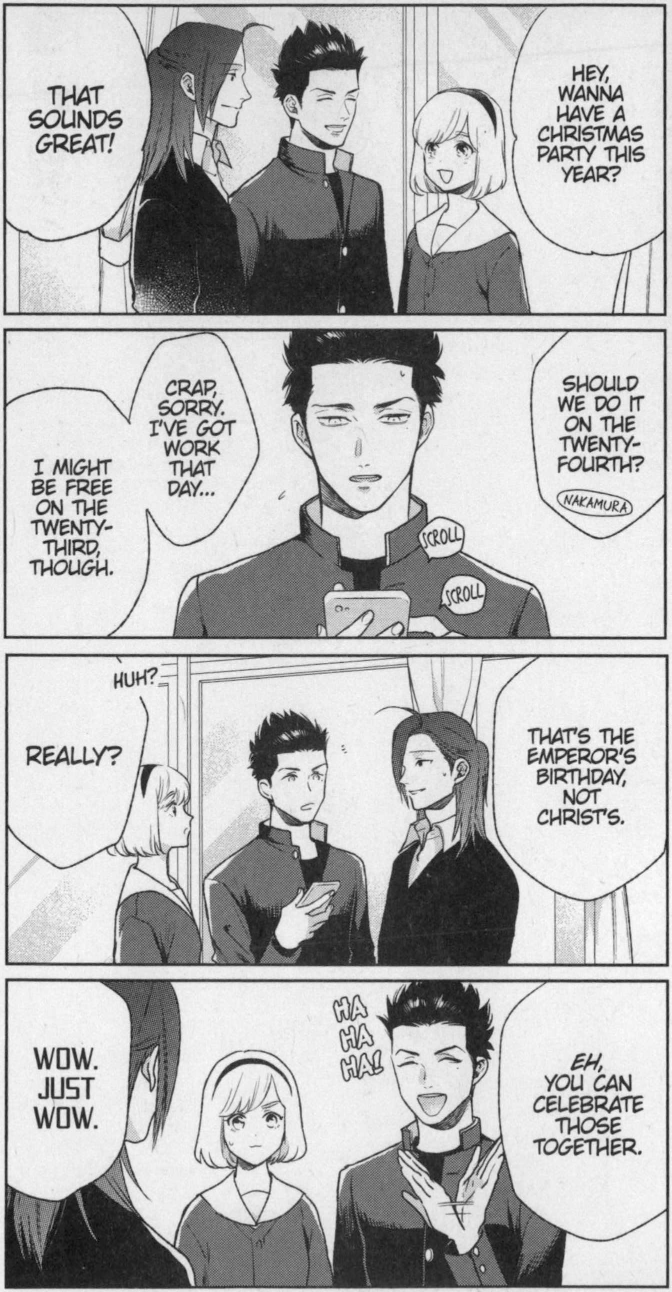
HEY, WANNA HAVE A CHRISTMAS PARTY THIS YEAR?
THAT SOUNDS GREAT!
SHOULD WE DO IT ON THE TWENTY-FOURTH?
NAKAMURA
SCROLL
SCROLL
CRAP, SORRY. I'VE GOT WORK THAT DAY...
I MIGHT BE FREE ON THE TWENTY-THIRD, THOUGH.
THAT'S THE EMPEROR'S BIRTHDAY, NOT CHRIST'S.
HUH?
REALLY?
*EH,* YOU CAN CELEBRATE THOSE TOGETHER.
HA HA HA!
WOW. JUST WOW.

## OUT OF THE RUNNING

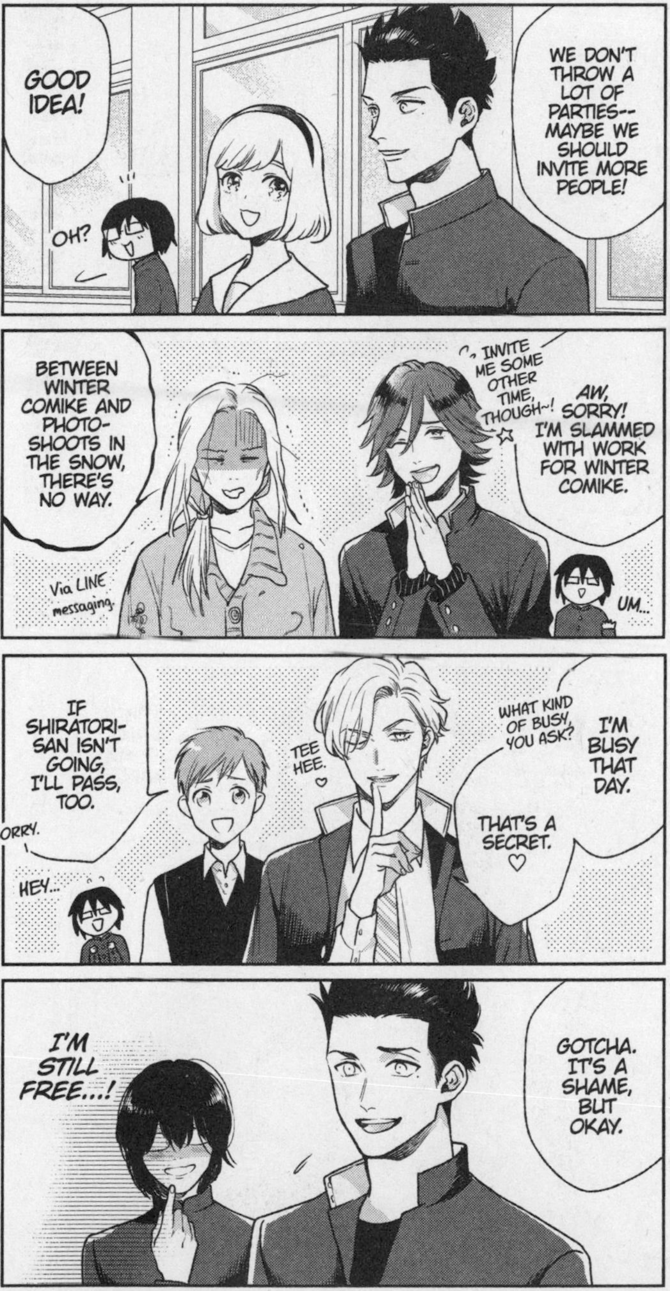

WE DON'T THROW A LOT OF PARTIES--MAYBE WE SHOULD INVITE MORE PEOPLE!
GOOD IDEA!
OH?
AW, SORRY! I'M SLAMMED WITH WORK FOR WINTER COMIKE.
INVITE ME SOME OTHER TIME, THOUGH~!
BETWEEN WINTER COMIKE AND PHOTO-SHOOTS IN THE SNOW, THERE'S NO WAY.
Via LINE messaging.
UM...
I'M BUSY THAT DAY.
WHAT KIND OF BUSY, YOU ASK?
THAT'S A SECRET.
TEE HEE.
IF SHIRATORI-SAN ISN'T GOING, I'LL PASS, TOO.
SORRY.
HEY...
GOTCHA. IT'S A SHAME, BUT OKAY.
I'M STILL FREE...!

# SHOUT IT LOUD AND PROUD

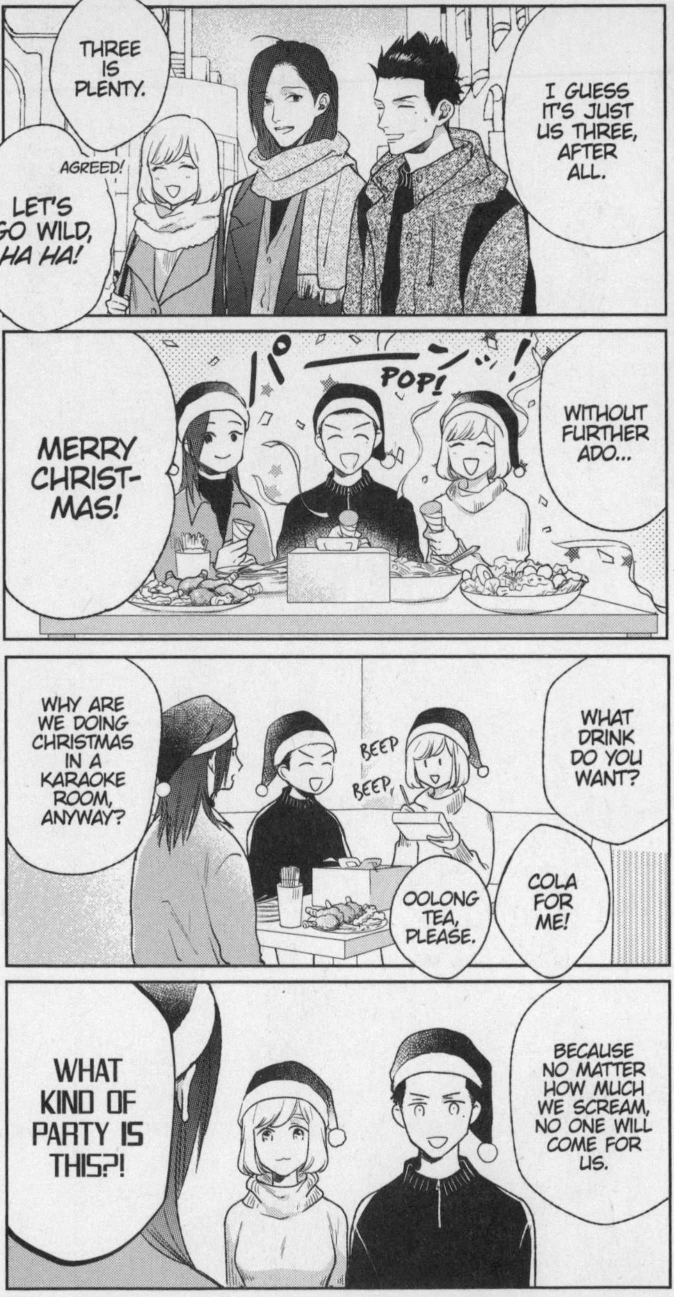
I GUESS IT'S JUST US THREE, AFTER ALL.
THREE IS PLENTY.
AGREED!
LET'S GO WILD, HA HA!
WITHOUT FURTHER ADO...
パーンッ!
POP!
MERRY CHRIST-MAS!
WHAT DRINK DO YOU WANT?
COLA FOR ME!
OOLONG TEA, PLEASE.
BEEP BEEP
WHY ARE WE DOING CHRISTMAS IN A KARAOKE ROOM, ANYWAY?
BECAUSE NO MATTER HOW MUCH WE SCREAM, NO ONE WILL COME FOR US.
WHAT KIND OF PARTY IS THIS?!

# THE BEST PART

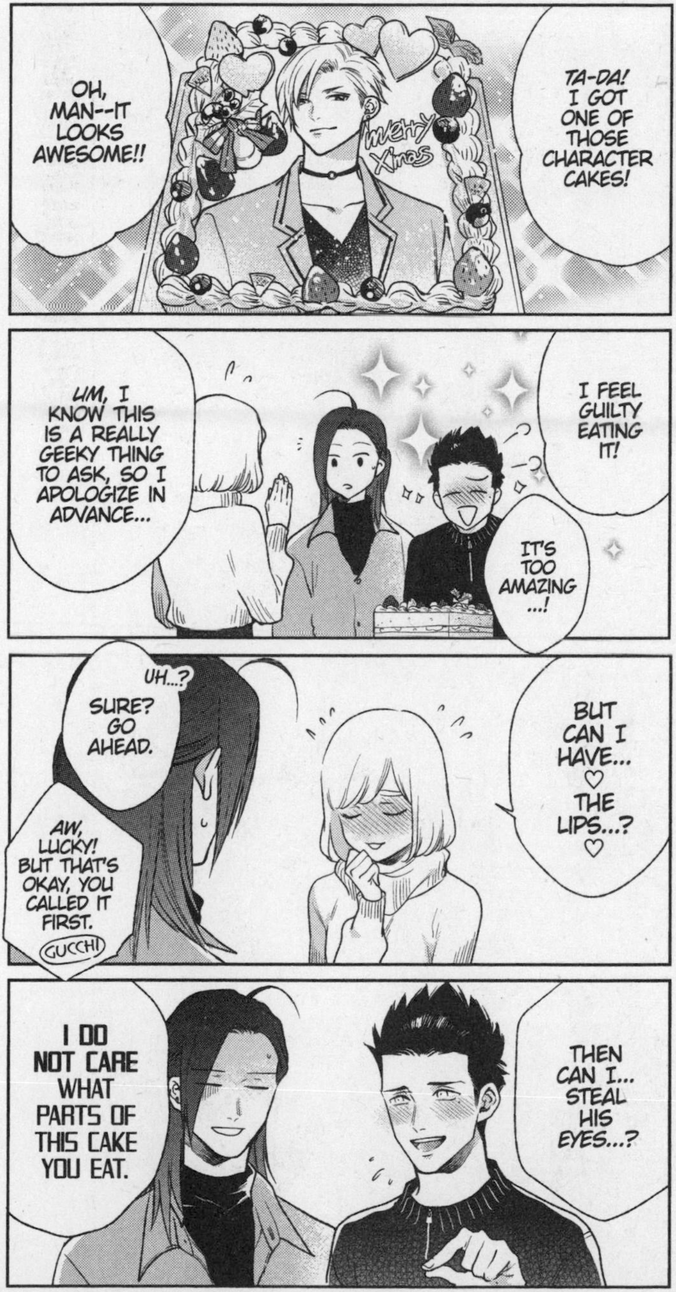
TA-DA! I GOT ONE OF THOSE CHARACTER CAKES!
OH, MAN--IT LOOKS AWESOME!!
Merry Xmas
I FEEL GUILTY EATING IT!
IT'S TOO AMAZING...!
UM, I KNOW THIS IS A REALLY GEEKY THING TO ASK, SO I APOLOGIZE IN ADVANCE...
BUT CAN I HAVE... ♡ THE LIPS...? ♡
UH...? SURE? GO AHEAD.
AW, LUCKY! BUT THAT'S OKAY, YOU CALLED IT FIRST.
GUCCHI
THEN CAN I... STEAL HIS EYES...?
I DO NOT CARE WHAT PARTS OF THIS CAKE YOU EAT.

# COMES WITH A BL VIDEO

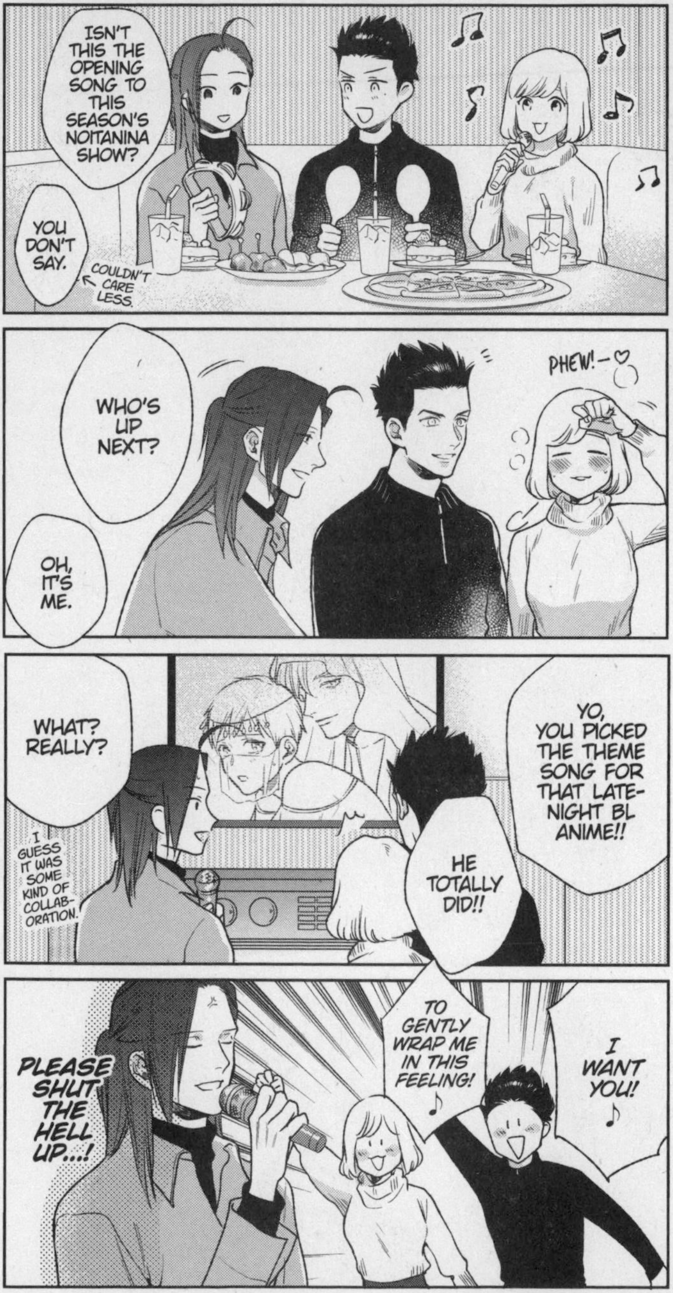
ISN'T THIS THE OPENING SONG TO THIS SEASON'S NOITANINA SHOW?
YOU DON'T SAY.
COULDN'T CARE LESS.
PHEW!
WHO'S UP NEXT?
OH, IT'S ME.
YO, YOU PICKED THE THEME SONG FOR THAT LATE-NIGHT BL ANIME!!
HE TOTALLY DID!!
WHAT? REALLY?
I GUESS IT WAS SOME KIND OF COLLABORATION.
I WANT YOU!
TO GENTLY WRAP ME IN THIS FEELING!
PLEASE SHUT THE HELL UP...!

# THE RIGHT MAN FOR THE RIGHT JOB

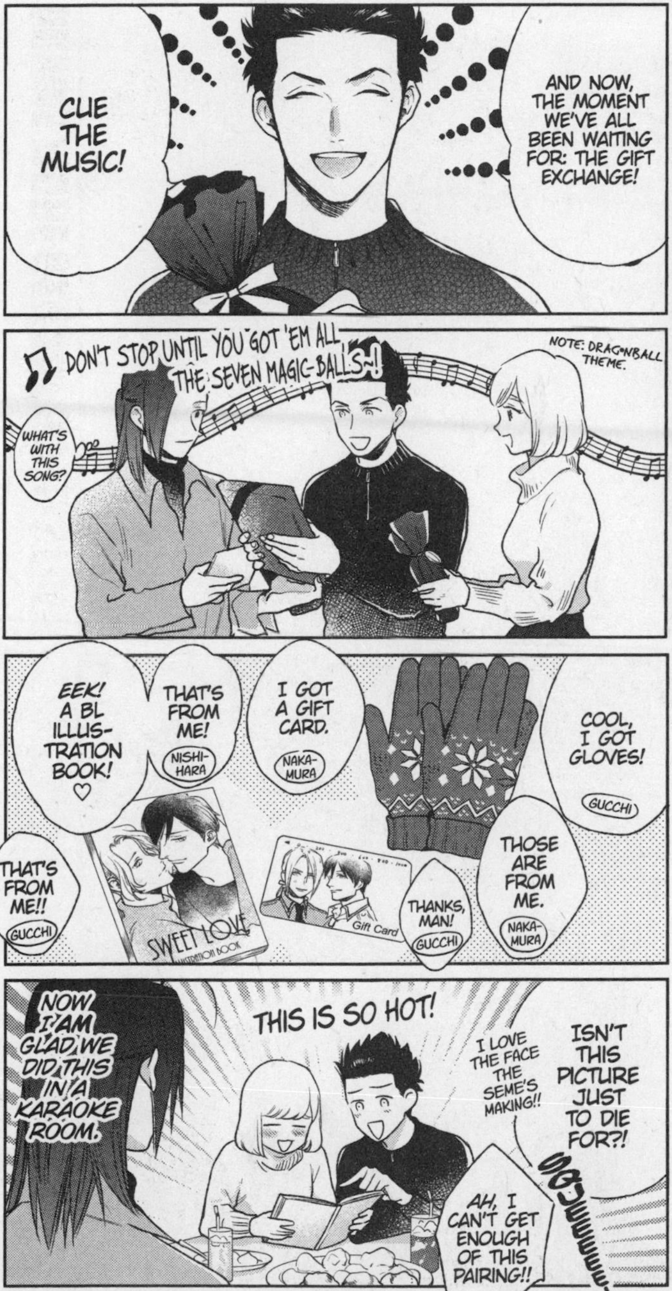
AND NOW, THE MOMENT WE'VE ALL BEEN WAITING FOR: THE GIFT EXCHANGE!
CUE THE MUSIC!
NOTE: DRAGONBALL THEME.
DON'T STOP UNTIL YOU GOT 'EM ALL THE SEVEN MAGIC-BALLS~!
WHAT'S WITH THIS SONG?
COOL, I GOT GLOVES!
GUCCHI
I GOT A GIFT CARD.
NAKAMURA
THAT'S FROM ME!
NISHIHARA
EEK! A BL ILLUSTRATION BOOK! ♡
THOSE ARE FROM ME.
NAKAMURA
THANKS, MAN!
GUCCHI
Gift Card
SWEET LOVE
ILLUSTRATION BOOK
THAT'S FROM ME!!
GUCCHI
ISN'T THIS PICTURE JUST TO DIE FOR?!
I LOVE THE FACE THE SEME'S MAKING!!
THIS IS SO HOT!
NOW I AM GLAD WE DID THIS IN A KARAOKE ROOM.
AH, I CAN'T GET ENOUGH OF THIS PAIRING!!

## GIMME MORE OF THAT GOOD STUFF

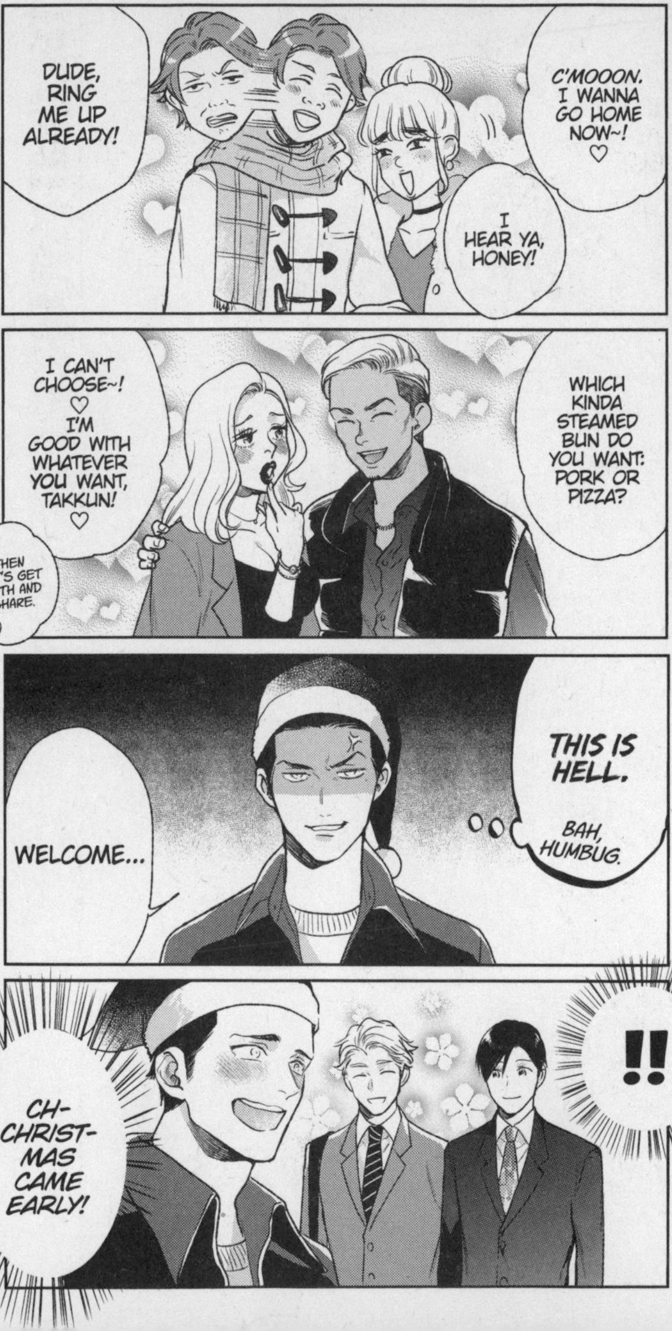
C'MOOON. I WANNA GO HOME NOW~! ♡
I HEAR YA, HONEY!
DUDE, RING ME UP ALREADY!
WHICH KINDA STEAMED BUN DO YOU WANT: PORK OR PIZZA?
I CAN'T CHOOSE~! ♡ I'M GOOD WITH WHATEVER YOU WANT, TAKKUN! ♡
THEN LET'S GET BOTH AND SHARE. ♡
THIS IS HELL.
BAH, HUMBUG.
WELCOME...
!!
CH-CHRISTMAS CAME EARLY!

# THE MOST LOVEABLE TIME OF THE YEAR

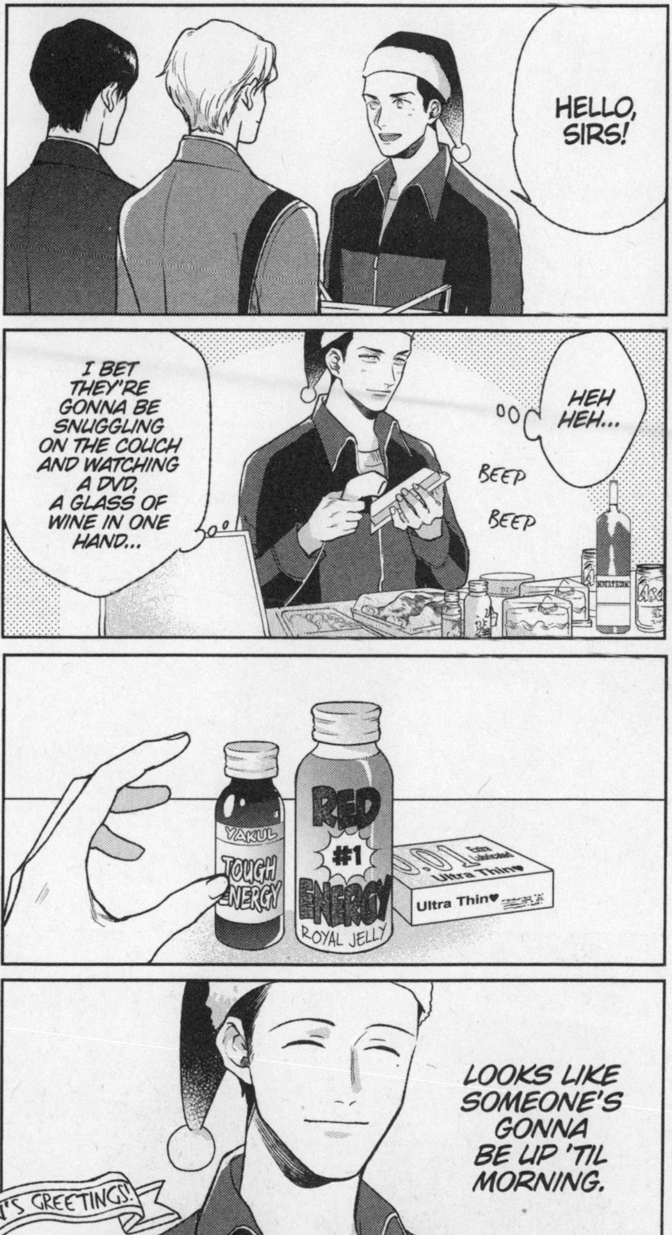
HELLO, SIRS!
HEH HEH...
BEEP
BEEP
I BET THEY'RE GONNA BE SNUGGLING ON THE COUCH AND WATCHING A DVD, A GLASS OF WINE IN ONE HAND...
YAKUL
TOUGH ENERGY
RED
#1
ENERGY
ROYAL JELLY
0.01
Ultra Thin♥
Ultra Thin♥
LOOKS LIKE SOMEONE'S GONNA BE UP 'TIL MORNING.
SEASON'S GREETINGS!

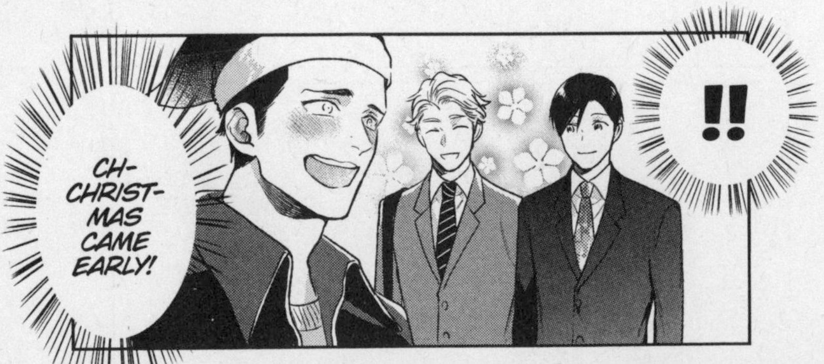
!!
CH- CHRIST- MAS CAME EARLY!

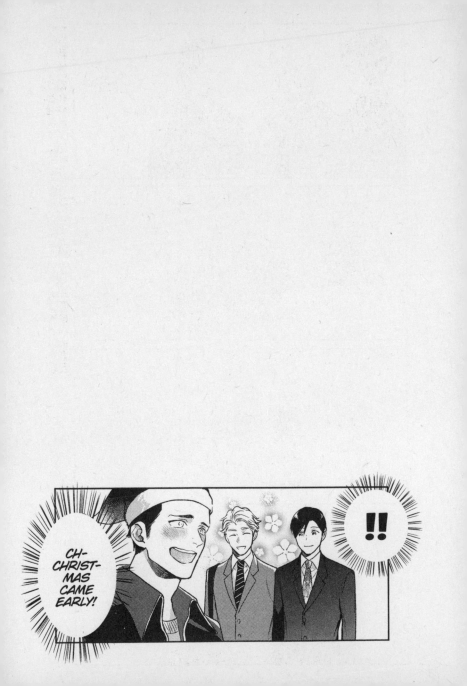

FKS

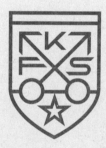

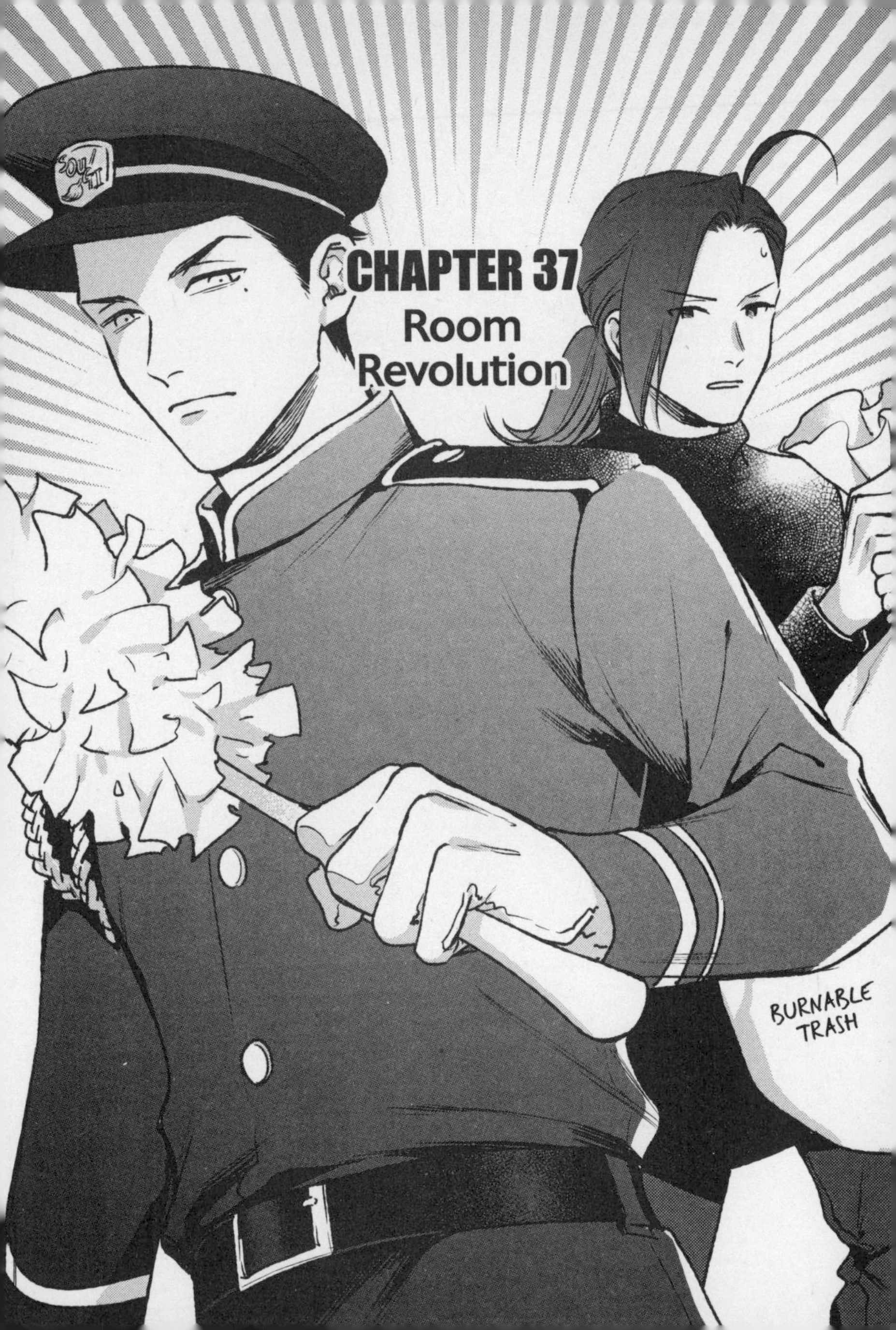
CHAPTER 37
Room Revolution
BURNABLE TRASH

# YEAR-END UPHEAVAL

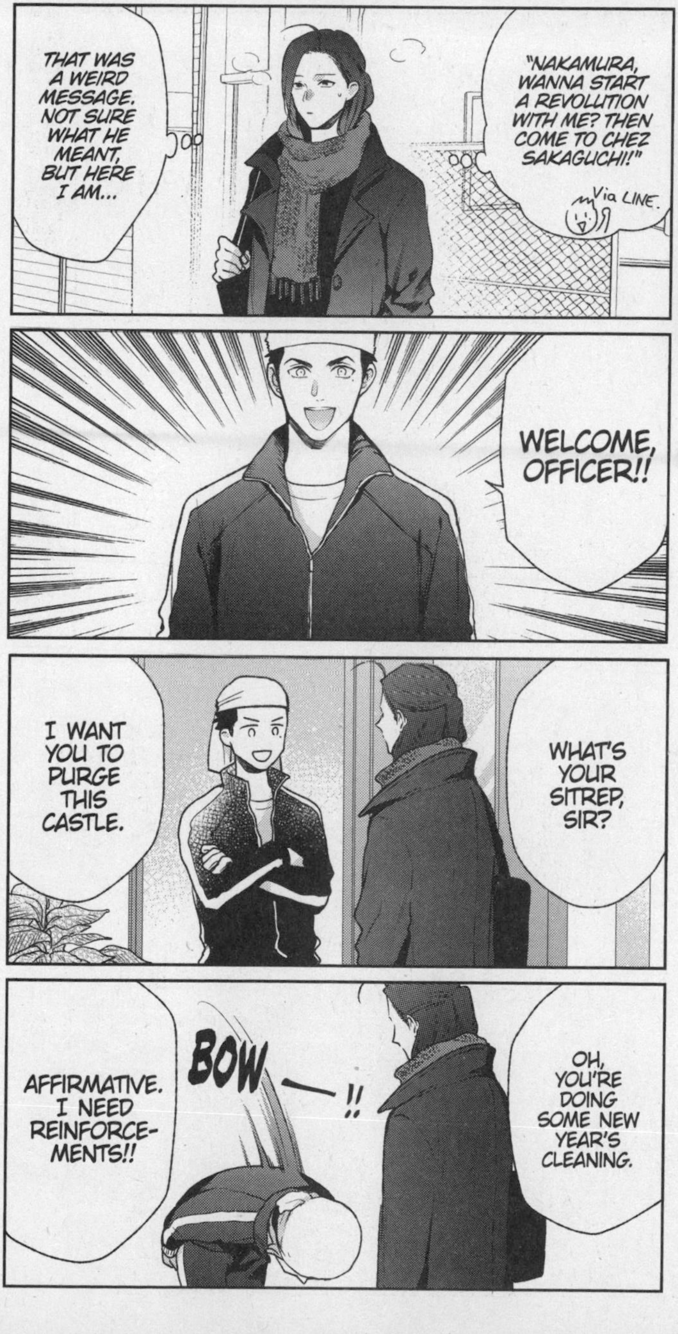
"NAKAMURA, WANNA START A REVOLUTION WITH ME? THEN COME TO CHEZ SAKAGUCHI!!"
Via LINE.
THAT WAS A WEIRD MESSAGE. NOT SURE WHAT HE MEANT, BUT HERE I AM...
WELCOME, OFFICER!!
WHAT'S YOUR SITREP, SIR?
I WANT YOU TO PURGE THIS CASTLE.
OH, YOU'RE DOING SOME NEW YEAR'S CLEANING.
BOW—!!
AFFIRMATIVE. I NEED REINFORCE-MENTS!!

# DANGER ZONE

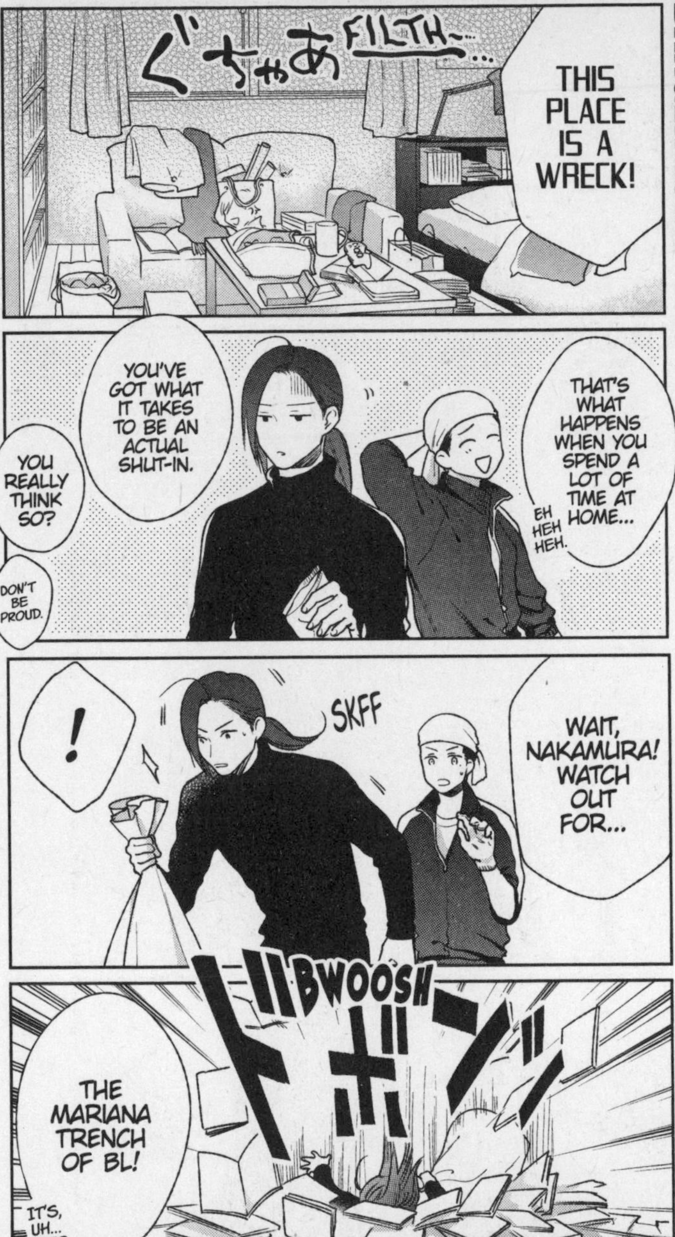
ぐちゃあ
FILTH~...
THIS PLACE IS A WRECK!
THAT'S WHAT HAPPENS WHEN YOU SPEND A LOT OF TIME AT HOME...
EH HEH HEH.
YOU'VE GOT WHAT IT TAKES TO BE AN ACTUAL SHUT-IN.
YOU REALLY THINK SO?
DON'T BE PROUD.
WAIT, NAKAMURA! WATCH OUT FOR...
SKFF
!
ドボーン
BWOOSH
THE MARIANA TRENCH OF BL!
IT'S, UH... DEEP.

## THE CHUB RETURNS

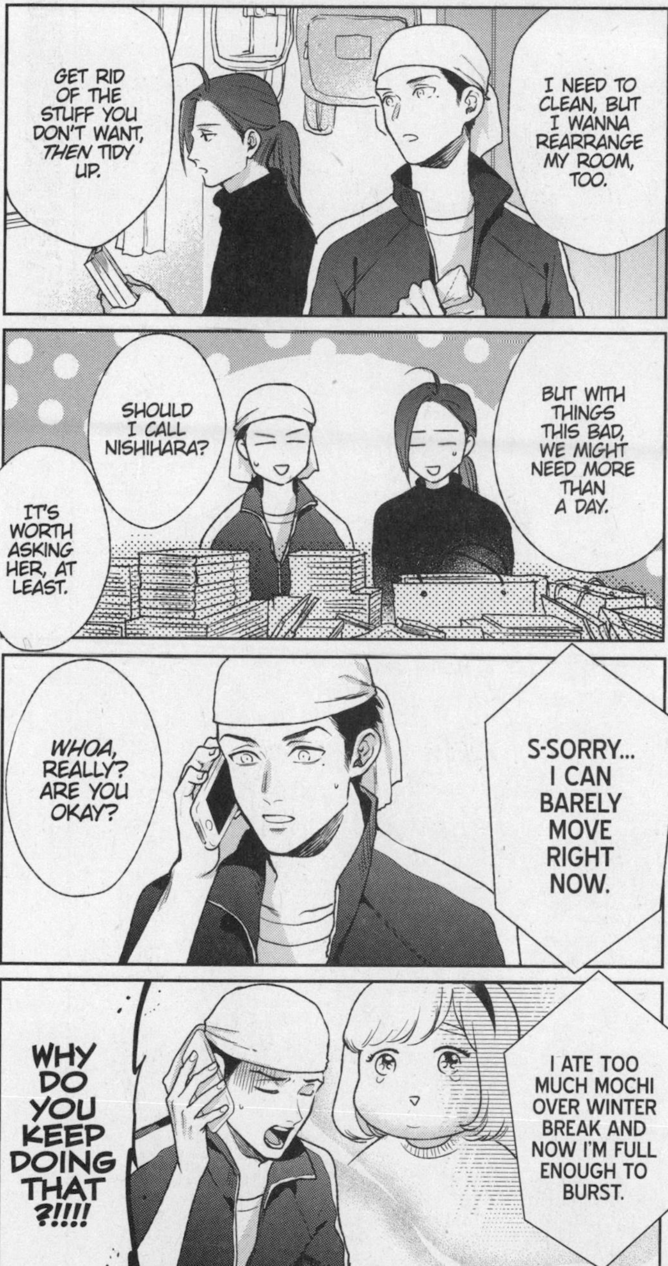
I NEED TO CLEAN, BUT I WANNA REARRANGE MY ROOM, TOO.
GET RID OF THE STUFF YOU DON'T WANT, *THEN* TIDY UP.
BUT WITH THINGS THIS BAD, WE MIGHT NEED MORE THAN A DAY.
SHOULD I CALL NISHIHARA?
IT'S WORTH ASKING HER, AT LEAST.
S-SORRY... I CAN BARELY MOVE RIGHT NOW.
*WHOA, REALLY? ARE YOU OKAY?*
I ATE TOO MUCH MOCHI OVER WINTER BREAK AND NOW I'M FULL ENOUGH TO BURST.
WHY DO YOU KEEP DOING THAT?!!!!

# PROGRESS DERAILED

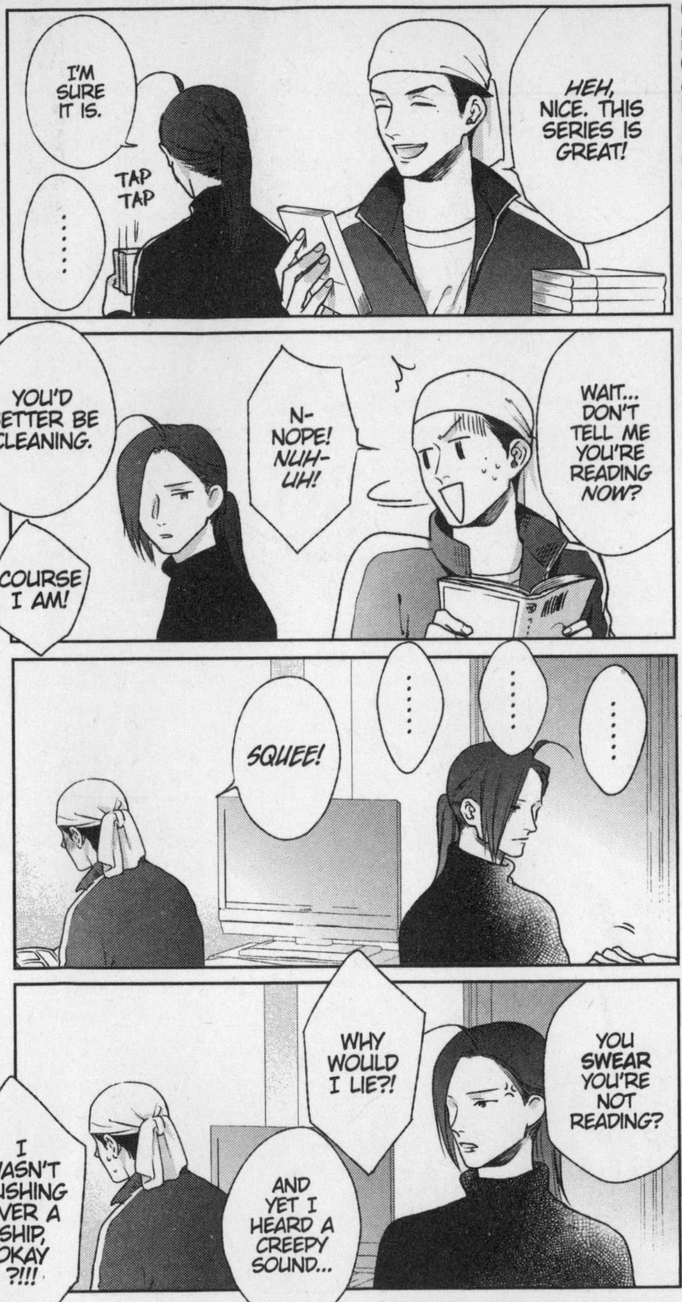
HEH, NICE. THIS SERIES IS GREAT!
I'M SURE IT IS.
TAP TAP
......
WAIT... DON'T TELL ME YOU'RE READING NOW?
N-NOPE! NUH-UH!
YOU'D BETTER BE CLEANING.
COURSE I AM!
......
......
......
SQUEE!
YOU SWEAR YOU'RE NOT READING?
WHY WOULD I LIE?!
AND YET I HEARD A CREEPY SOUND...
I WASN'T GUSHING OVER A SHIP, OKAY?!!!

# THINGS CAN'T GO BACK TO THE WAY THEY WERE

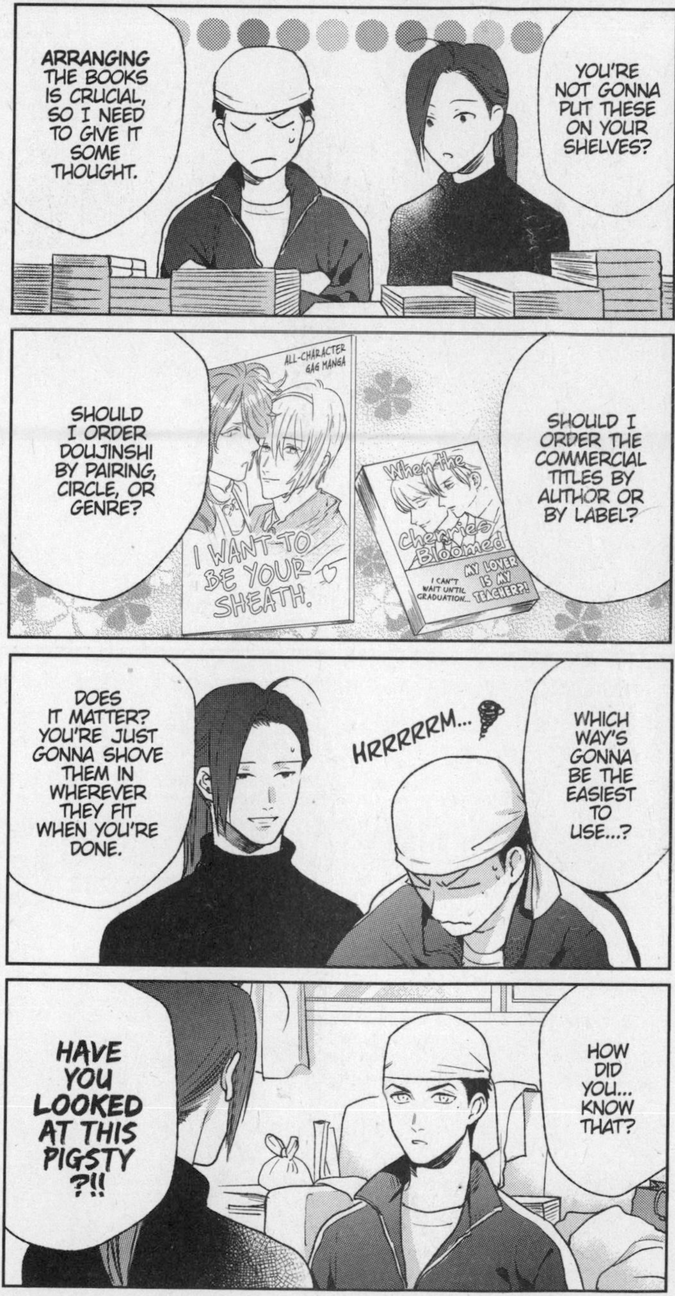
YOU'RE NOT GONNA PUT THESE ON YOUR SHELVES?
ARRANGING THE BOOKS IS CRUCIAL, SO I NEED TO GIVE IT SOME THOUGHT.
SHOULD I ORDER THE COMMERCIAL TITLES BY AUTHOR OR BY LABEL?
When the Cherries Bloomed
MY LOVER IS MY TEACHER?!
I CAN'T WAIT UNTIL GRADUATION...
ALL-CHARACTER GAG MANGA
I WANT TO BE YOUR SHEATH.
SHOULD I ORDER DOUJINSHI BY PAIRING, CIRCLE, OR GENRE?
WHICH WAY'S GONNA BE THE EASIEST TO USE...?
HRRRRRM...
DOES IT MATTER? YOU'RE JUST GONNA SHOVE THEM IN WHEREVER THEY FIT WHEN YOU'RE DONE.
HOW DID YOU... KNOW THAT?
HAVE YOU LOOKED AT THIS PIGSTY?!!

# I DON'T GET IT

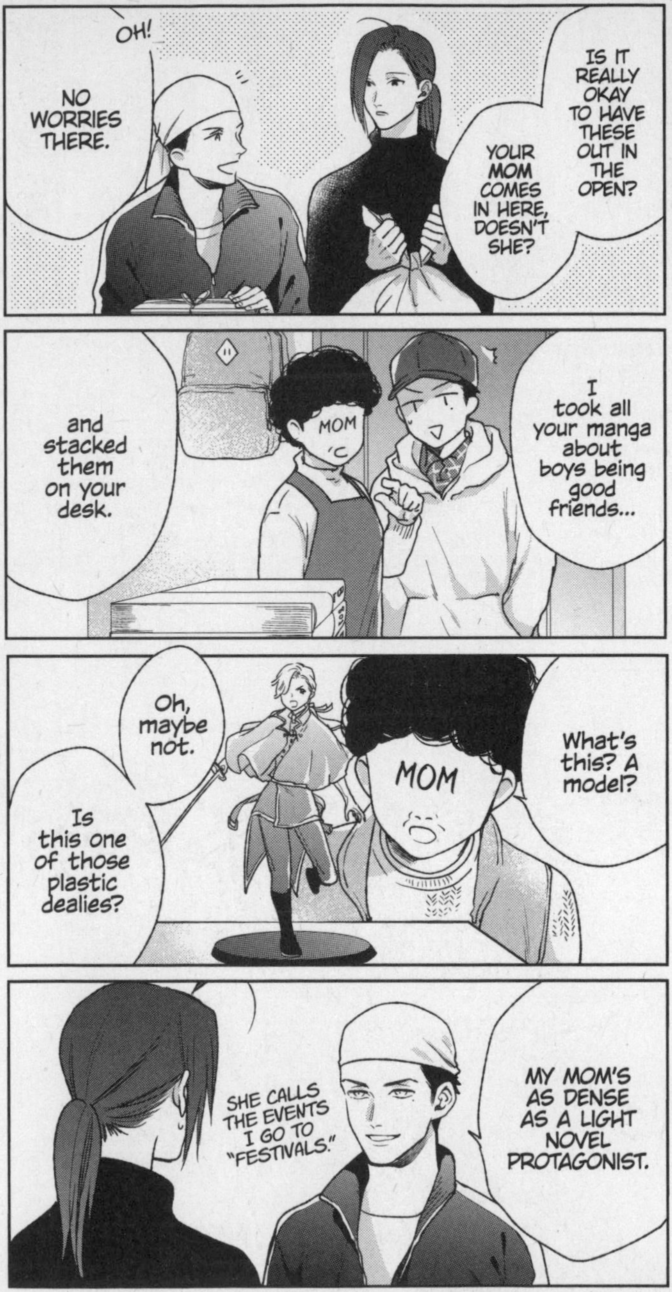
IS IT REALLY OKAY TO HAVE THESE OUT IN THE OPEN?
YOUR MOM COMES IN HERE, DOESN'T SHE?
OH!
NO WORRIES THERE.
I took all your manga about boys being good friends...
MOM
and stacked them on your desk.
What's this? A model?
MOM
Oh, maybe not.
Is this one of those plastic dealies?
MY MOM'S AS DENSE AS A LIGHT NOVEL PROTAGONIST.
SHE CALLS THE EVENTS I GO TO "FESTIVALS."

# ALWAYS AT HAND

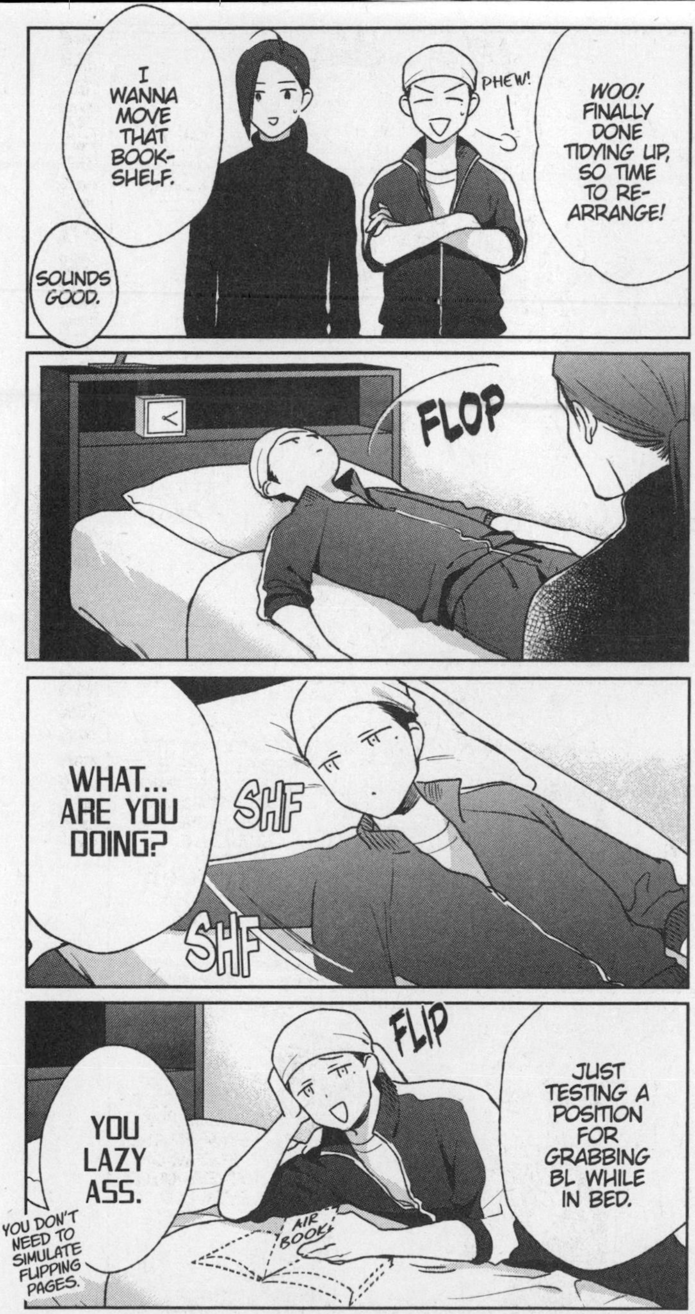
WOO! FINALLY DONE TIDYING UP, SO TIME TO RE-ARRANGE!
PHEW!
I WANNA MOVE THAT BOOK-SHELF.
SOUNDS GOOD.
FLOP
SHF
WHAT... ARE YOU DOING?
SHF
FLIP
JUST TESTING A POSITION FOR GRABBING BL WHILE IN BED.
AIR BOOK
YOU LAZY ASS.
YOU DON'T NEED TO SIMULATE FLIPPING PAGES.

# TAKING THE RELATIONSHIP TO THE NEXT LEVEL

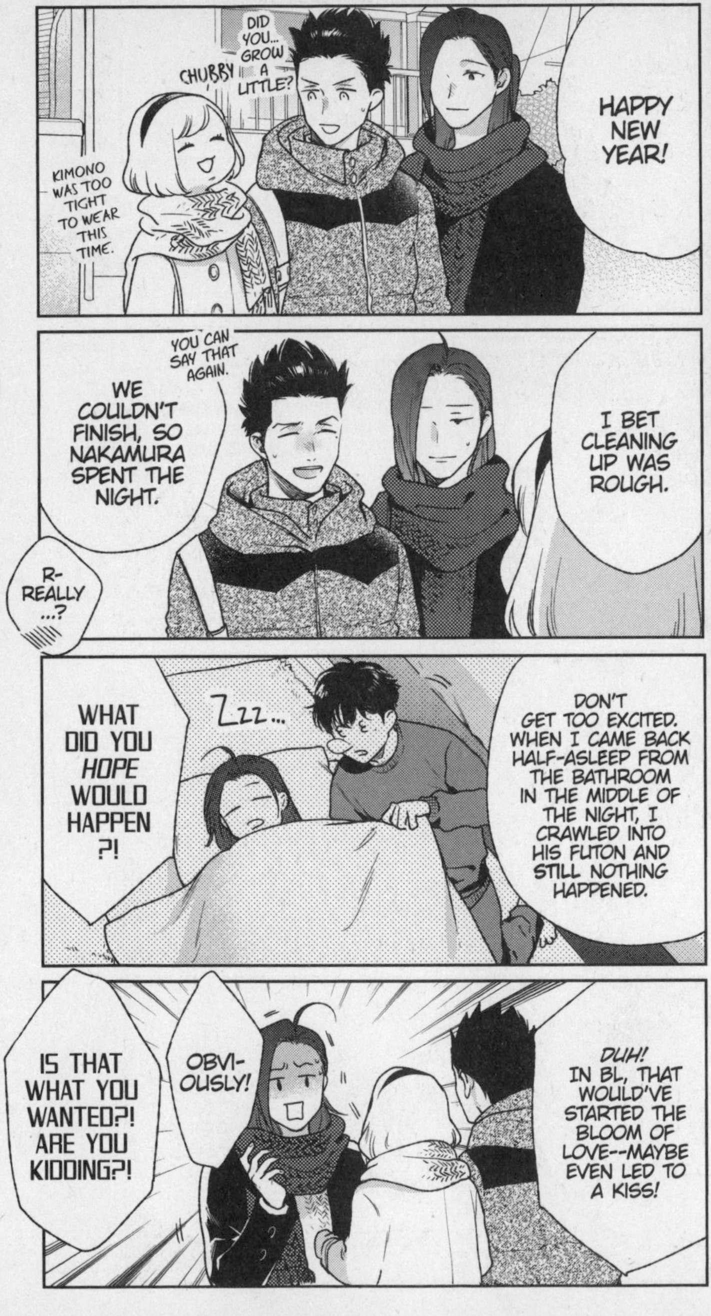
HAPPY NEW YEAR!
DID YOU... GROW A LITTLE?
CHUBBY
KIMONO WAS TOO TIGHT TO WEAR THIS TIME.
I BET CLEANING UP WAS ROUGH.
YOU CAN SAY THAT AGAIN.
WE COULDN'T FINISH, SO NAKAMURA SPENT THE NIGHT.
R-REALLY ...?
DON'T GET TOO EXCITED. WHEN I CAME BACK HALF-ASLEEP FROM THE BATHROOM IN THE MIDDLE OF THE NIGHT, I CRAWLED INTO HIS FUTON AND STILL NOTHING HAPPENED.
Zzz...
WHAT DID YOU *HOPE* WOULD HAPPEN ?!
*DUH!* IN BL, THAT WOULD'VE STARTED THE BLOOM OF LOVE--MAYBE EVEN LED TO A KISS!
OBVI-OUSLY!
IS THAT WHAT YOU WANTED?! ARE YOU KIDDING?!

# THE GODS ARE BUSY

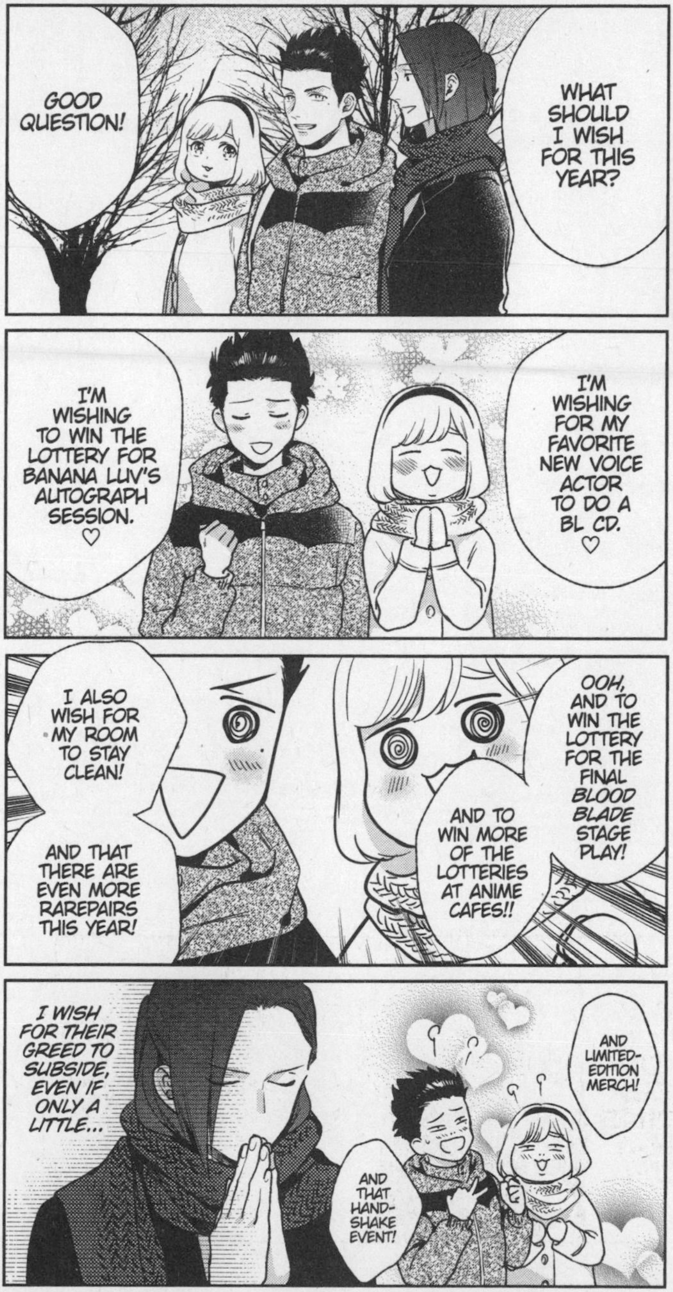
WHAT SHOULD I WISH FOR THIS YEAR?
GOOD QUESTION!
I'M WISHING FOR MY FAVORITE NEW VOICE ACTOR TO DO A BL CD. ♡
I'M WISHING TO WIN THE LOTTERY FOR BANANA LUV'S AUTOGRAPH SESSION. ♡
OOH, AND TO WIN THE LOTTERY FOR THE FINAL *BLOOD BLADE* STAGE PLAY!
AND TO WIN MORE OF THE LOTTERIES AT ANIME CAFES!!
I ALSO WISH FOR MY ROOM TO STAY CLEAN!
AND THAT THERE ARE EVEN MORE RAREPAIRS THIS YEAR!
AND LIMITED-EDITION MERCH!
AND THAT HAND-SHAKE EVENT!
I WISH FOR THEIR GREED TO SUBSIDE, EVEN IF ONLY A LITTLE...

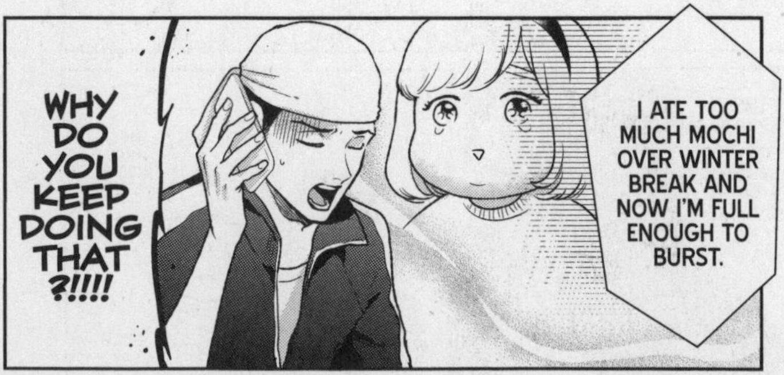
I ATE TOO MUCH MOCHI OVER WINTER BREAK AND NOW I'M FULL ENOUGH TO BURST.
WHY DO YOU KEEP DOING THAT ?!!!!

FKS

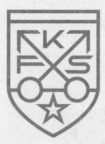

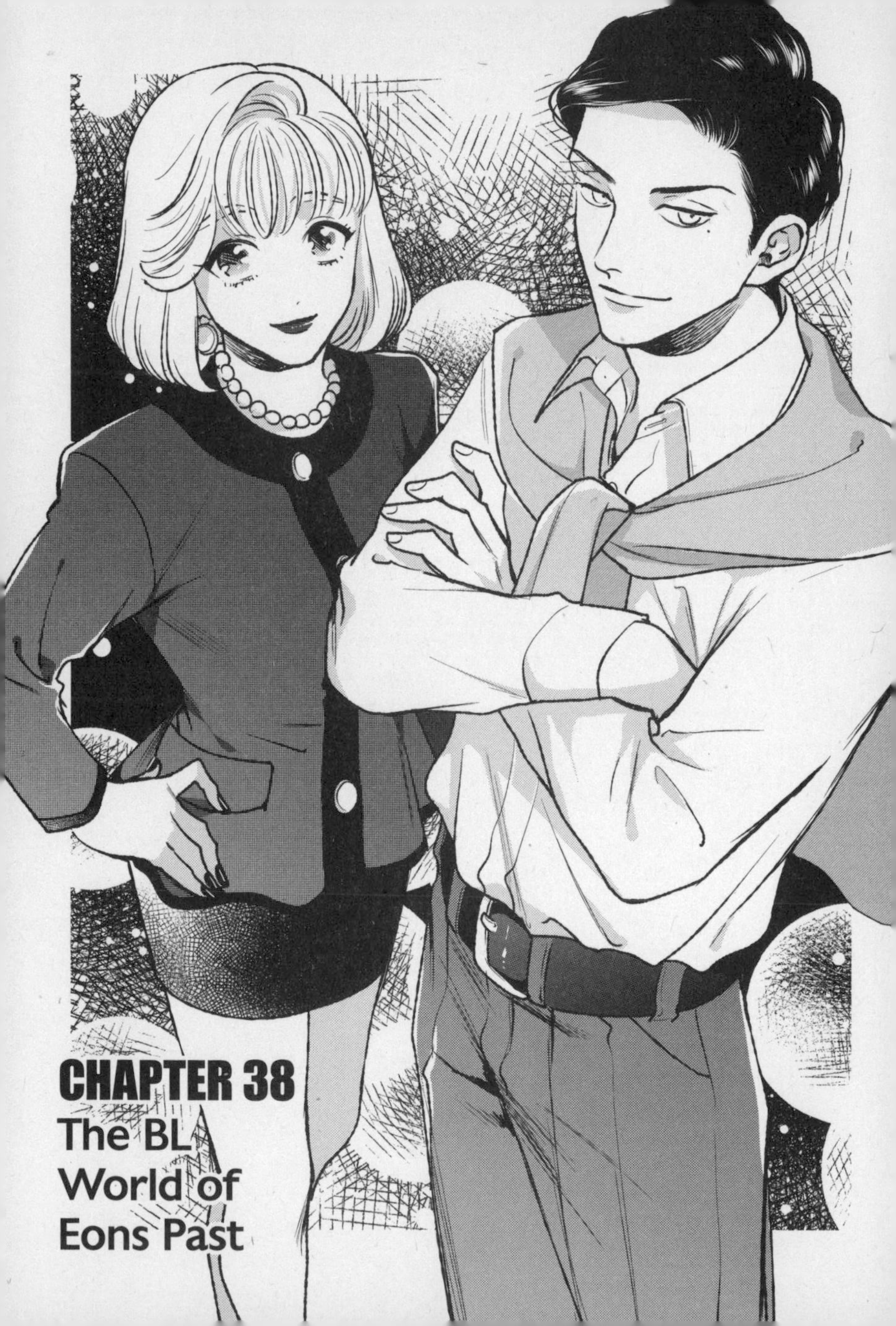

# CHAPTER 38

## The BL World of Eons Past

THE SEXY SCENE YOU'VE BEEN WAITING FOR

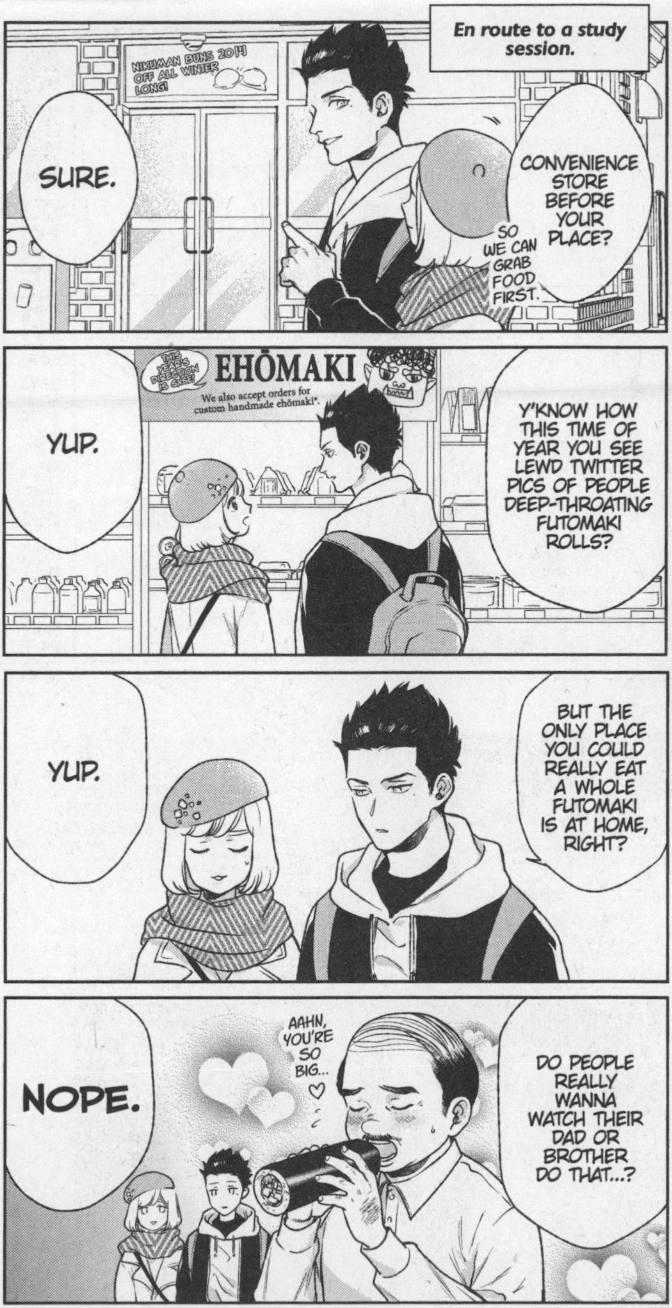
En route to a study session.
CONVENIENCE STORE BEFORE YOUR PLACE?
SO WE CAN GRAB FOOD FIRST.
SURE.
NIKUMAN BUNS 20円 OFF ALL WINTER LONG!
Y'KNOW HOW THIS TIME OF YEAR YOU SEE LEWD TWITTER PICS OF PEOPLE DEEP-THROATING FUTOMAKI ROLLS?
YUP.
EHŌMAKI
THIS YEAR'S DIRECTION IS SxSE!
We also accept orders for custom handmade ehōmaki*.
BUT THE ONLY PLACE YOU COULD REALLY EAT A WHOLE FUTOMAKI IS AT HOME, RIGHT?
YUP.
DO PEOPLE REALLY WANNA WATCH THEIR DAD OR BROTHER DO THAT...?
AAHN, YOU'RE SO BIG... ♡
NOPE.

*A roll composed of seven ingredients considered to be lucky. It's eaten for the Setsubun holiday while facing the direction considered to be auspicious that year. Setsubun is the holiday where oni are chased away, which explains the leap in topics on the next page.

# THE GULF BETWEEN MEN AND WOMEN

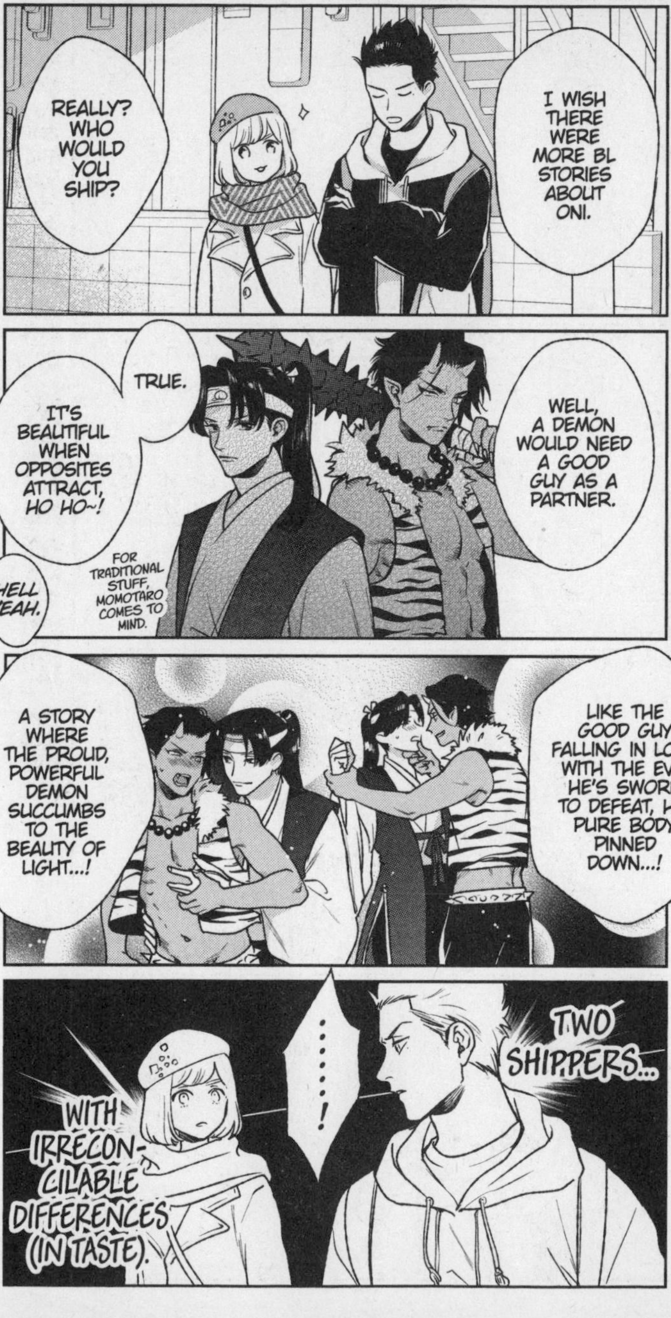
I WISH THERE WERE MORE BL STORIES ABOUT ONI.
REALLY? WHO WOULD YOU SHIP?
WELL, A DEMON WOULD NEED A GOOD GUY AS A PARTNER.
TRUE.
IT'S BEAUTIFUL WHEN OPPOSITES ATTRACT, HO HO~!
FOR TRADITIONAL STUFF, MOMOTARO COMES TO MIND.
HELL YEAH.
LIKE THE GOOD GUY FALLING IN LOVE WITH THE EVIL HE'S SWORN TO DEFEAT, HIS PURE BODY PINNED DOWN...!
A STORY WHERE THE PROUD, POWERFUL DEMON SUCCUMBS TO THE BEAUTY OF LIGHT...!
TWO SHIPPERS...
......!
WITH IRRECON-CILABLE DIFFERENCES (IN TASTE).

## RESCALING THE CATEGORY

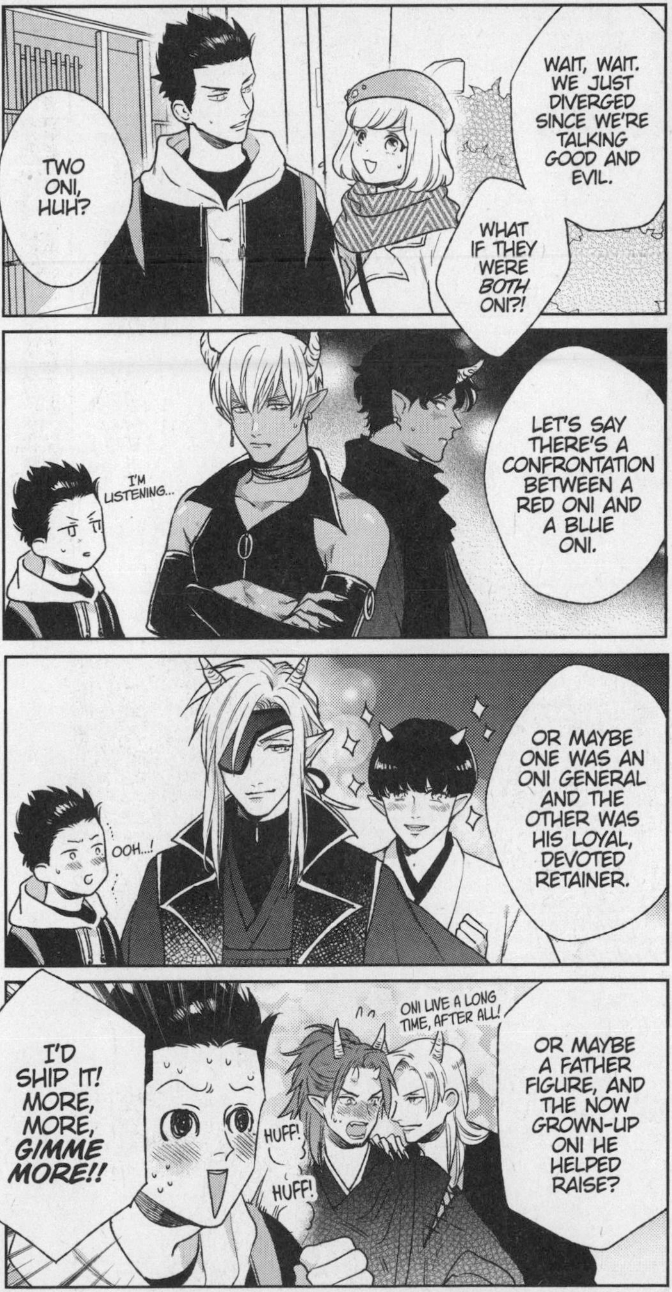
WAIT, WAIT. WE JUST DIVERGED SINCE WE'RE TALKING GOOD AND EVIL.
WHAT IF THEY WERE *BOTH* ONI?!
TWO ONI, HUH?
LET'S SAY THERE'S A CONFRONTATION BETWEEN A RED ONI AND A BLUE ONI.
I'M LISTENING...
OR MAYBE ONE WAS AN ONI GENERAL AND THE OTHER WAS HIS LOYAL, DEVOTED RETAINER.
OOH...!
OR MAYBE A FATHER FIGURE, AND THE NOW GROWN-UP ONI HE HELPED RAISE?
ONI LIVE A LONG TIME, AFTER ALL!
HUFF!
HUFF!
I'D SHIP IT! MORE, MORE, **GIMME MORE!!**

# DADS DON'T UNDERSTAND

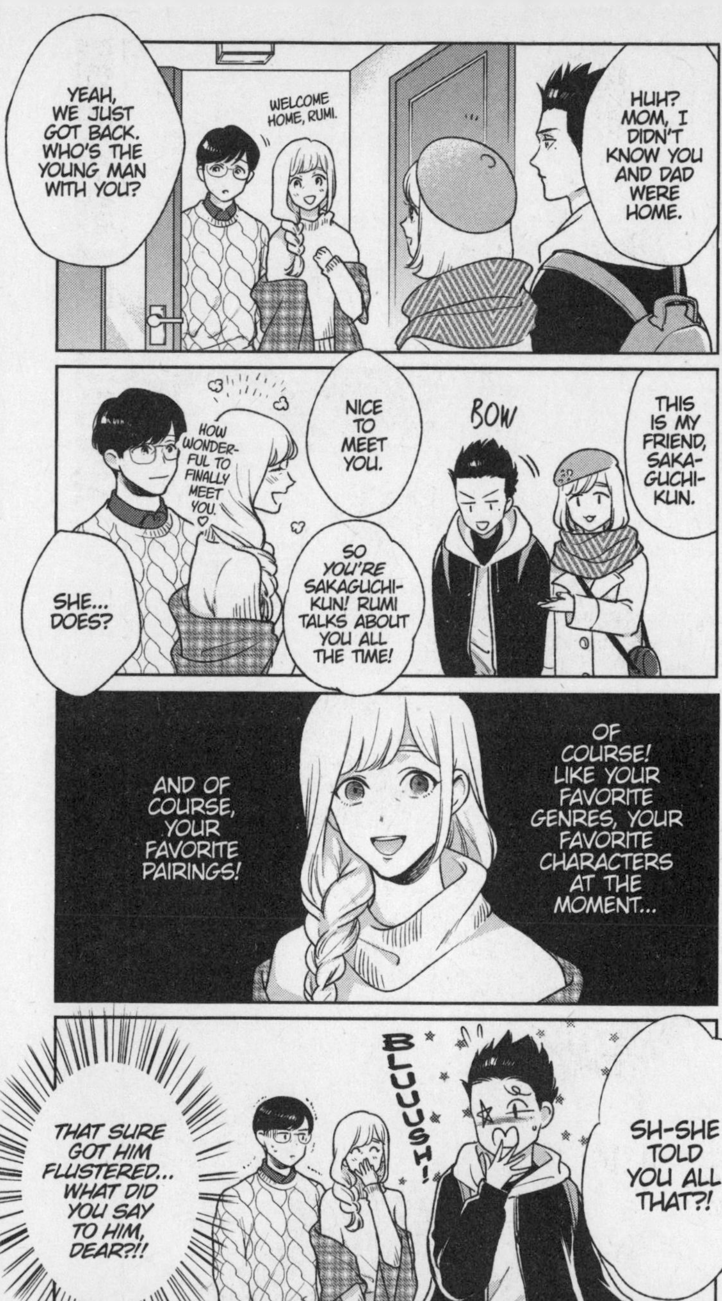

HUH? MOM, I DIDN'T KNOW YOU AND DAD WERE HOME.
WELCOME HOME, RUMI.
YEAH, WE JUST GOT BACK. WHO'S THE YOUNG MAN WITH YOU?
THIS IS MY FRIEND, SAKAGUCHI-KUN.
BOW
NICE TO MEET YOU.
SO YOU'RE SAKAGUCHI-KUN! RUMI TALKS ABOUT YOU ALL THE TIME!
HOW WONDERFUL TO FINALLY MEET YOU.
SHE... DOES?
OF COURSE! LIKE YOUR FAVORITE GENRES, YOUR FAVORITE CHARACTERS AT THE MOMENT...
AND OF COURSE, YOUR FAVORITE PAIRINGS!
SH-SHE TOLD YOU ALL THAT?!
BLUUUSH!
THAT SURE GOT HIM FLUSTERED... WHAT DID YOU SAY TO HIM, DEAR?!!

# WHERE IS THAT FUDANSHI NOW?

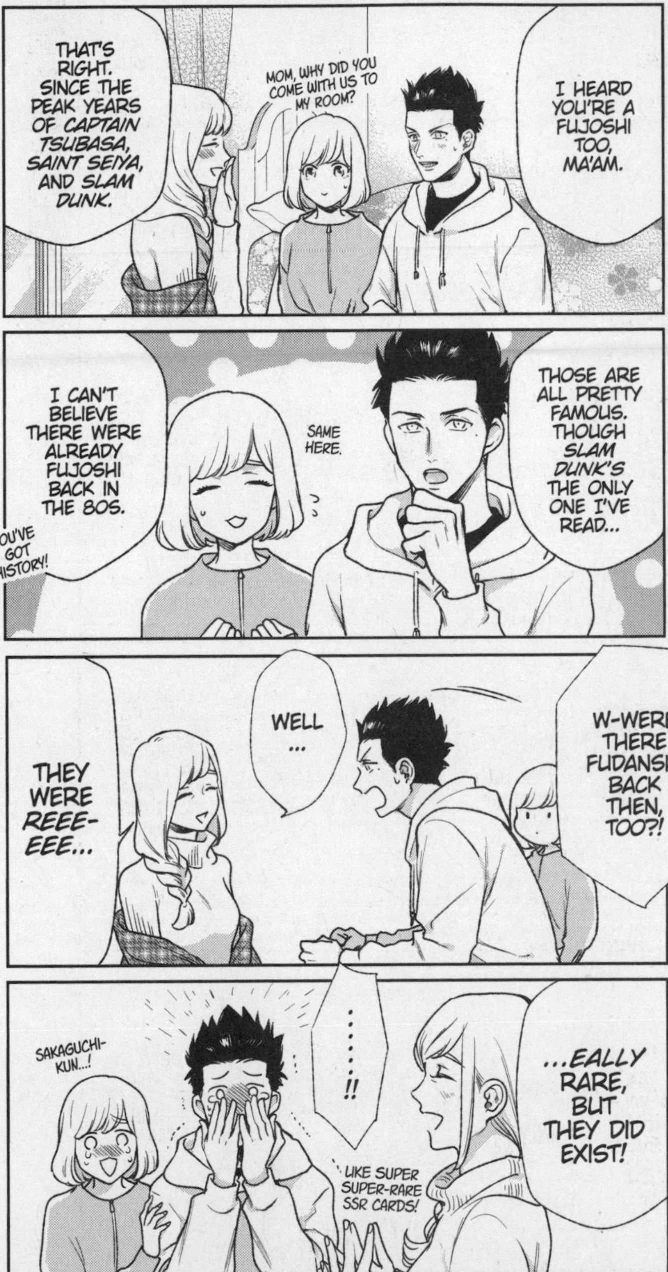
I HEARD YOU'RE A FUJOSHI TOO, MA'AM.
MOM, WHY DID YOU COME WITH US TO MY ROOM?
THAT'S RIGHT. SINCE THE PEAK YEARS OF *CAPTAIN TSUBASA*, *SAINT SEIYA*, AND *SLAM DUNK*.
THOSE ARE ALL PRETTY FAMOUS. THOUGH *SLAM DUNK*'S THE ONLY ONE I'VE READ...
SAME HERE.
I CAN'T BELIEVE THERE WERE ALREADY FUJOSHI BACK IN THE 80S.
YOU'VE GOT HISTORY!
W-WERE THERE FUDANSHI BACK THEN, TOO?!
WELL ...
THEY WERE REEE-EEE...
...EALLY RARE, BUT THEY DID EXIST!
......!!
LIKE SUPER SUPER-RARE SSR CARDS!
SAKAGUCHI-KUN...!

# THE DECADENT 80S

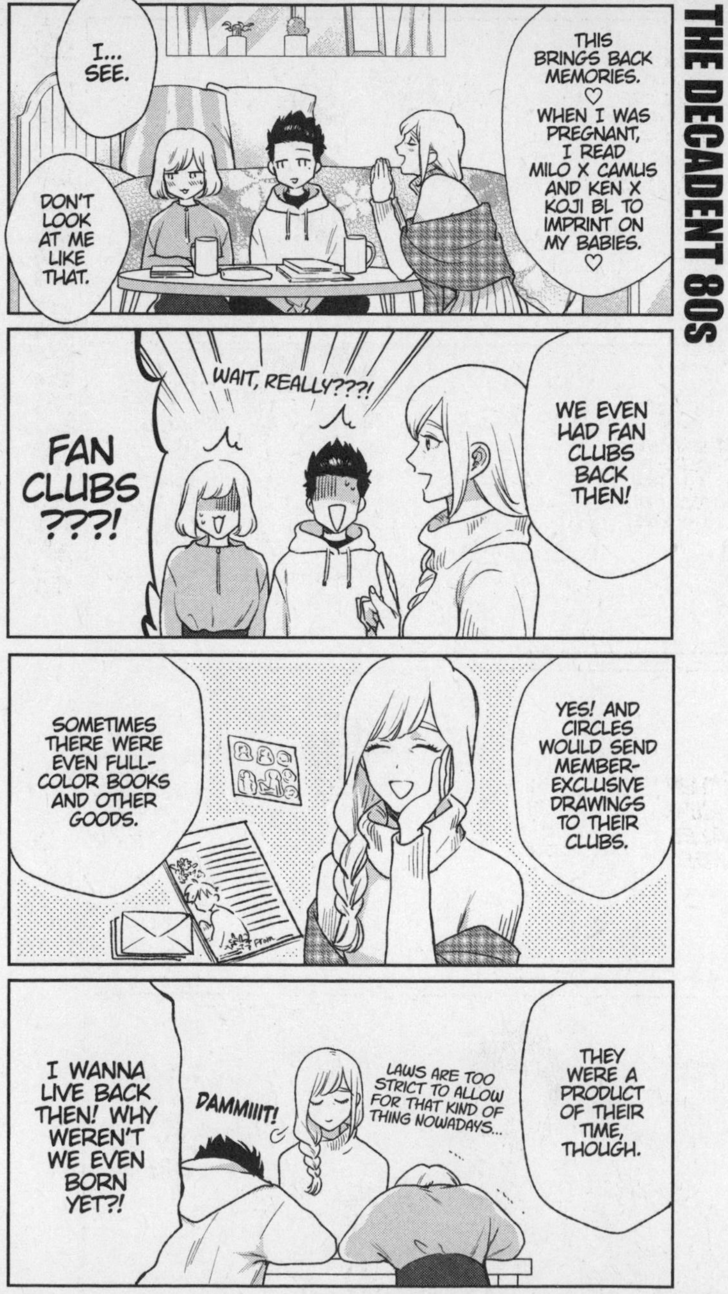
THIS BRINGS BACK MEMORIES. ♡ WHEN I WAS PREGNANT, I READ MILO X CAMUS AND KEN X KOJI BL TO IMPRINT ON MY BABIES. ♡
I... SEE.
DON'T LOOK AT ME LIKE THAT.
WE EVEN HAD FAN CLUBS BACK THEN!
WAIT, REALLY???!
FAN CLUBS???!
YES! AND CIRCLES WOULD SEND MEMBER-EXCLUSIVE DRAWINGS TO THEIR CLUBS.
SOMETIMES THERE WERE EVEN FULL-COLOR BOOKS AND OTHER GOODS.
THEY WERE A PRODUCT OF THEIR TIME, THOUGH.
LAWS ARE TOO STRICT TO ALLOW FOR THAT KIND OF THING NOWADAYS...
DAMMIIIT!
I WANNA LIVE BACK THEN! WHY WEREN'T WE EVEN BORN YET?!

## LAVISH

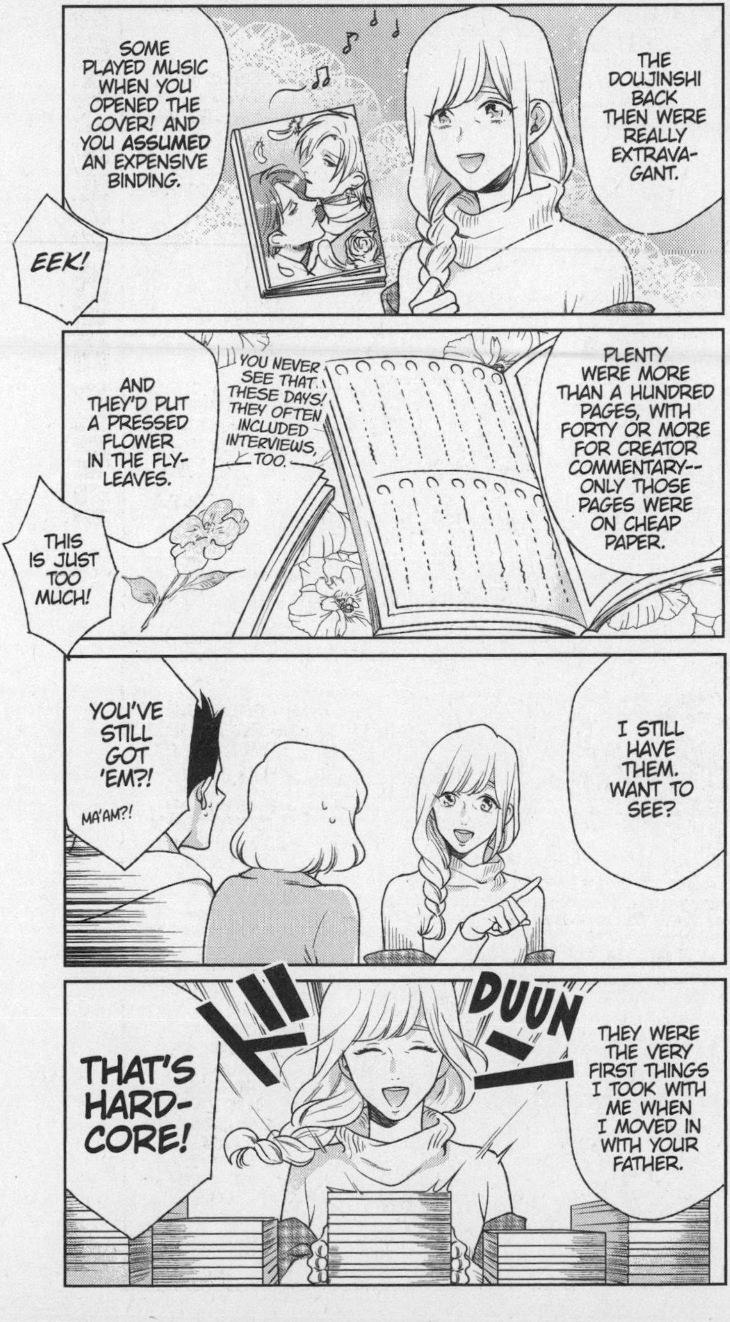
THE DOUJINSHI BACK THEN WERE REALLY EXTRAVAGANT.
SOME PLAYED MUSIC WHEN YOU OPENED THE COVER! AND YOU ASSUMED AN EXPENSIVE BINDING.
EEK!
PLENTY WERE MORE THAN A HUNDRED PAGES, WITH FORTY OR MORE FOR CREATOR COMMENTARY--ONLY THOSE PAGES WERE ON CHEAP PAPER.
YOU NEVER SEE THAT THESE DAYS! THEY OFTEN INCLUDED INTERVIEWS, TOO.
AND THEY'D PUT A PRESSED FLOWER IN THE FLY-LEAVES.
THIS IS JUST TOO MUCH!
I STILL HAVE THEM. WANT TO SEE?
YOU'VE STILL GOT 'EM?!
MA'AM?!
DUUN
THEY WERE THE VERY FIRST THINGS I TOOK WITH ME WHEN I MOVED IN WITH YOUR FATHER.
THAT'S HARD-CORE!

SOME THINGS NEVER CHANGE

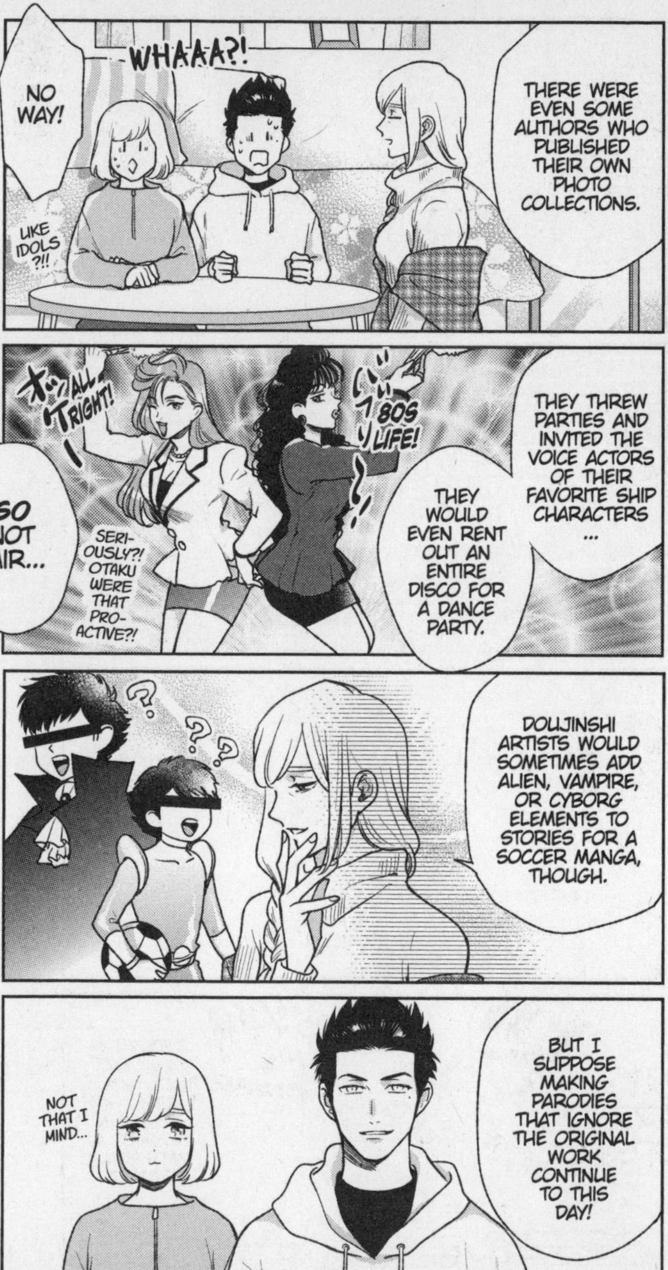
THERE WERE EVEN SOME AUTHORS WHO PUBLISHED THEIR OWN PHOTO COLLECTIONS.
WHAAA?!
NO WAY!
LIKE IDOLS?!!
THEY THREW PARTIES AND INVITED THE VOICE ACTORS OF THEIR FAVORITE SHIP CHARACTERS...
THEY WOULD EVEN RENT OUT AN ENTIRE DISCO FOR A DANCE PARTY.
80S LIFE!
ALL RIGHT!
SERIOUSLY?! OTAKU WERE THAT PROACTIVE?!
SO NOT FAIR...
DOUJINSHI ARTISTS WOULD SOMETIMES ADD ALIEN, VAMPIRE, OR CYBORG ELEMENTS TO STORIES FOR A SOCCER MANGA, THOUGH.
BUT I SUPPOSE MAKING PARODIES THAT IGNORE THE ORIGINAL WORK CONTINUE TO THIS DAY!
NOT THAT I MIND...

## WELCOME TO THE NISHIHARA RESIDENCE

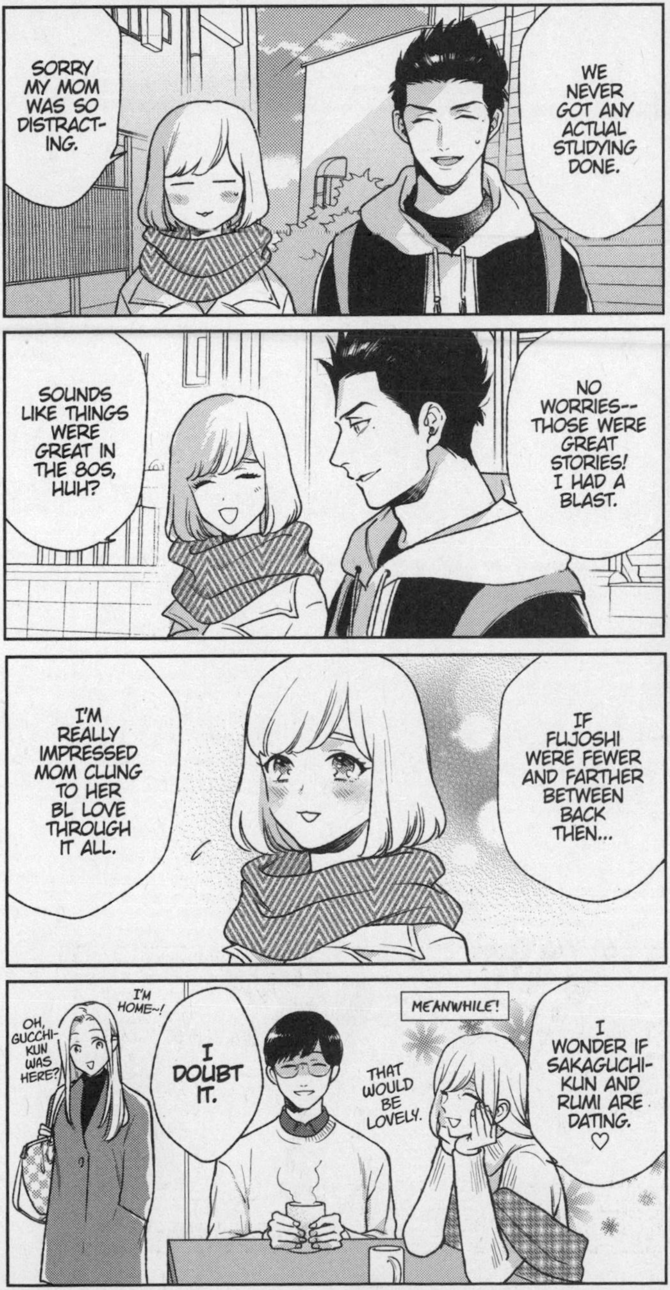
WE NEVER GOT ANY ACTUAL STUDYING DONE.
SORRY MY MOM WAS SO DISTRACTING.
NO WORRIES--THOSE WERE GREAT STORIES! I HAD A BLAST.
SOUNDS LIKE THINGS WERE GREAT IN THE 80S, HUH?
IF FUJOSHI WERE FEWER AND FARTHER BETWEEN BACK THEN...
I'M REALLY IMPRESSED MOM CLUNG TO HER BL LOVE THROUGH IT ALL.
MEANWHILE!
I WONDER IF SAKAGUCHI-KUN AND RUMI ARE DATING. ♡
THAT WOULD BE LOVELY.
I DOUBT IT.
I'M HOME~!
OH, GUCCHI-KUN WAS HERE?

K
F S

# CHAPTER 39
## Today's the Perfect Day for a Date

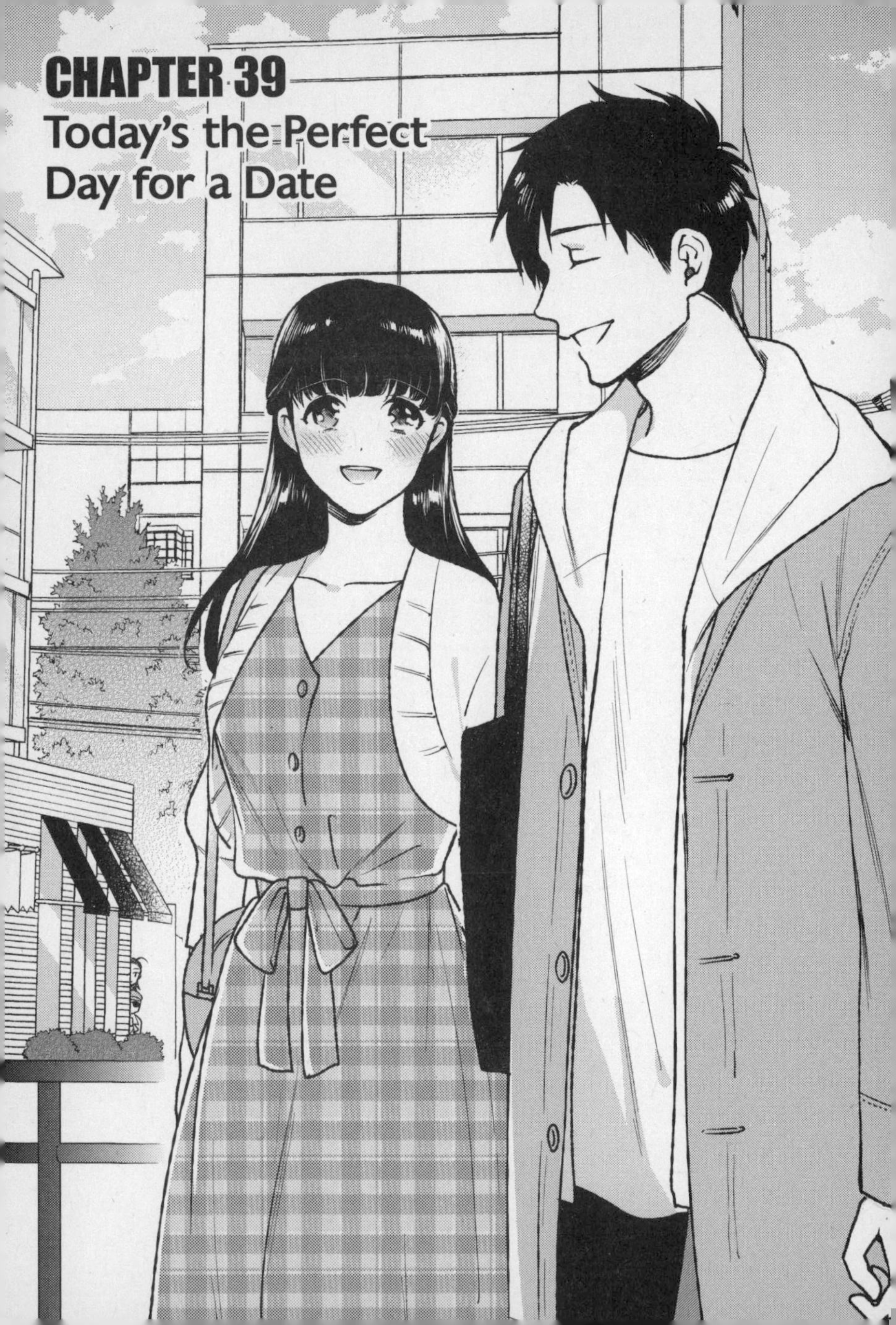

SOMETHING ANY (BL-LOVING) BOY WOULD LOVE

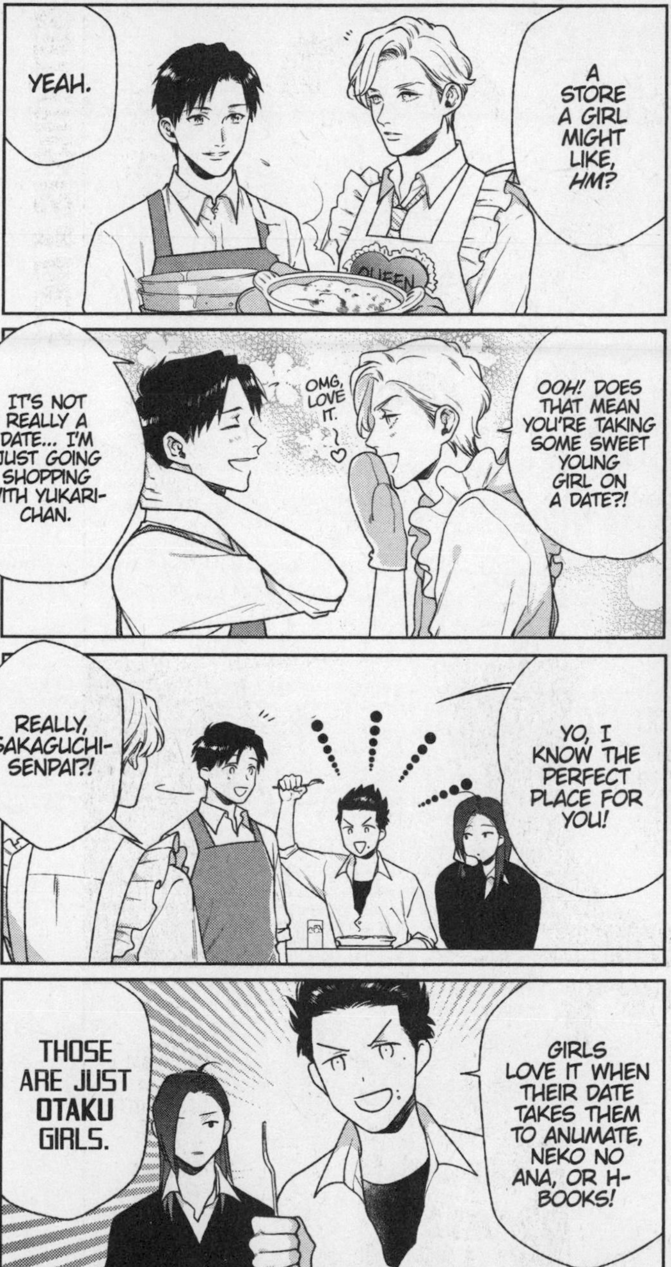
A STORE A GIRL MIGHT LIKE, HM?
YEAH.
OOH! DOES THAT MEAN YOU'RE TAKING SOME SWEET YOUNG GIRL ON A DATE?!
OMG, LOVE IT.
IT'S NOT REALLY A DATE... I'M JUST GOING SHOPPING WITH YUKARI-CHAN.
YO, I KNOW THE PERFECT PLACE FOR YOU!
REALLY, SAKAGUCHI-SENPAI?!
GIRLS LOVE IT WHEN THEIR DATE TAKES THEM TO ANUMATE, NEKO NO ANA, OR H-BOOKS!
THOSE ARE JUST OTAKU GIRLS.

## BUT THIS IS A DATE

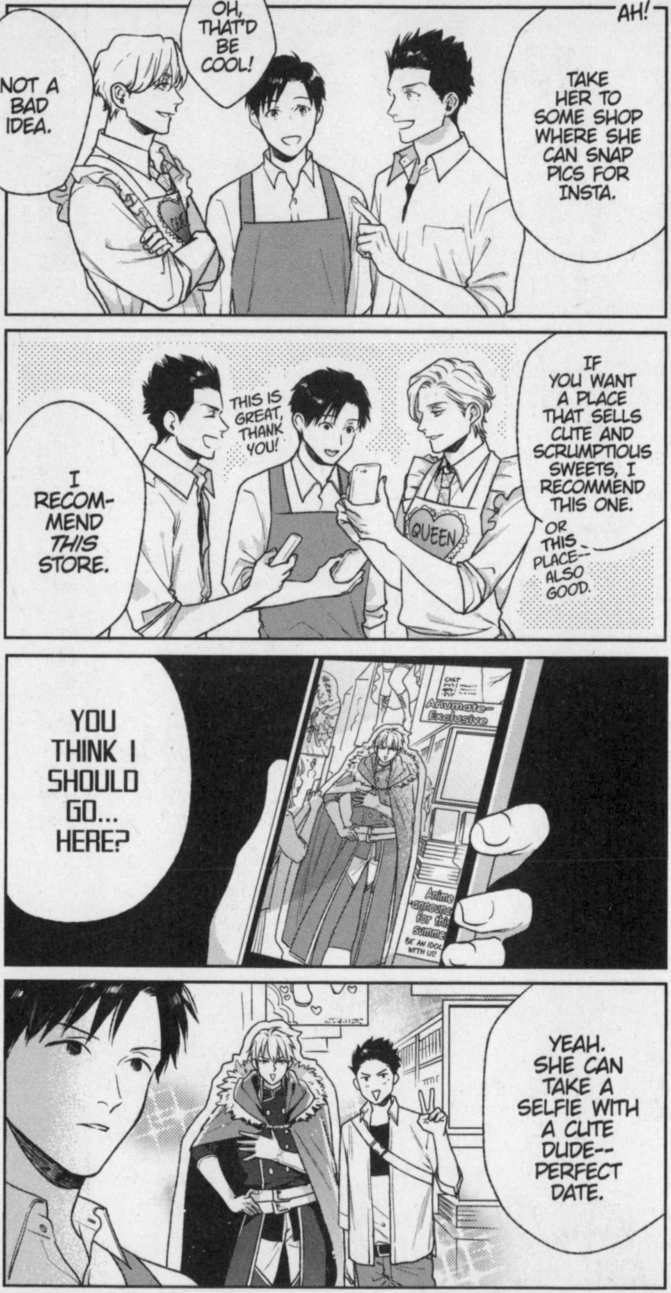
AH!
TAKE HER TO SOME SHOP WHERE SHE CAN SNAP PICS FOR INSTA.
OH, THAT'D BE COOL!
NOT A BAD IDEA.
IF YOU WANT A PLACE THAT SELLS CUTE AND SCRUMPTIOUS SWEETS, I RECOMMEND THIS ONE.
OR THIS PLACE-- ALSO GOOD.
THIS IS GREAT, THANK YOU!
I RECOMMEND *THIS* STORE.
Anumate-Exclusive
BE AN IDOL WITH US!
YOU THINK I SHOULD GO... HERE?
YEAH. SHE CAN TAKE A SELFIE WITH A CUTE DUDE-- PERFECT DATE.

## WALKING AHEAD OF MASTER

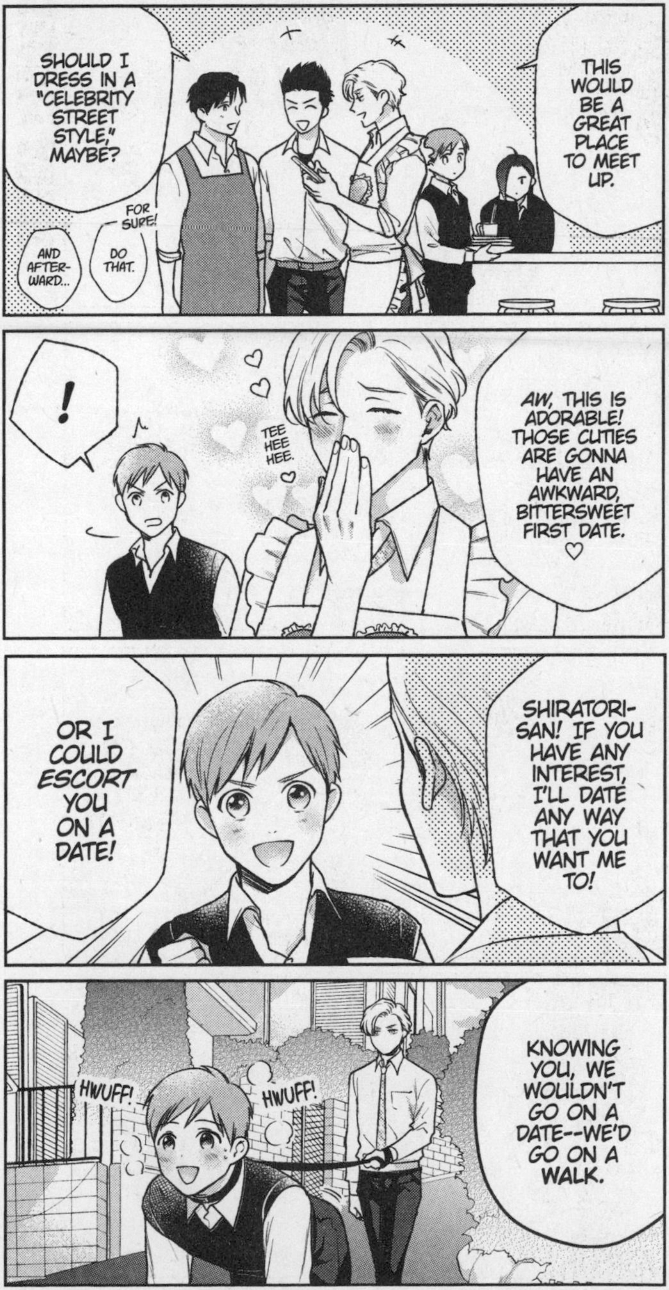
THIS WOULD BE A GREAT PLACE TO MEET UP.
SHOULD I DRESS IN A "CELEBRITY STREET STYLE," MAYBE?
FOR SURE!
DO THAT.
AND AFTER-WARD...
AW, THIS IS ADORABLE! THOSE CUTIES ARE GONNA HAVE AN AWKWARD, BITTERSWEET FIRST DATE. ♡
TEE HEE HEE.
!
SHIRATORI-SAN! IF YOU HAVE ANY INTEREST, I'LL DATE ANY WAY THAT YOU WANT ME TO!
OR I COULD ESCORT YOU ON A DATE!
KNOWING YOU, WE WOULDN'T GO ON A DATE--WE'D GO ON A WALK.
HWUFF!
HWUFF!

# SECRET AGENT

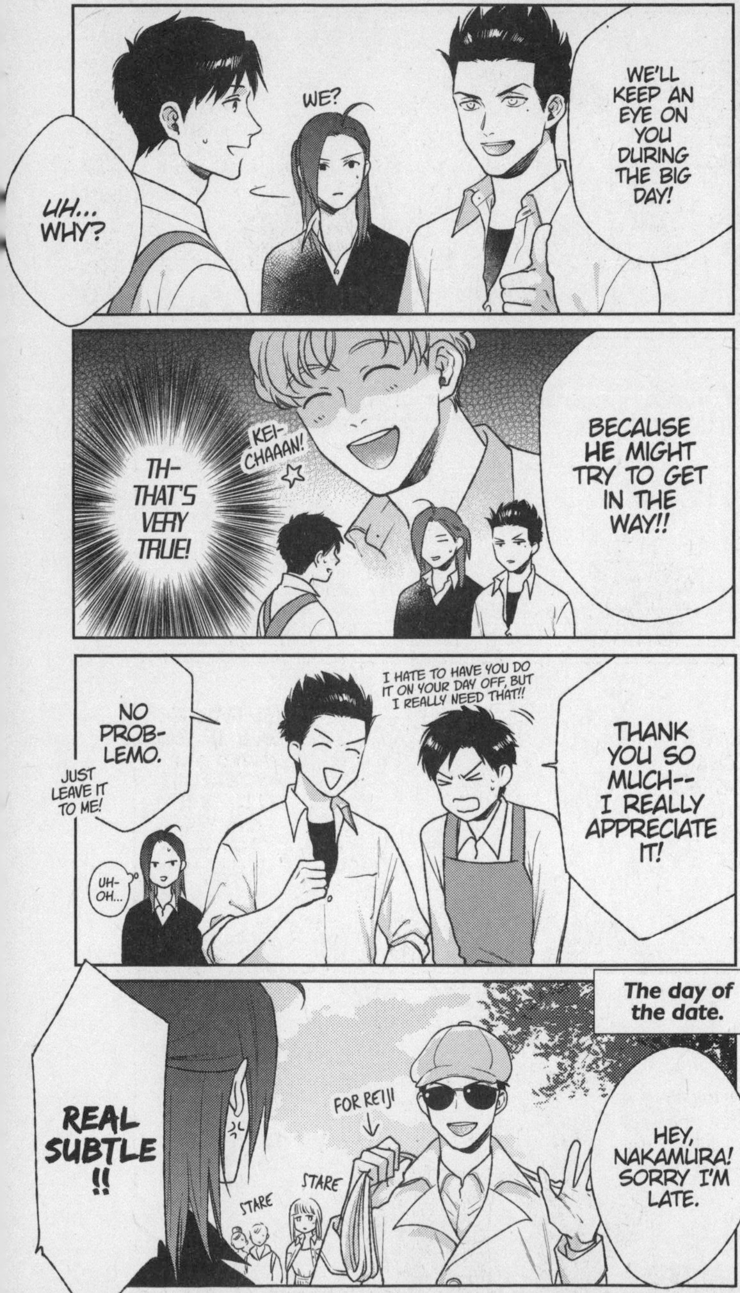
WE'LL KEEP AN EYE ON YOU DURING THE BIG DAY!
WE?
UH... WHY?
BECAUSE HE MIGHT TRY TO GET IN THE WAY!!
KEI-CHAAAN!
TH-THAT'S VERY TRUE!
THANK YOU SO MUCH-- I REALLY APPRECIATE IT!
I HATE TO HAVE YOU DO IT ON YOUR DAY OFF, BUT I REALLY NEED THAT!!
NO PROB-LEMO.
JUST LEAVE IT TO ME!
UH-OH...
The day of the date.
HEY, NAKAMURA! SORRY I'M LATE.
FOR REIJI
STARE
STARE
REAL SUBTLE!!

# AVOIDANCE

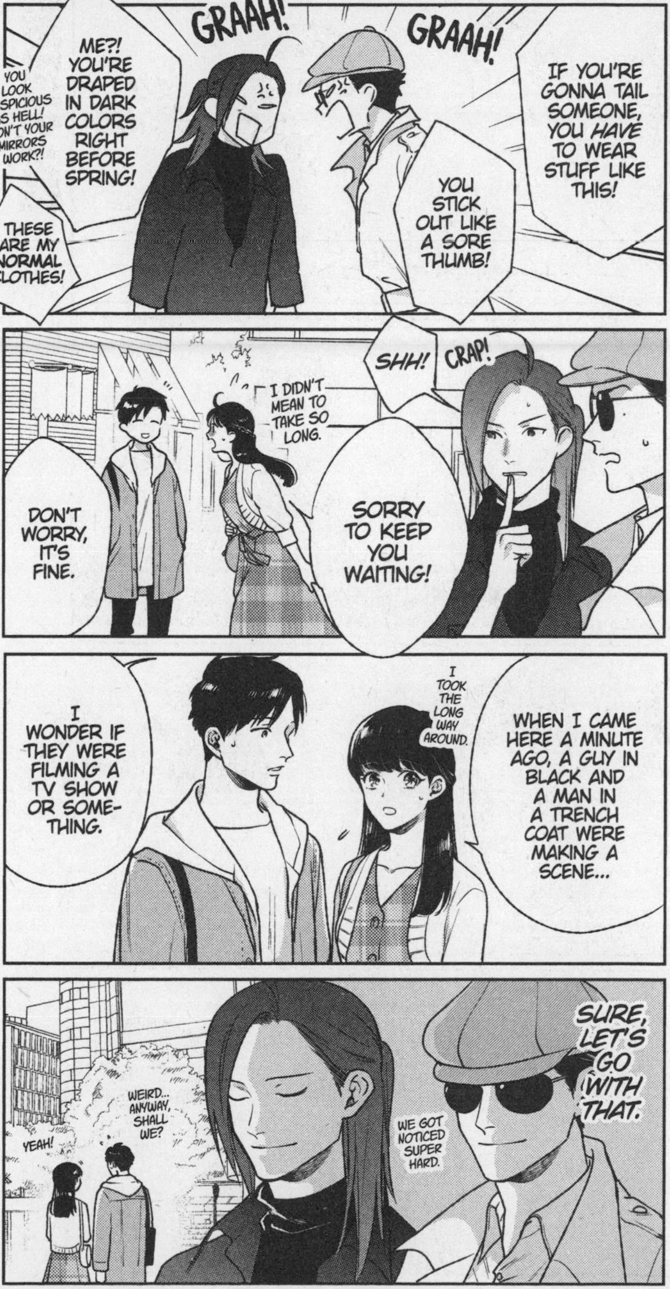
IF YOU'RE GONNA TAIL SOMEONE, YOU *HAVE* TO WEAR STUFF LIKE THIS!
GRAAH!
YOU STICK OUT LIKE A SORE THUMB!
GRAAH!
ME?! YOU'RE DRAPED IN DARK COLORS RIGHT BEFORE SPRING!
YOU LOOK SUSPICIOUS AS HELL! DON'T YOUR MIRRORS WORK?!
THESE ARE MY NORMAL CLOTHES!
CRAP!
SHH!
SORRY TO KEEP YOU WAITING!
I DIDN'T MEAN TO TAKE SO LONG.
DON'T WORRY, IT'S FINE.
WHEN I CAME HERE A MINUTE AGO, A GUY IN BLACK AND A MAN IN A TRENCH COAT WERE MAKING A SCENE...
I TOOK THE LONG WAY AROUND.
I WONDER IF THEY WERE FILMING A TV SHOW OR SOME-THING.
SURE, LET'S GO WITH THAT.
WE GOT NOTICED SUPER HARD.
WEIRD... ANYWAY, SHALL WE?
YEAH!

# SWEETS FAN

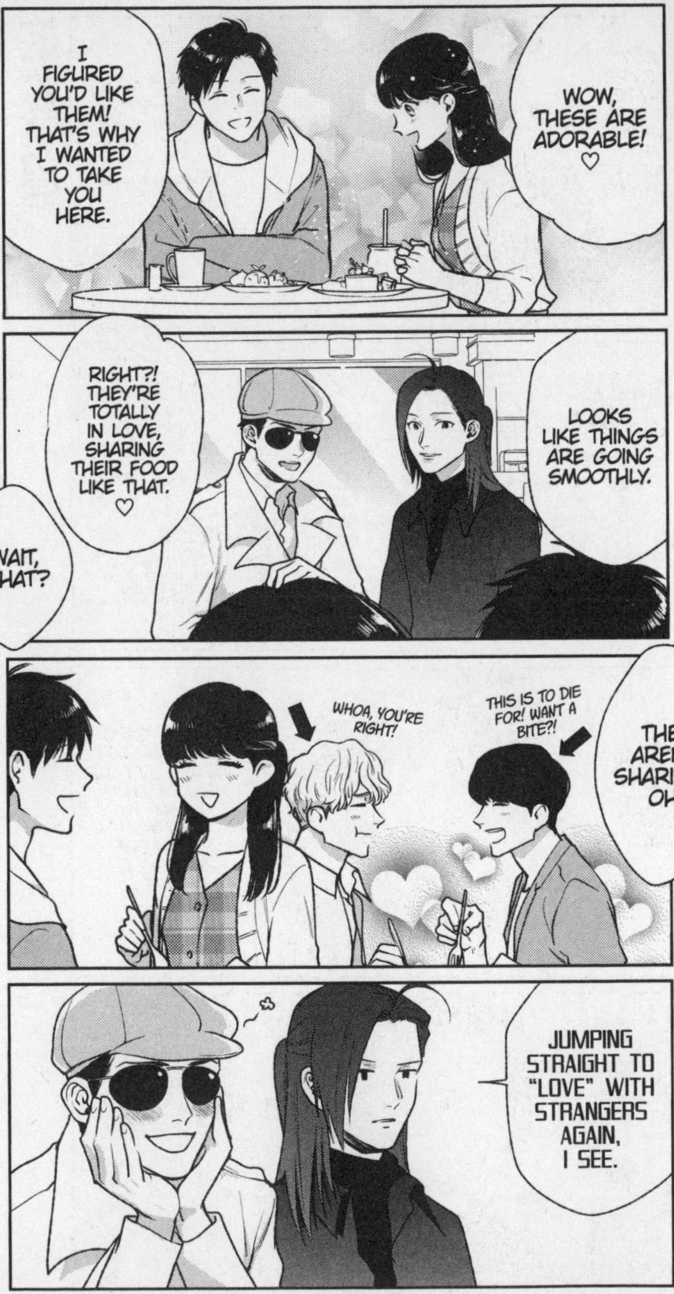
WOW, THESE ARE ADORABLE! ♡
I FIGURED YOU'D LIKE THEM! THAT'S WHY I WANTED TO TAKE YOU HERE.
LOOKS LIKE THINGS ARE GOING SMOOTHLY.
RIGHT?! THEY'RE TOTALLY IN LOVE, SHARING THEIR FOOD LIKE THAT. ♡
WAIT, WHAT?
THEY AREN'T SHARING... OH.
THIS IS TO DIE FOR! WANT A BITE?!
WHOA, YOU'RE RIGHT!
JUMPING STRAIGHT TO "LOVE" WITH STRANGERS AGAIN, I SEE.

# PRIORITIES

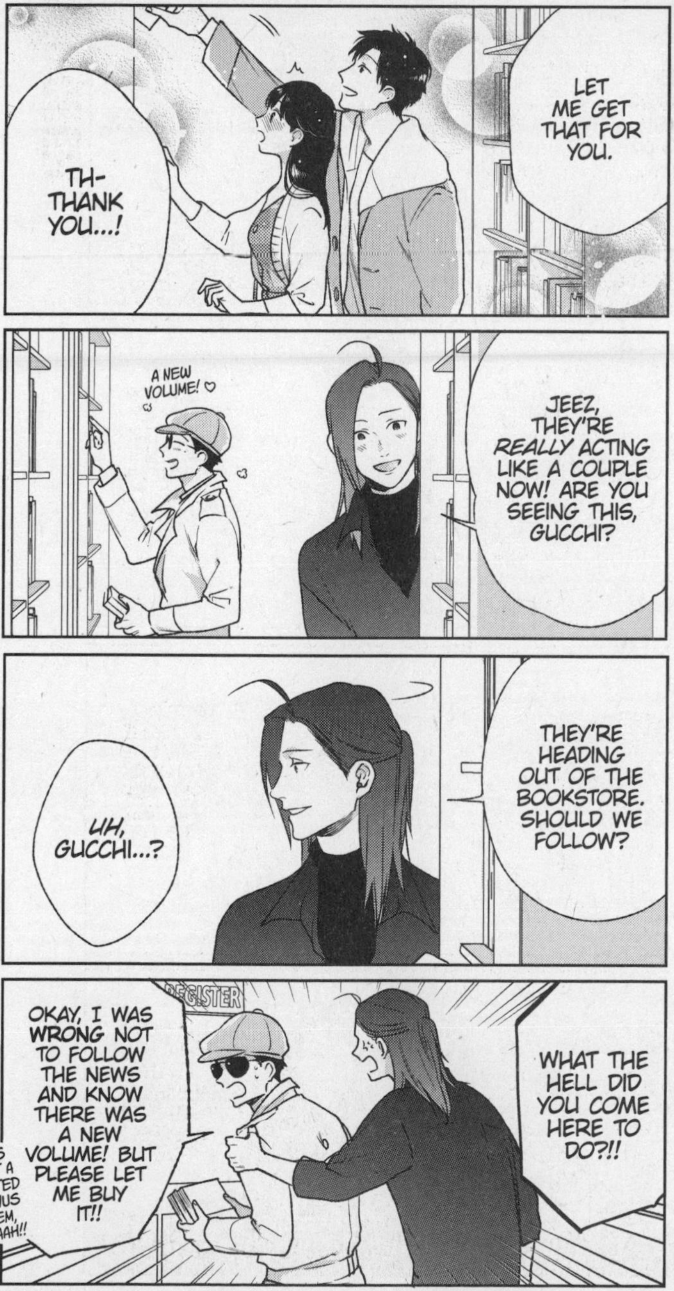
LET ME GET THAT FOR YOU.
TH-THANK YOU...!
JEEZ, THEY'RE *REALLY* ACTING LIKE A COUPLE NOW! ARE YOU SEEING THIS, GUCCHI?
A NEW VOLUME! ♡
THEY'RE HEADING OUT OF THE BOOKSTORE. SHOULD WE FOLLOW?
UH, GUCCHI...?
REGISTER
WHAT THE HELL DID YOU COME HERE TO DO?!!
OKAY, I WAS WRONG NOT TO FOLLOW THE NEWS AND KNOW THERE WAS A NEW VOLUME! BUT PLEASE LET ME BUY IT!!
IT'S GOT A LIMITED BONUS ITEM, WAAAH!!

# TOO CRUEL

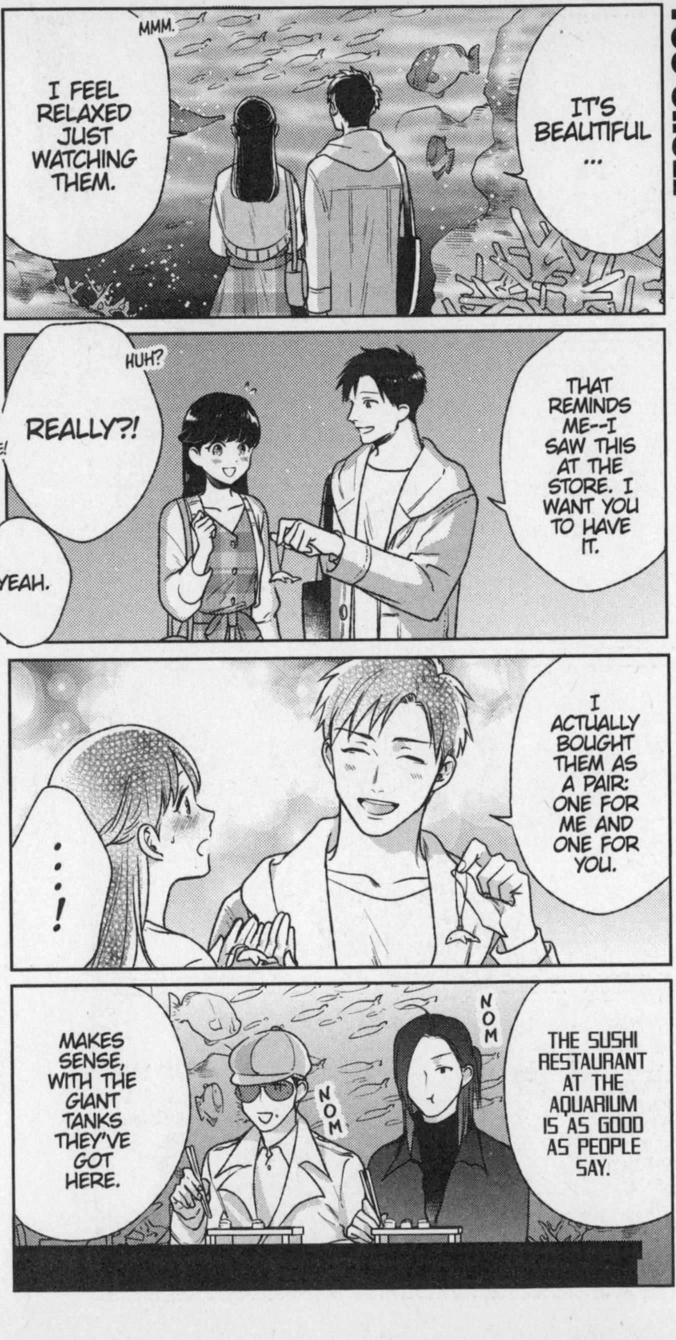
IT'S BEAUTIFUL ...
MMM.
I FEEL RELAXED JUST WATCHING THEM.
THAT REMINDS ME--I SAW THIS AT THE STORE. I WANT YOU TO HAVE IT.
HUH?
REALLY?!
IT'S SO CUTE! ♡
YEAH.
I ACTUALLY BOUGHT THEM AS A PAIR: ONE FOR ME AND ONE FOR YOU.
...!
THE SUSHI RESTAURANT AT THE AQUARIUM IS AS GOOD AS PEOPLE SAY.
NOM
NOM
MAKES SENSE, WITH THE GIANT TANKS THEY'VE GOT HERE.

# THE TROPES HE'S DREAMED OF WOULD COME TRUE

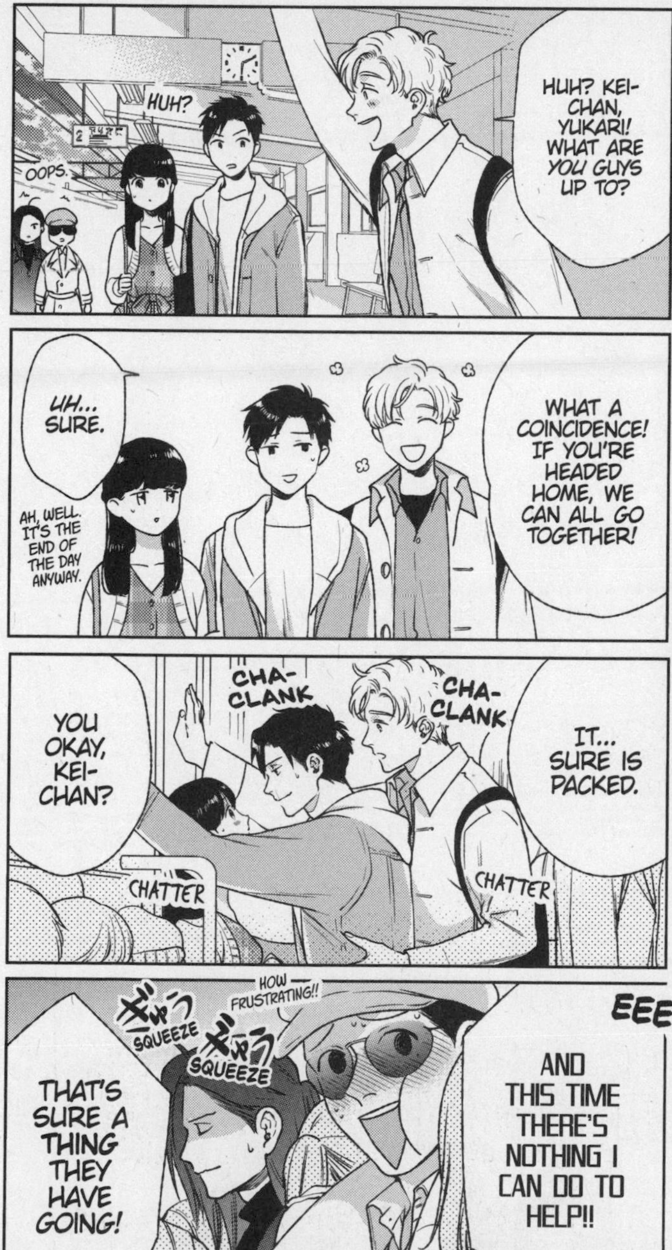
HUH? KEI-CHAN, YUKARI! WHAT ARE YOU GUYS UP TO?
HUH?
OOPS.
WHAT A COINCIDENCE! IF YOU'RE HEADED HOME, WE CAN ALL GO TOGETHER!
UH... SURE.
AH, WELL. IT'S THE END OF THE DAY ANYWAY.
IT... SURE IS PACKED.
CHA-CLANK
CHA-CLANK
YOU OKAY, KEI-CHAN?
CHATTER
CHATTER
EEEE~
AND THIS TIME THERE'S NOTHING I CAN DO TO HELP!!
HOW FRUSTRATING!!
ぎゅう SQUEEZE
ぎゅう SQUEEZE
THAT'S SURE A THING THEY HAVE GOING!

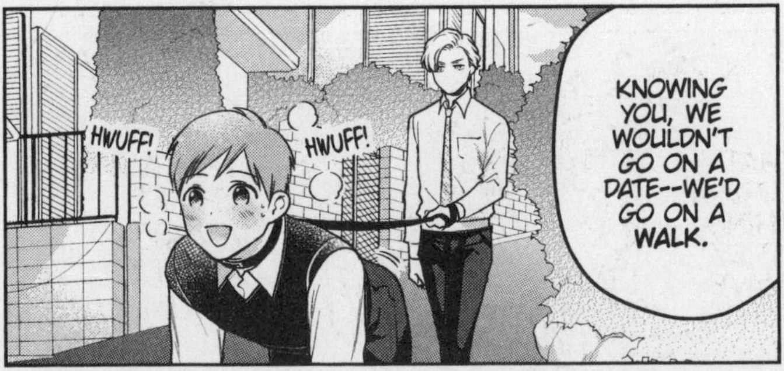
KNOWING YOU, WE WOULDN'T GO ON A DATE--WE'D GO ON A WALK.
HWUFF!
HWUFF!

KFS

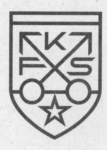

# RYUSEI ☆ HIKARU

**CHAPTER 40**
## Daigo Makes His Commercial Debut

YAOI PUBLISHERS

# THE BIG TIME

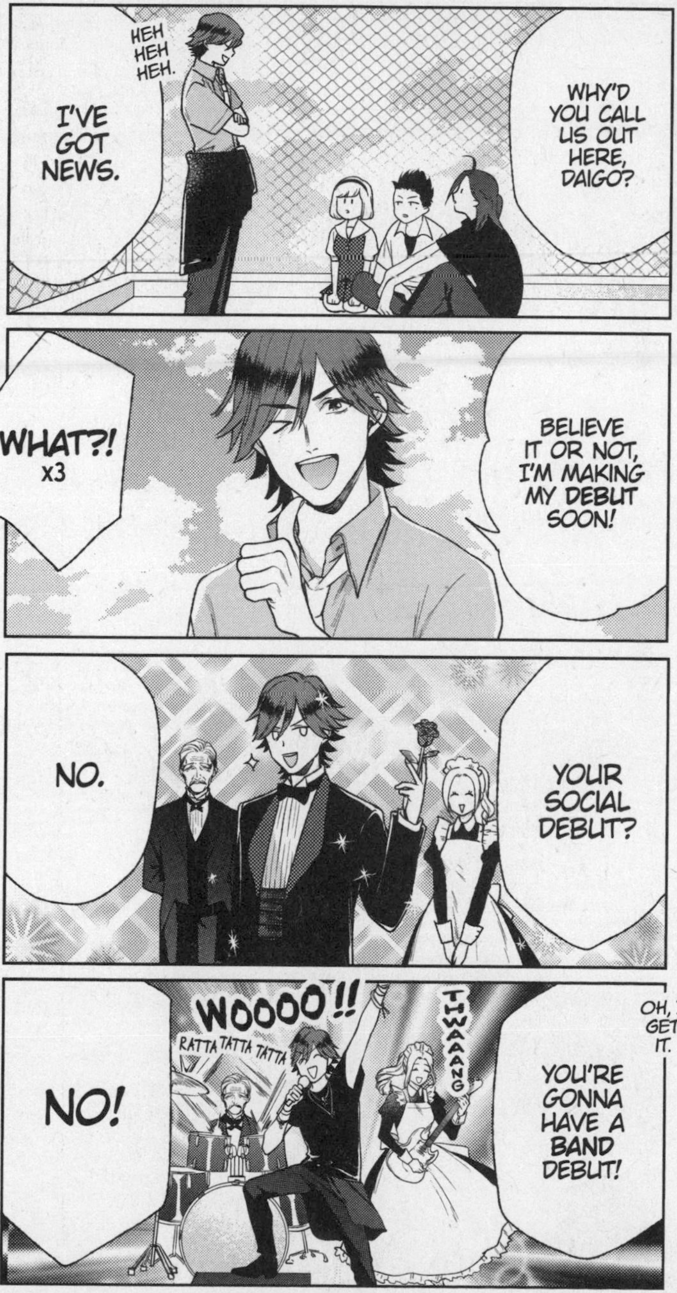
WHY'D YOU CALL US OUT HERE, DAIGO?
HEH HEH HEH.
I'VE GOT NEWS.
BELIEVE IT OR NOT, I'M MAKING MY DEBUT SOON!
WHAT?! x3
YOUR SOCIAL DEBUT?
NO.
OH, I GET IT.
YOU'RE GONNA HAVE A BAND DEBUT!
THWAAANG
WOOOO!!
RATTA TATTA TATTA
NO!

## MOVING UP TO THE MAJORS

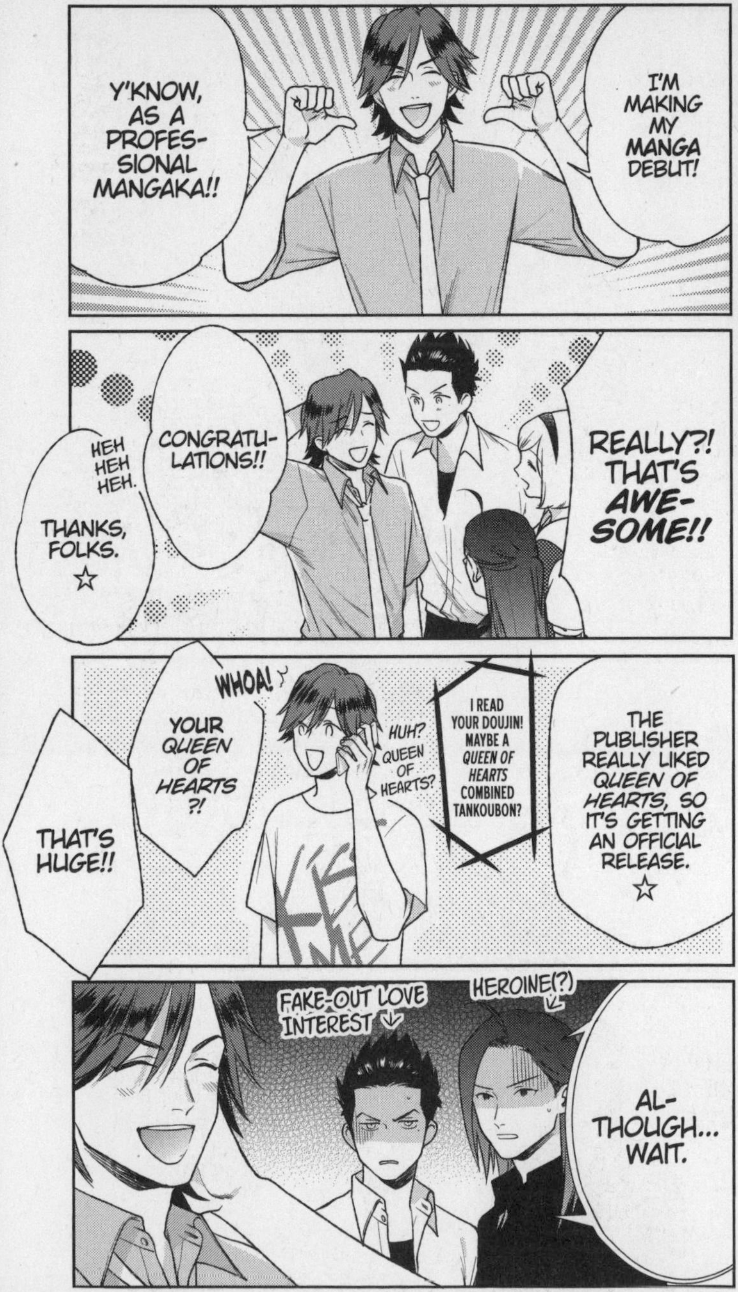
I'M MAKING MY MANGA DEBUT!
Y'KNOW, AS A PROFES-SIONAL MANGAKA!!
REALLY?! THAT'S *AWE-SOME!!*
CONGRATU-LATIONS!!
HEH HEH HEH.
THANKS, FOLKS. ☆
THE PUBLISHER REALLY LIKED *QUEEN OF HEARTS*, SO IT'S GETTING AN OFFICIAL RELEASE. ☆
I READ YOUR DOUJIN! MAYBE A *QUEEN OF HEARTS* COMBINED TANKOUBON?
HUH? *QUEEN OF HEARTS?*
WHOA!
YOUR *QUEEN OF HEARTS* ?!
THAT'S HUGE!!
AL-THOUGH... WAIT.
HEROINE(?)
FAKE-OUT LOVE INTEREST

## SPREADABILITY

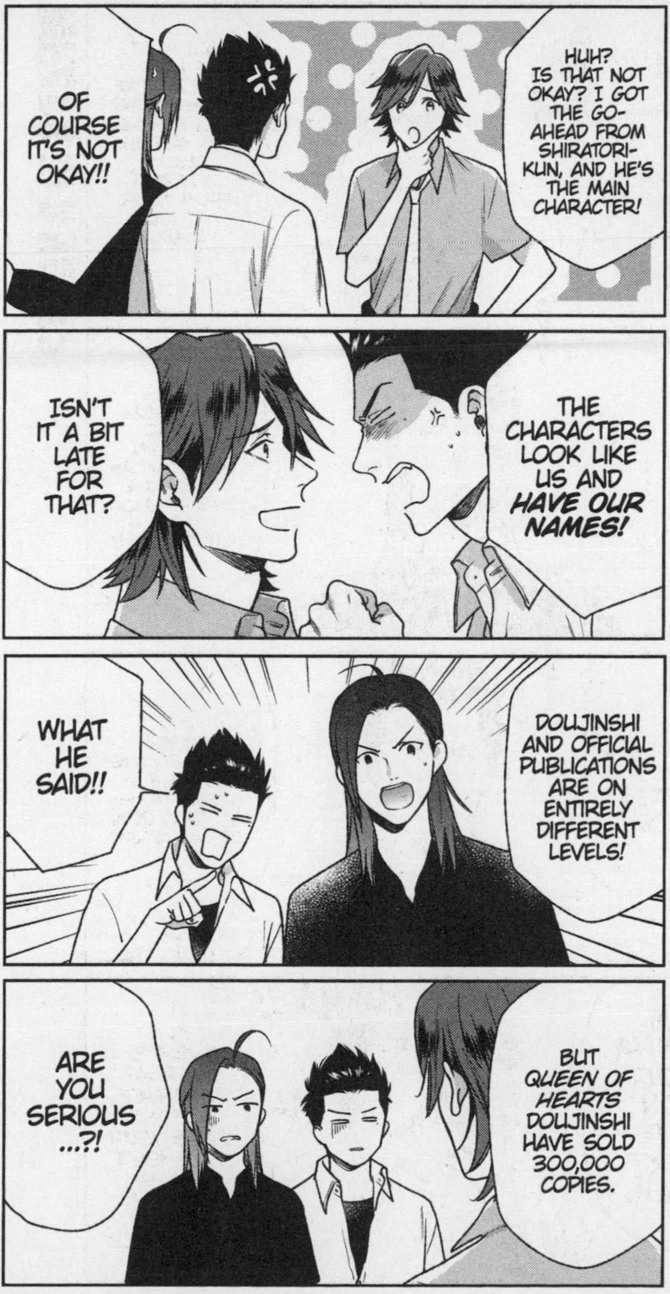
HUH? IS THAT NOT OKAY? I GOT THE GO-AHEAD FROM SHIRATORI-KUN, AND HE'S THE MAIN CHARACTER!
OF COURSE IT'S NOT OKAY!!
THE CHARACTERS LOOK LIKE US AND *HAVE OUR NAMES!*
ISN'T IT A BIT LATE FOR THAT?
DOUJINSHI AND OFFICIAL PUBLICATIONS ARE ON ENTIRELY DIFFERENT LEVELS!
WHAT HE SAID!!
BUT *QUEEN OF HEARTS* DOUJINSHI HAVE SOLD 300,000 COPIES.
ARE YOU SERIOUS ...?!

# WHAT'S IN A NAME?

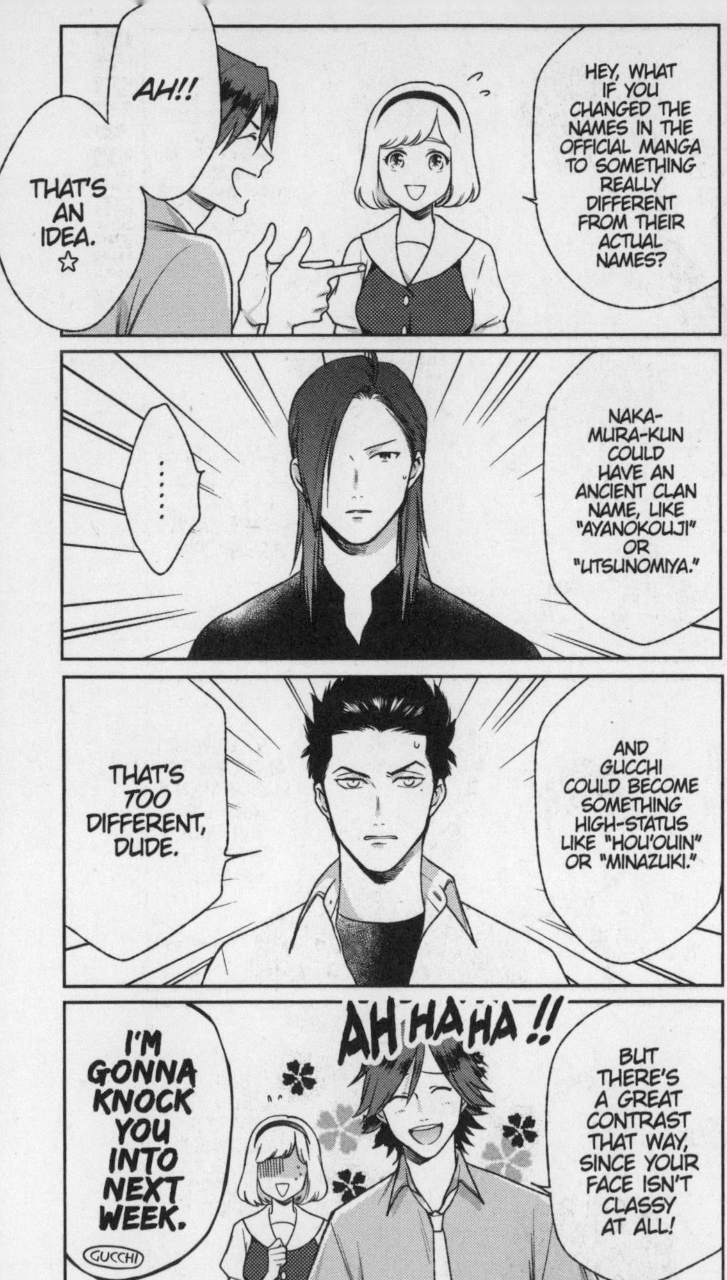

HEY, WHAT IF YOU CHANGED THE NAMES IN THE OFFICIAL MANGA TO SOMETHING REALLY DIFFERENT FROM THEIR ACTUAL NAMES?
AH!!
THAT'S AN IDEA. ☆
NAKA-MURA-KUN COULD HAVE AN ANCIENT CLAN NAME, LIKE "AYANOKOUJI" OR "UTSUNOMIYA."
......
AND GUCCHI COULD BECOME SOMETHING HIGH-STATUS LIKE "HOU'OUIN" OR "MINAZUKI."
THAT'S *TOO* DIFFERENT, DUDE.
AH HA HA!!
BUT THERE'S A GREAT CONTRAST THAT WAY, SINCE YOUR FACE ISN'T CLASSY AT ALL!
I'M GONNA KNOCK YOU INTO NEXT WEEK.
GUCCHI

# WHAT HE DOESN'T KNOW WON'T HURT HIM

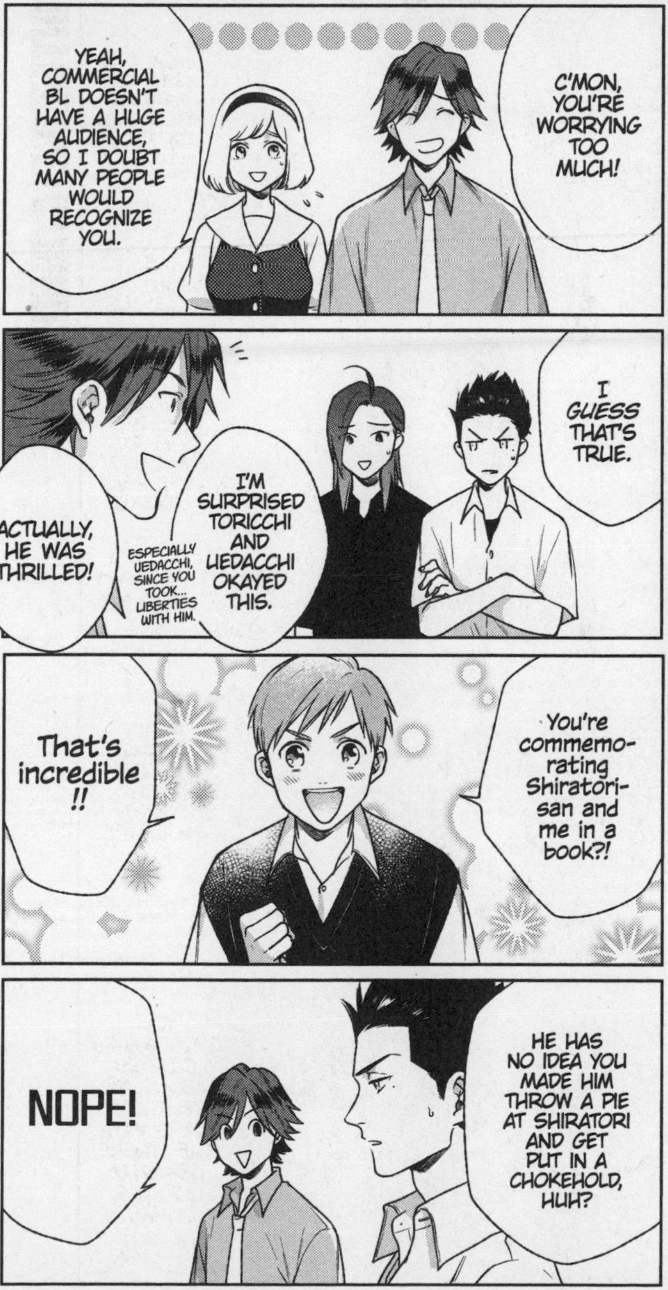
C'MON, YOU'RE WORRYING TOO MUCH!
YEAH, COMMERCIAL BL DOESN'T HAVE A HUGE AUDIENCE, SO I DOUBT MANY PEOPLE WOULD RECOGNIZE YOU.
I GUESS THAT'S TRUE.
I'M SURPRISED TORICCHI AND UEDACCHI OKAYED THIS.
ESPECIALLY UEDACCHI, SINCE YOU TOOK... LIBERTIES WITH HIM.
ACTUALLY, HE WAS THRILLED!
You're commemo-rating Shiratori-san and me in a book?!
That's incredible !!
HE HAS NO IDEA YOU MADE HIM THROW A PIE AT SHIRATORI AND GET PUT IN A CHOKEHOLD, HUH?
NOPE!

# INTERPRETATIONING

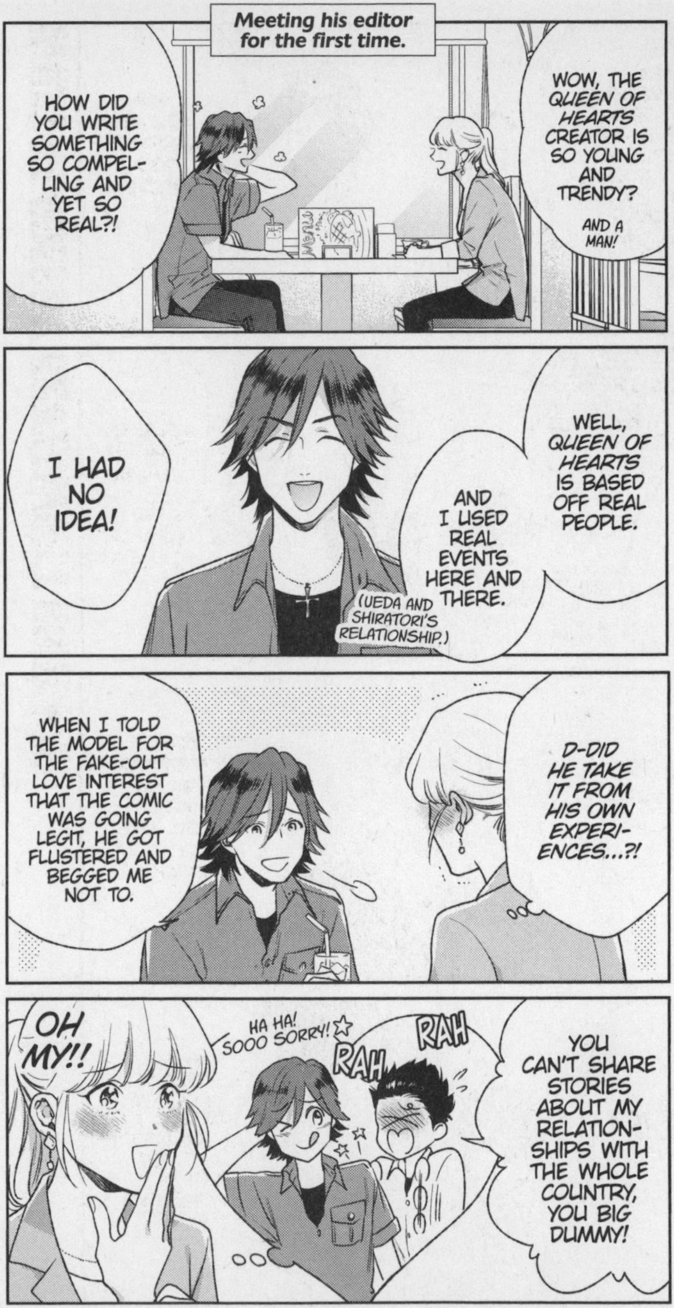
Meeting his editor for the first time.
WOW, THE QUEEN OF HEARTS CREATOR IS SO YOUNG AND TRENDY?
AND A MAN!
HOW DID YOU WRITE SOMETHING SO COMPEL-LING AND YET SO REAL?!
WELL, QUEEN OF HEARTS IS BASED OFF REAL PEOPLE.
AND I USED REAL EVENTS HERE AND THERE.
(UEDA AND SHIRATORI'S RELATIONSHIP.)
I HAD NO IDEA!
D-DID HE TAKE IT FROM HIS OWN EXPERI-ENCES...?!
WHEN I TOLD THE MODEL FOR THE FAKE-OUT LOVE INTEREST THAT THE COMIC WAS GOING LEGIT, HE GOT FLUSTERED AND BEGGED ME NOT TO.
YOU CAN'T SHARE STORIES ABOUT MY RELATION-SHIPS WITH THE WHOLE COUNTRY, YOU BIG DUMMY!
RAH
RAH
HA HA! SOOO SORRY! ☆
OH MY!!

# HIS ANSWER TO EVERYTHING

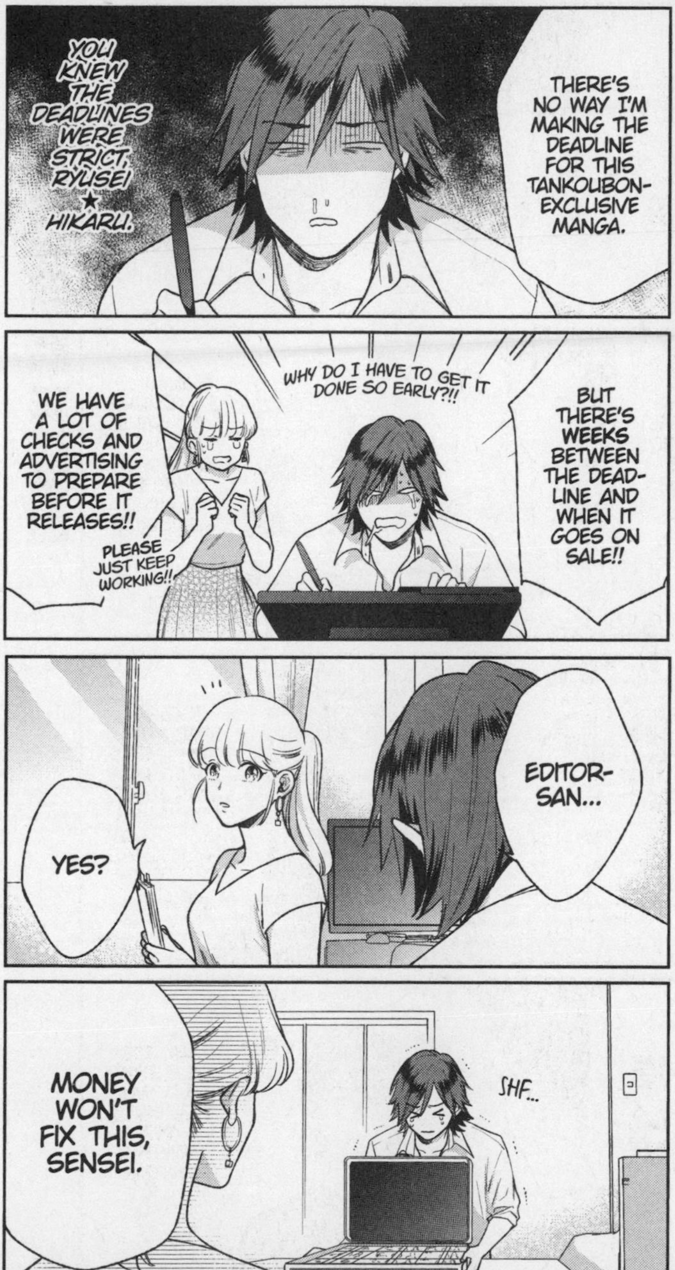

THERE'S NO WAY I'M MAKING THE DEADLINE FOR THIS TANKOUBON-EXCLUSIVE MANGA.
YOU KNEW THE DEADLINES WERE STRICT, RYUSEI★HIKARU.
BUT THERE'S WEEKS BETWEEN THE DEAD-LINE AND WHEN IT GOES ON SALE!!
WHY DO I HAVE TO GET IT DONE SO EARLY?!!
WE HAVE A LOT OF CHECKS AND ADVERTISING TO PREPARE BEFORE IT RELEASES!!
PLEASE JUST KEEP WORKING!!
EDITOR-SAN...
YES?
SHF...
MONEY WON'T FIX THIS, SENSEI.

# THINGS NEVER GO AS PLANNED

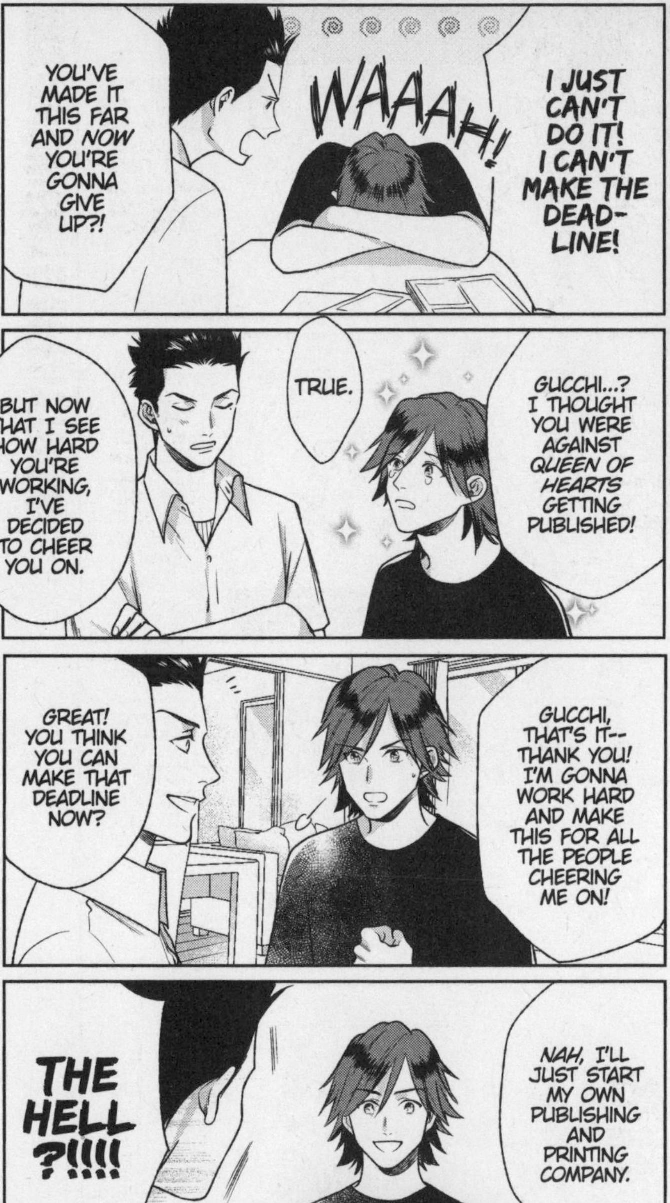
I JUST CAN'T DO IT! I CAN'T MAKE THE DEADLINE!
WAAAAH!
YOU'VE MADE IT THIS FAR AND *NOW* YOU'RE GONNA GIVE UP?!
GUCCHI...? I THOUGHT YOU WERE AGAINST *QUEEN OF HEARTS* GETTING PUBLISHED!
TRUE.
BUT NOW THAT I SEE HOW HARD YOU'RE WORKING, I'VE DECIDED TO CHEER YOU ON.
GUCCHI, THAT'S IT--THANK YOU! I'M GONNA WORK HARD AND MAKE THIS FOR ALL THE PEOPLE CHEERING ME ON!
GREAT! YOU THINK YOU CAN MAKE THAT DEADLINE NOW?
*NAH,* I'LL JUST START MY OWN PUBLISHING AND PRINTING COMPANY.
THE HELL?!!!!

# ULTERIOR MOTIVES

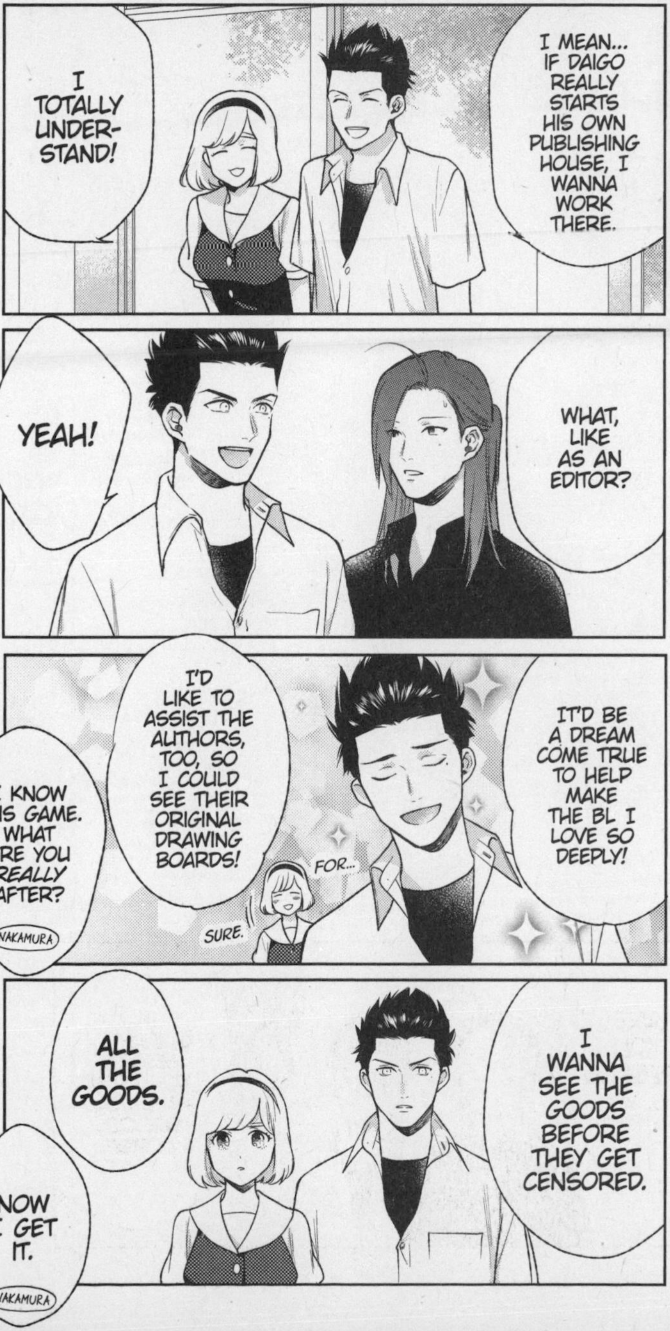
I MEAN... IF DAIGO REALLY STARTS HIS OWN PUBLISHING HOUSE, I WANNA WORK THERE.
I TOTALLY UNDER-STAND!
WHAT, LIKE AS AN EDITOR?
YEAH!
IT'D BE A DREAM COME TRUE TO HELP MAKE THE BL I LOVE SO DEEPLY!
FOR...
I'D LIKE TO ASSIST THE AUTHORS, TOO, SO I COULD SEE THEIR ORIGINAL DRAWING BOARDS!
SURE.
I KNOW THIS GAME. WHAT ARE YOU *REALLY* AFTER?
NAKAMURA
I WANNA SEE THE GOODS BEFORE THEY GET CENSORED.
ALL THE GOODS.
NOW I GET IT.
NAKAMURA

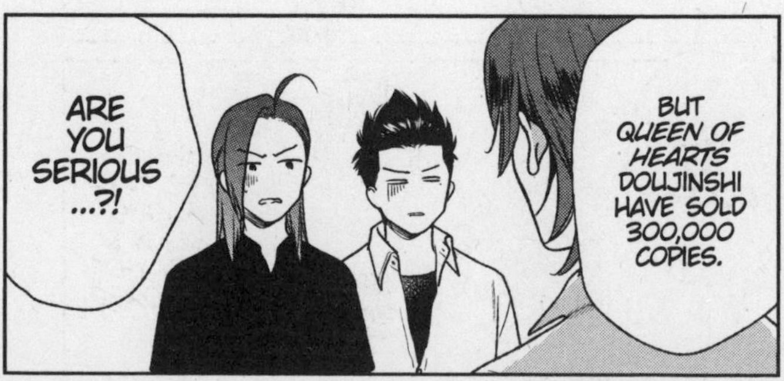
BUT QUEEN OF HEARTS DOUJINSHI HAVE SOLD 300,000 COPIES.
ARE YOU SERIOUS ...?!

K

F S

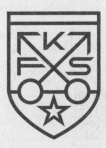

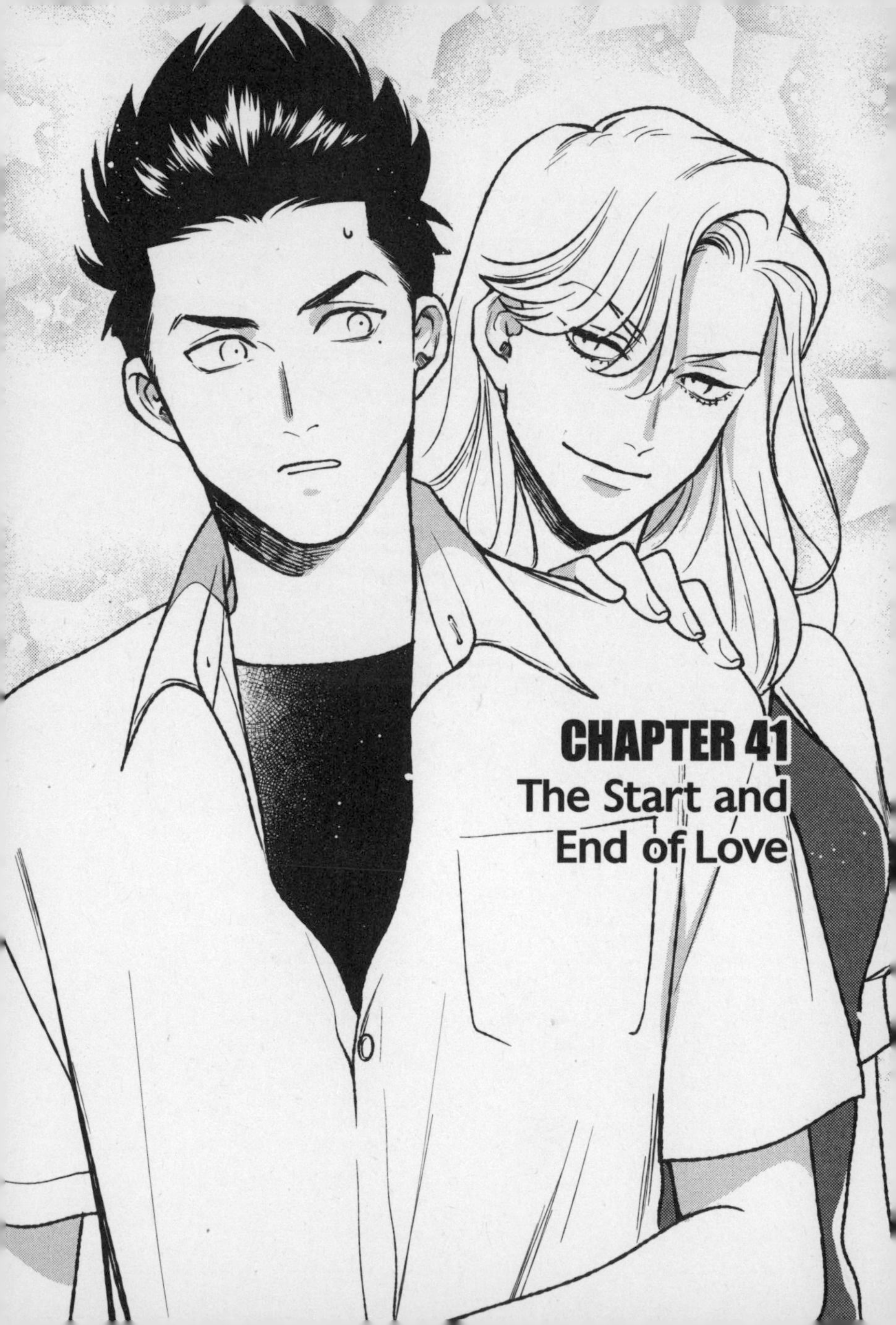
CHAPTER 41
The Start and End of Love

## FEAR NOT

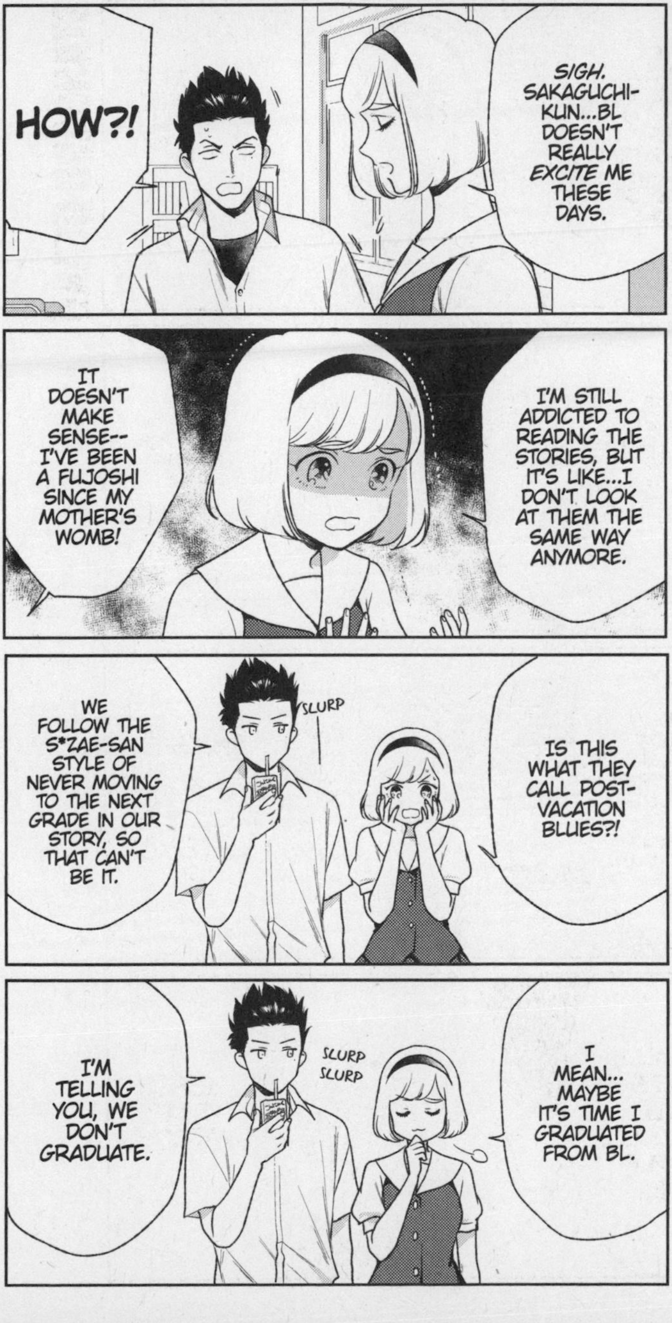
SIGH. SAKAGUCHI-KUN...BL DOESN'T REALLY *EXCITE* ME THESE DAYS.
HOW?!
I'M STILL ADDICTED TO READING THE STORIES, BUT IT'S LIKE...I DON'T LOOK AT THEM THE SAME WAY ANYMORE.
IT DOESN'T MAKE SENSE--I'VE BEEN A FUJOSHI SINCE MY MOTHER'S WOMB!
IS THIS WHAT THEY CALL POST-VACATION BLUES?!
SLURP
WE FOLLOW THE S*ZAE-SAN STYLE OF NEVER MOVING TO THE NEXT GRADE IN OUR STORY, SO THAT CAN'T BE IT.
I MEAN... MAYBE IT'S TIME I GRADUATED FROM BL.
SLURP SLURP
I'M TELLING YOU, WE DON'T GRADUATE.

STANDARD OTAKU

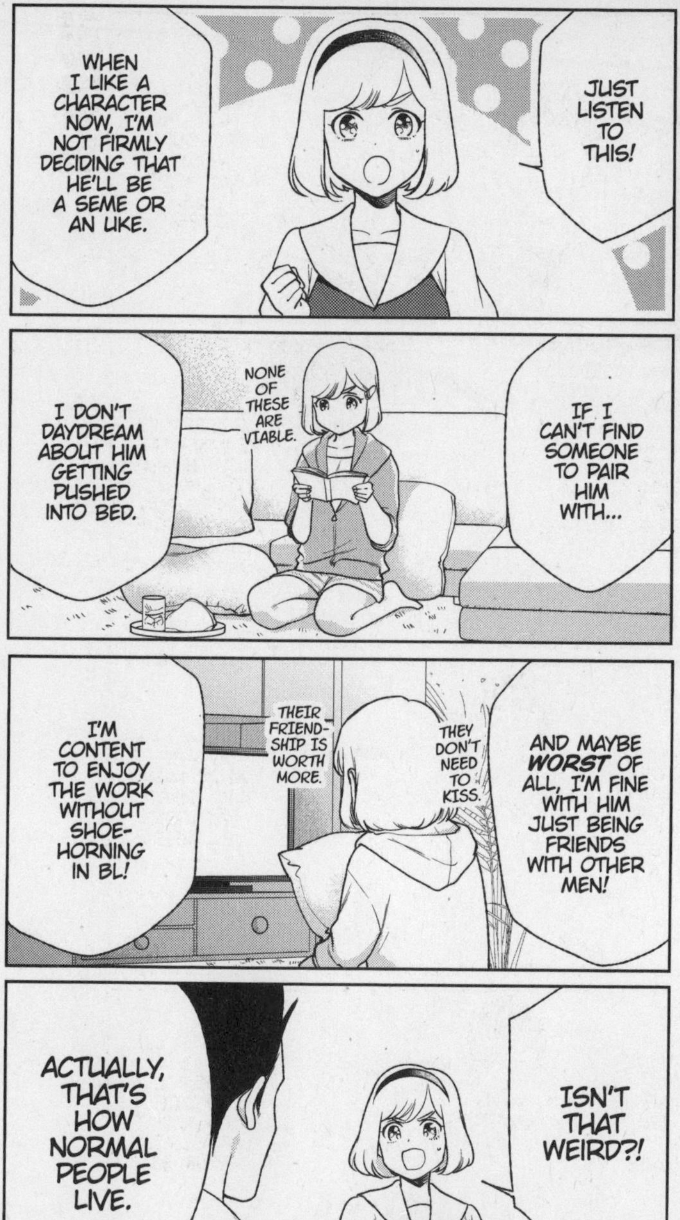
JUST LISTEN TO THIS!
WHEN I LIKE A CHARACTER NOW, I'M NOT FIRMLY DECIDING THAT HE'LL BE A SEME OR AN UKE.
IF I CAN'T FIND SOMEONE TO PAIR HIM WITH...
NONE OF THESE ARE VIABLE.
I DON'T DAYDREAM ABOUT HIM GETTING PUSHED INTO BED.
AND MAYBE WORST OF ALL, I'M FINE WITH HIM JUST BEING FRIENDS WITH OTHER MEN!
THEY DON'T NEED TO KISS.
THEIR FRIENDSHIP IS WORTH MORE.
I'M CONTENT TO ENJOY THE WORK WITHOUT SHOE-HORNING IN BL!
ISN'T THAT WEIRD?!
ACTUALLY, THAT'S HOW NORMAL PEOPLE LIVE.

# THE STAR GUY

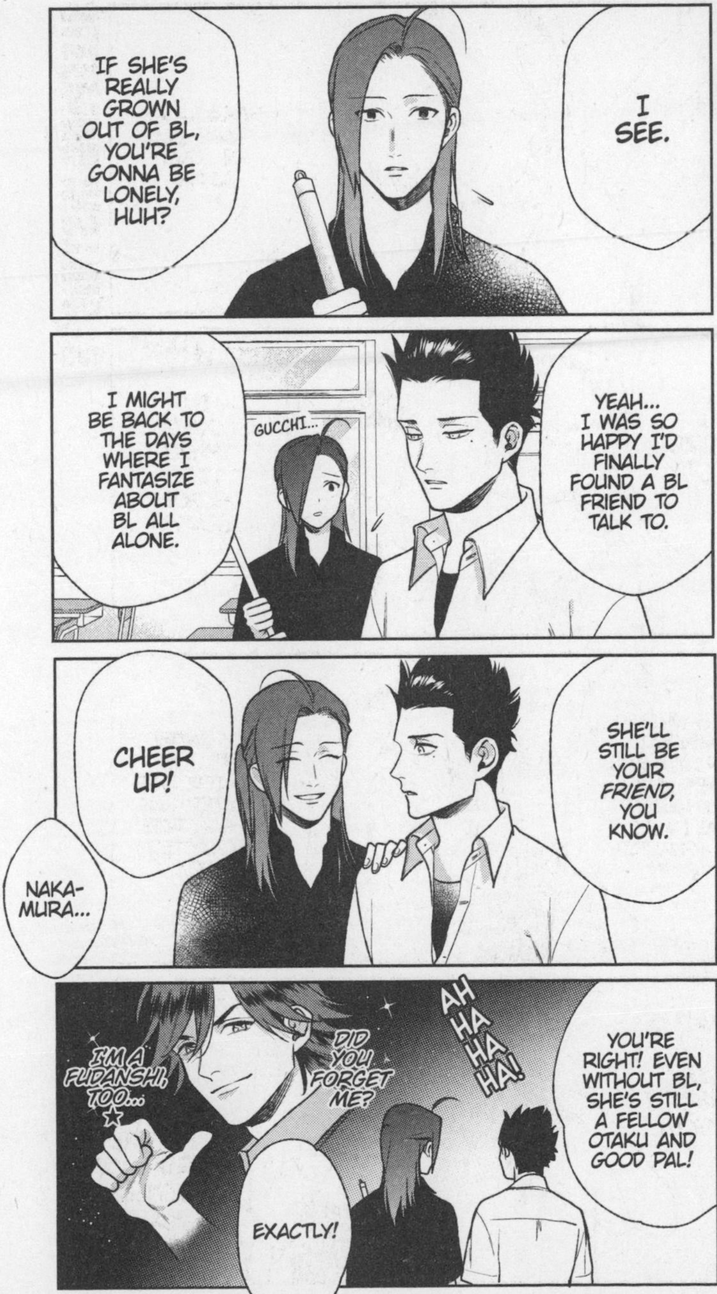
I SEE.
IF SHE'S REALLY GROWN OUT OF BL, YOU'RE GONNA BE LONELY, HUH?
YEAH... I WAS SO HAPPY I'D FINALLY FOUND A BL FRIEND TO TALK TO.
GUCCHI...
I MIGHT BE BACK TO THE DAYS WHERE I FANTASIZE ABOUT BL ALL ALONE.
SHE'LL STILL BE YOUR *FRIEND*, YOU KNOW.
CHEER UP!
NAKA-MURA...
YOU'RE RIGHT! EVEN WITHOUT BL, SHE'S STILL A FELLOW OTAKU AND GOOD PAL!
AH HA HA HA HA!
DID YOU FORGET ME?
I'M A FUDANSHI, TOO...☆
EXACTLY!

## SLEEPING INSTINCTS

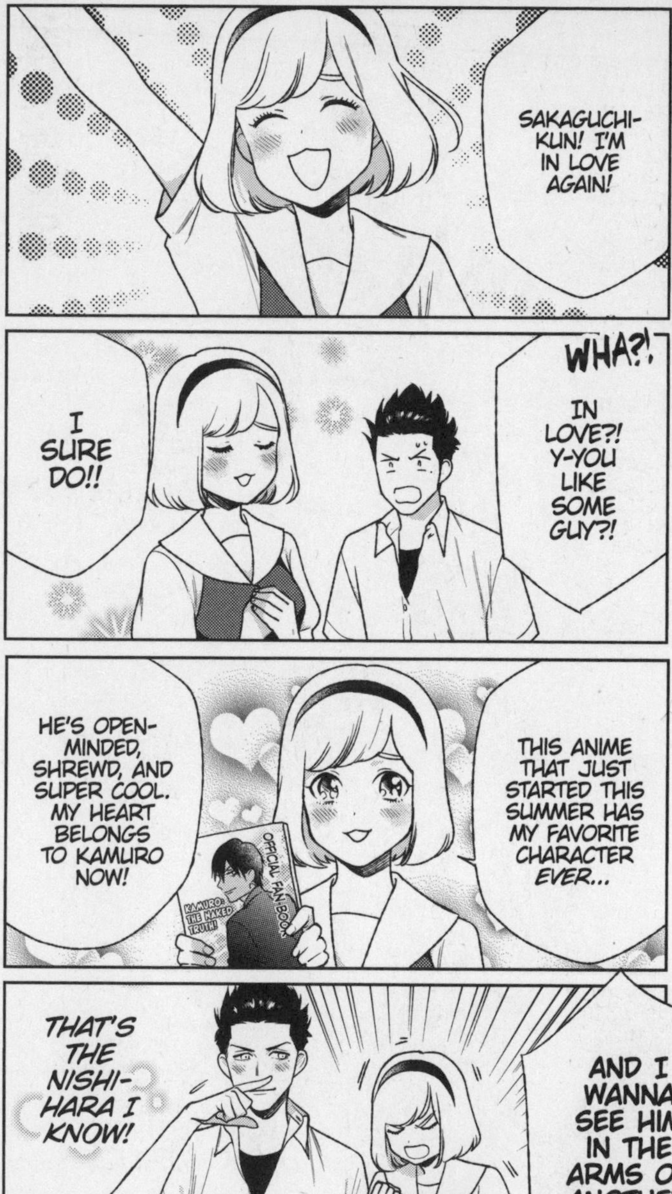
SAKAGUCHI-KUN! I'M IN LOVE AGAIN!
WHA?!
IN LOVE?! Y-YOU LIKE SOME GUY?!
I SURE DO!!
THIS ANIME THAT JUST STARTED THIS SUMMER HAS MY FAVORITE CHARACTER EVER...
HE'S OPEN-MINDED, SHREWD, AND SUPER COOL. MY HEART BELONGS TO KAMURO NOW!
OFFICIAL FAN BOOK
KAMURO: THE NAKED TRUTH!
AND I WANNA SEE HIM IN THE ARMS OF ANOTHER MAN!!
THAT'S THE NISHIHARA I KNOW!

# A RAY OF HOPE

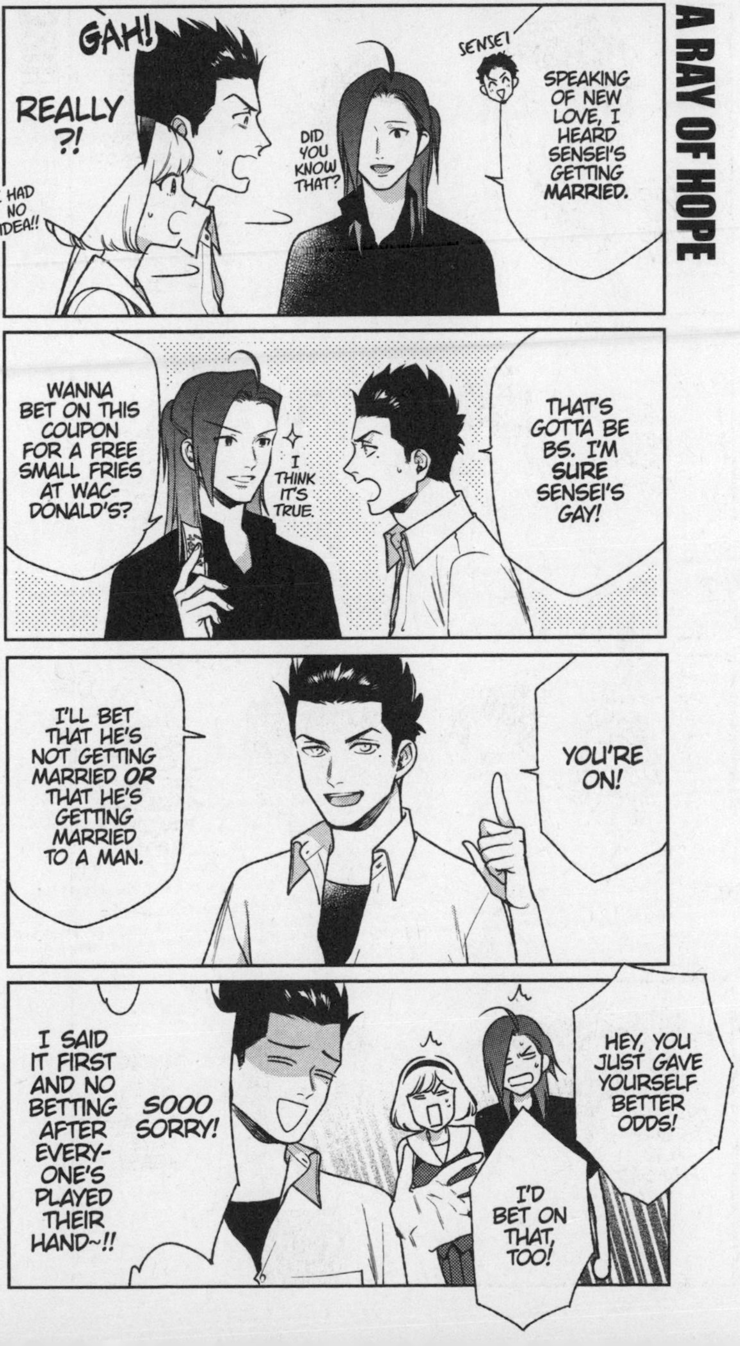
SENSEI
SPEAKING OF NEW LOVE, I HEARD SENSEI'S GETTING MARRIED.
DID YOU KNOW THAT?
GAH!
REALLY ?!
I HAD NO IDEA!!
THAT'S GOTTA BE BS. I'M SURE SENSEI'S GAY!
I THINK IT'S TRUE.
WANNA BET ON THIS COUPON FOR A FREE SMALL FRIES AT WAC-DONALD'S?
YOU'RE ON!
I'LL BET THAT HE'S NOT GETTING MARRIED *OR* THAT HE'S GETTING MARRIED TO A MAN.
HEY, YOU JUST GAVE YOURSELF BETTER ODDS!
I'D BET ON THAT, TOO!
SOOO SORRY!
I SAID IT FIRST AND NO BETTING AFTER EVERYONE'S PLAYED THEIR HAND~!!

320円

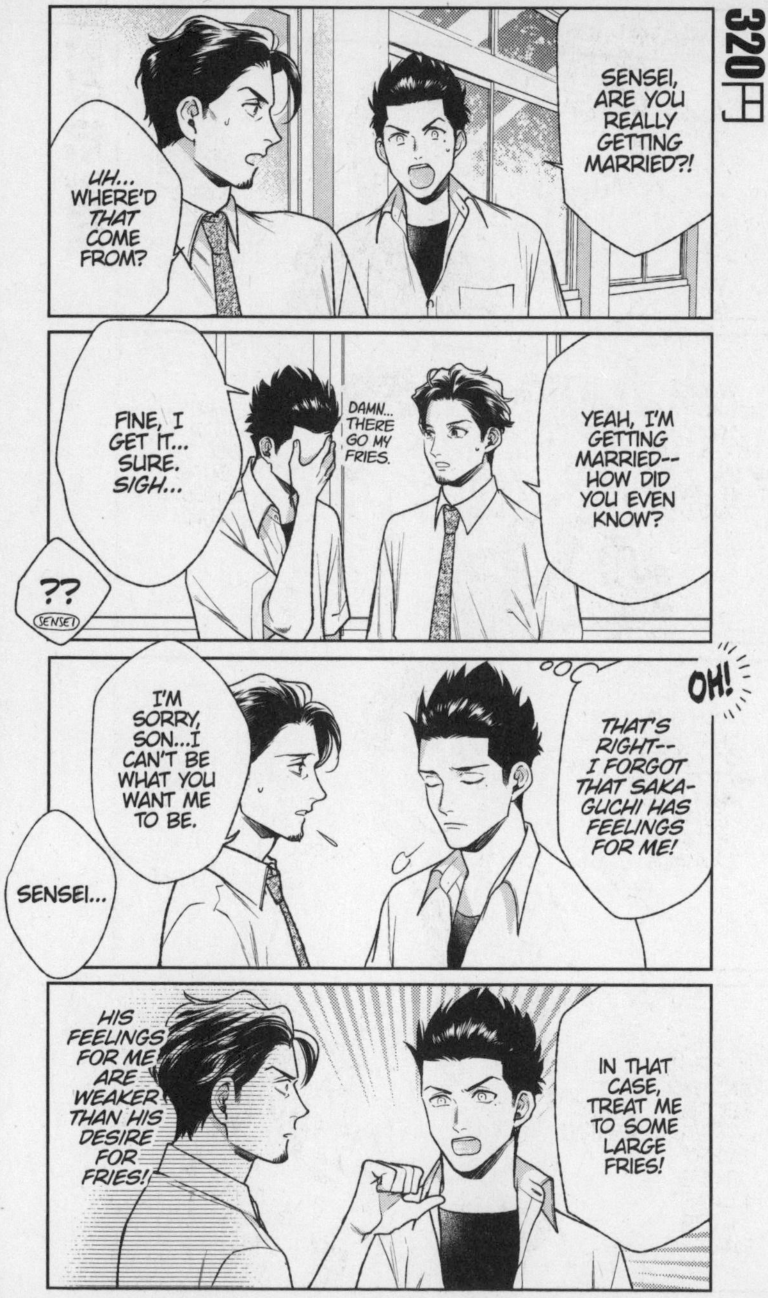
SENSEI, ARE YOU REALLY GETTING MARRIED?!
UH... WHERE'D THAT COME FROM?
YEAH, I'M GETTING MARRIED-- HOW DID YOU EVEN KNOW?
DAMN... THERE GO MY FRIES.
FINE, I GET IT... SURE. SIGH...
??
SENSEI
OH!
THAT'S RIGHT-- I FORGOT THAT SAKAGUCHI HAS FEELINGS FOR ME!
I'M SORRY, SON...I CAN'T BE WHAT YOU WANT ME TO BE.
SENSEI...
IN THAT CASE, TREAT ME TO SOME LARGE FRIES!
HIS FEELINGS FOR ME ARE WEAKER THAN HIS DESIRE FOR FRIES!

# POPULAR GUY

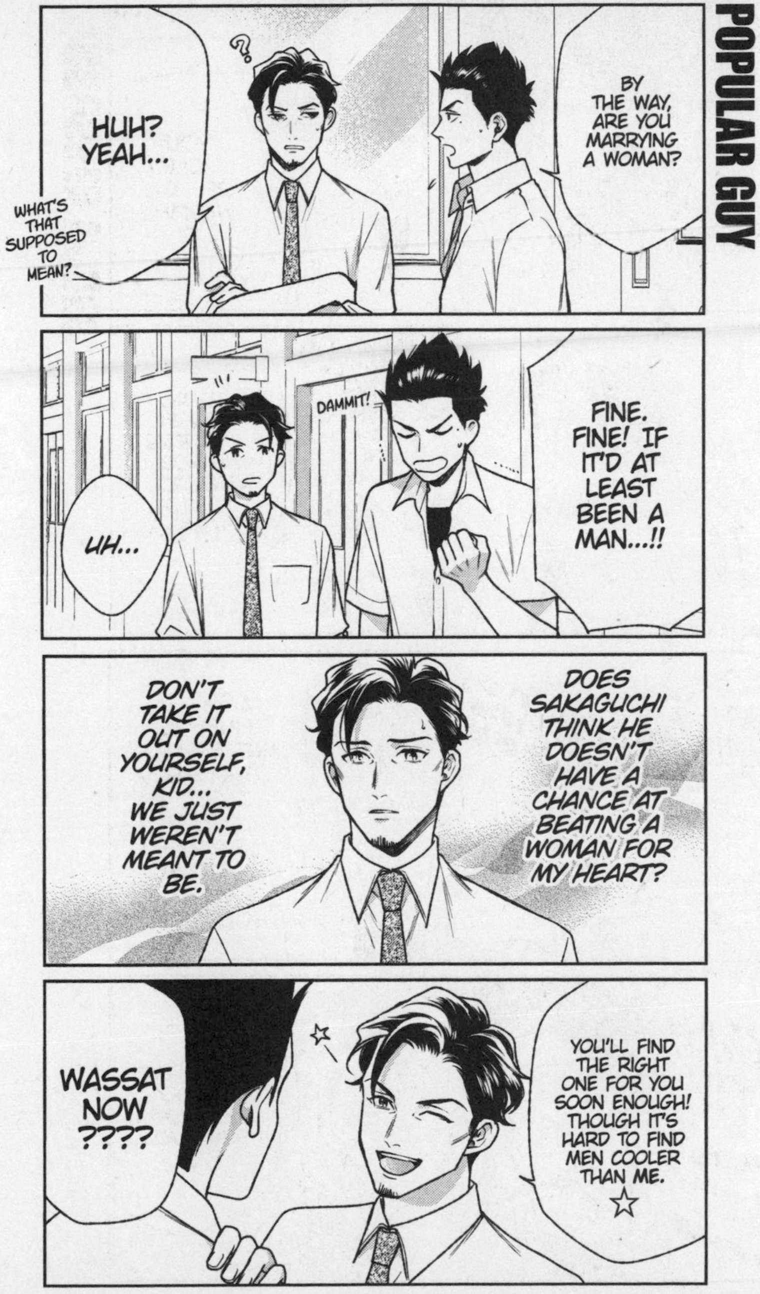
BY THE WAY, ARE YOU MARRYING A WOMAN?
HUH? YEAH...
WHAT'S THAT SUPPOSED TO MEAN?
FINE. FINE! IF IT'D AT LEAST BEEN A MAN...!!
DAMMIT!
UH...
DOES SAKAGUCHI THINK HE DOESN'T HAVE A CHANCE AT BEATING A WOMAN FOR MY HEART?
DON'T TAKE IT OUT ON YOURSELF, KID... WE JUST WEREN'T MEANT TO BE.
YOU'LL FIND THE RIGHT ONE FOR YOU SOON ENOUGH! THOUGH IT'S HARD TO FIND MEN COOLER THAN ME. ☆
WASSAT NOW ????

# CROSSED WIRES

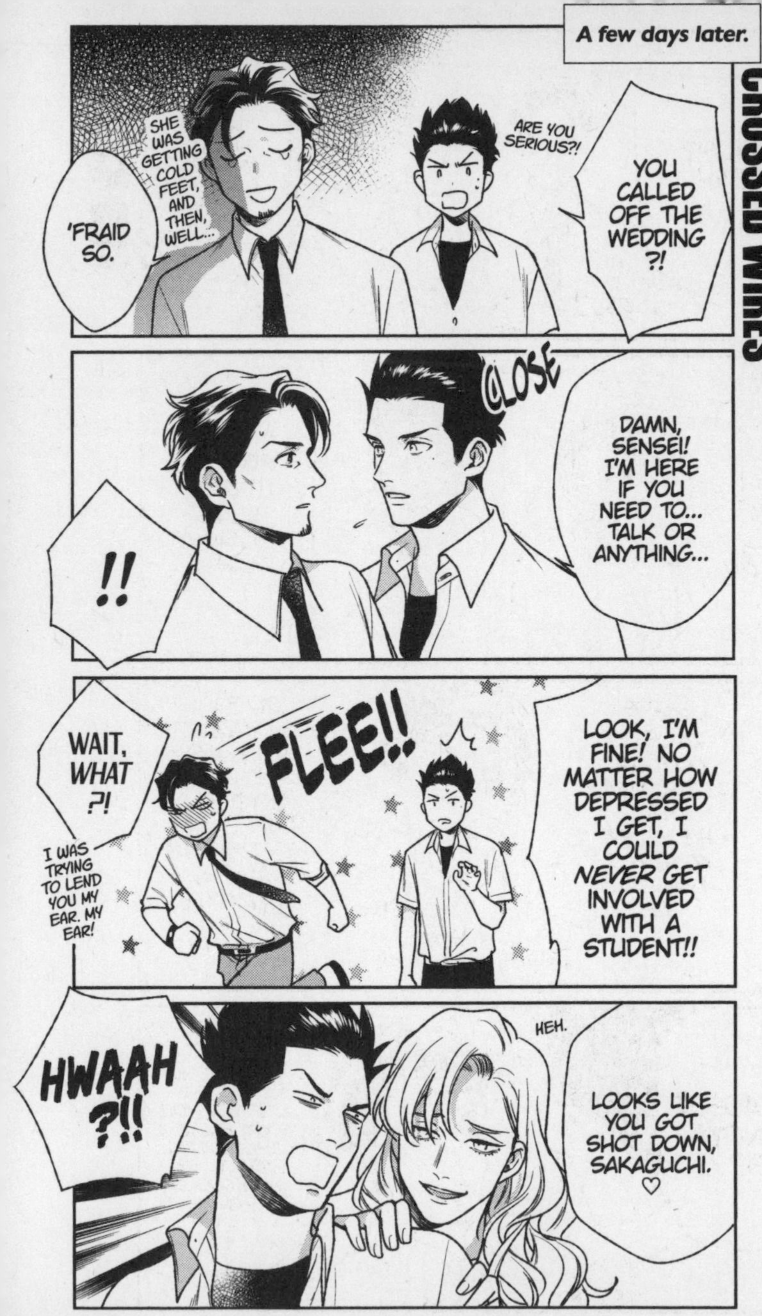
A few days later.
YOU CALLED OFF THE WEDDING?!
ARE YOU SERIOUS?!
SHE WAS GETTING COLD FEET, AND THEN, WELL...
'FRAID SO.
DAMN, SENSEI! I'M HERE IF YOU NEED TO... TALK OR ANYTHING...
CLOSE
!!
LOOK, I'M FINE! NO MATTER HOW DEPRESSED I GET, I COULD *NEVER* GET INVOLVED WITH A STUDENT!!
FLEE!!
WAIT, WHAT?!
I WAS TRYING TO LEND YOU MY EAR. MY EAR!
LOOKS LIKE YOU GOT SHOT DOWN, SAKAGUCHI. ♡
HEH.
HWAAH?!!

## I TAKE IT BACK

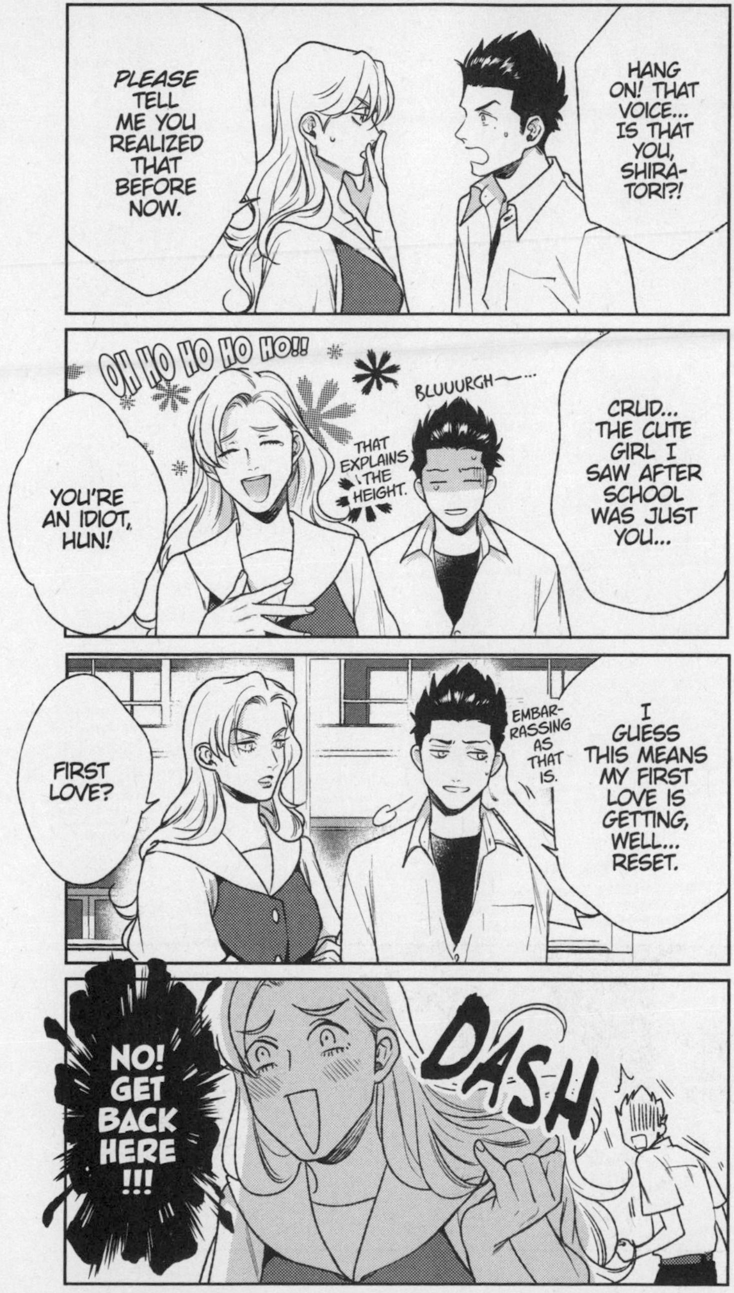
HANG ON! THAT VOICE... IS THAT YOU, SHIRATORI?!
PLEASE TELL ME YOU REALIZED THAT BEFORE NOW.
CRUD... THE CUTE GIRL I SAW AFTER SCHOOL WAS JUST YOU...
BLUUURGH~...
OH HO HO HO HO!!
THAT EXPLAINS THE HEIGHT.
YOU'RE AN IDIOT, HUN!
I GUESS THIS MEANS MY FIRST LOVE IS GETTING, WELL... RESET.
EMBARRASSING AS THAT IS.
FIRST LOVE?
DASH
NO! GET BACK HERE!!!

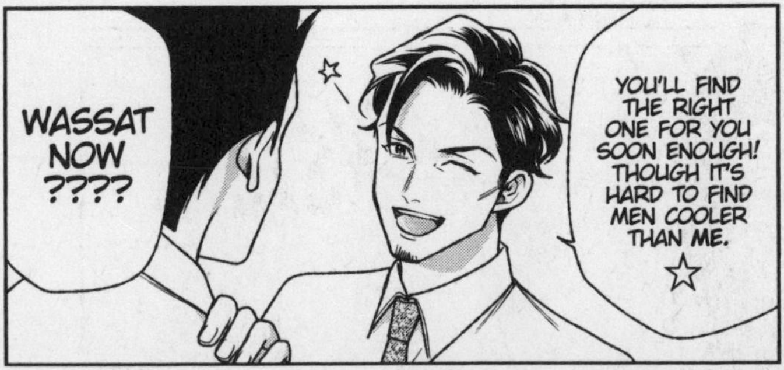
YOU'LL FIND THE RIGHT ONE FOR YOU SOON ENOUGH! THOUGH IT'S HARD TO FIND MEN COOLER THAN ME. ☆
WASSAT NOW ????

KFS

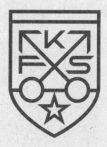

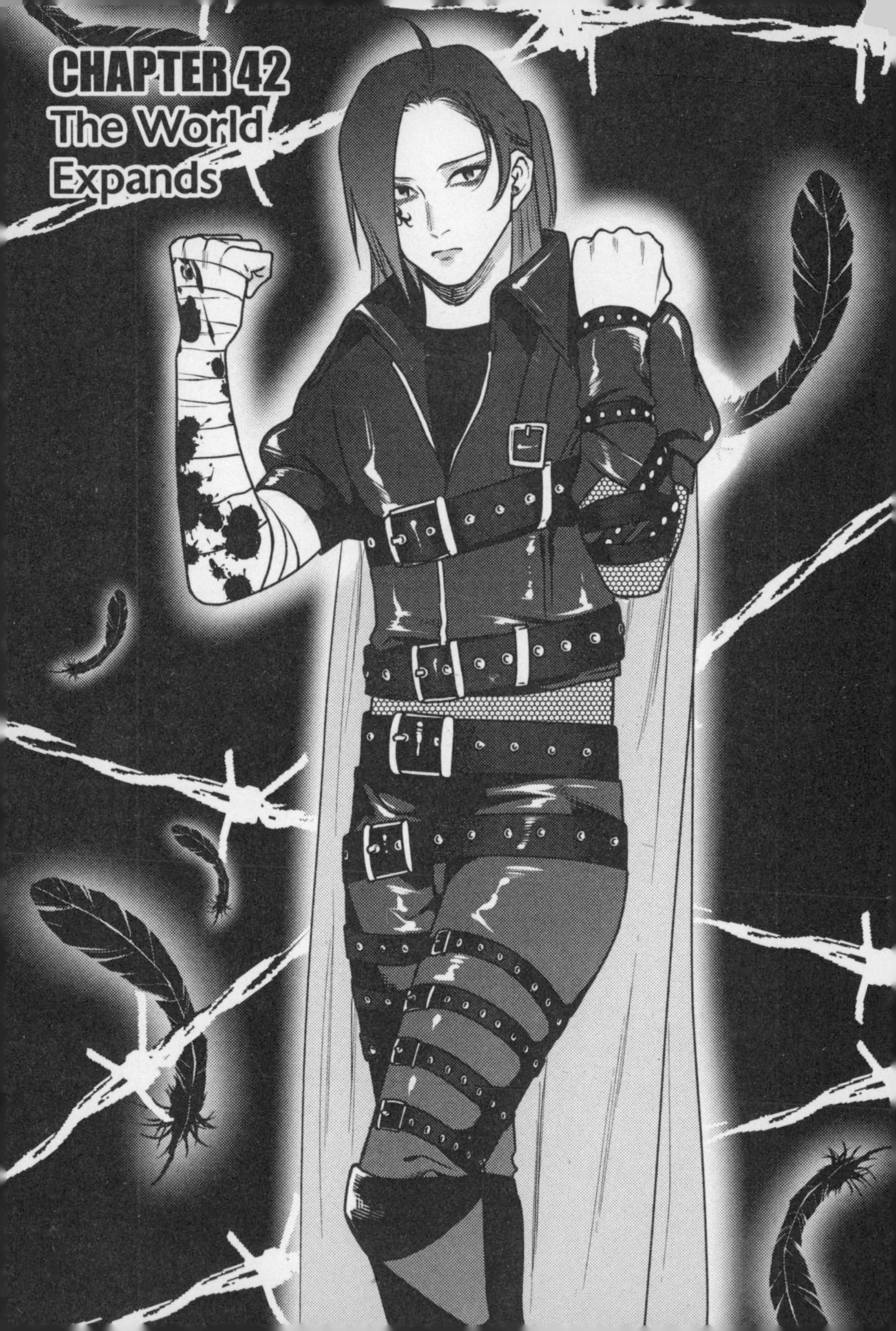
CHAPTER 42
The World Expands

I STARTED A BAND

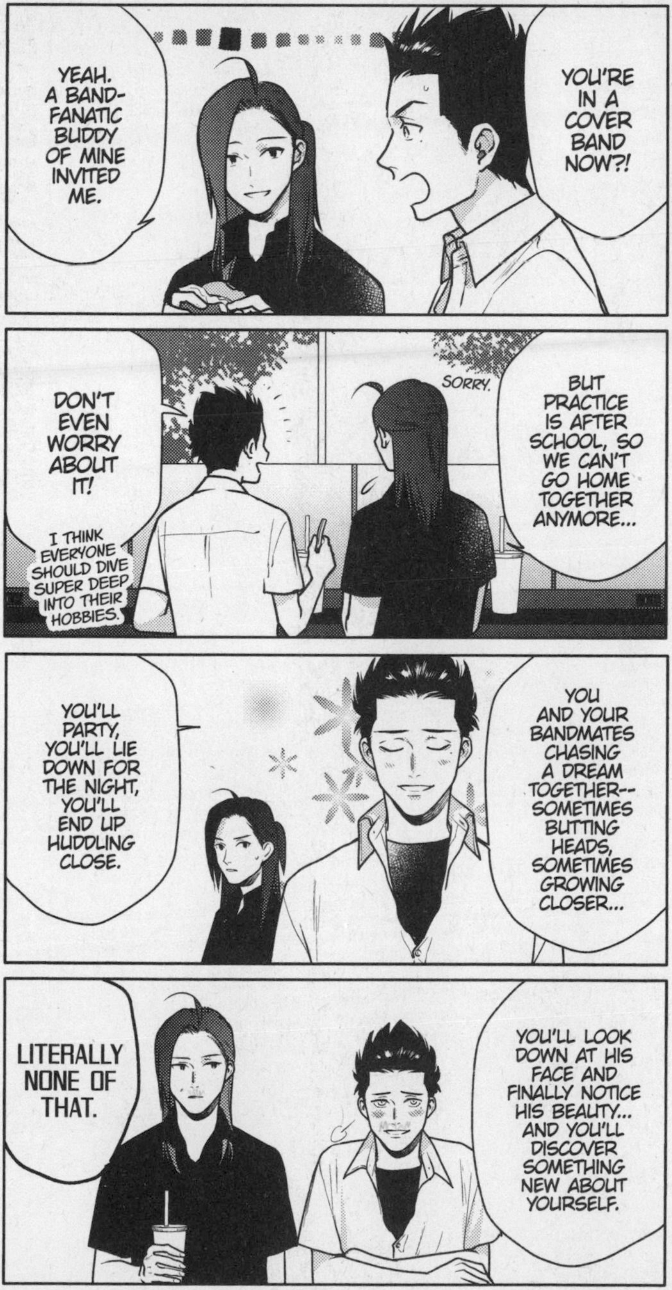
YOU'RE IN A COVER BAND NOW?!
YEAH. A BAND-FANATIC BUDDY OF MINE INVITED ME.
BUT PRACTICE IS AFTER SCHOOL, SO WE CAN'T GO HOME TOGETHER ANYMORE...
SORRY.
DON'T EVEN WORRY ABOUT IT!
I THINK EVERYONE SHOULD DIVE SUPER DEEP INTO THEIR HOBBIES.
YOU AND YOUR BANDMATES CHASING A DREAM TOGETHER--SOMETIMES BUTTING HEADS, SOMETIMES GROWING CLOSER...
YOU'LL PARTY, YOU'LL LIE DOWN FOR THE NIGHT, YOU'LL END UP HUDDLING CLOSE.
YOU'LL LOOK DOWN AT HIS FACE AND FINALLY NOTICE HIS BEAUTY... AND YOU'LL DISCOVER SOMETHING NEW ABOUT YOURSELF.
LITERALLY NONE OF THAT.

Meeting face to face.

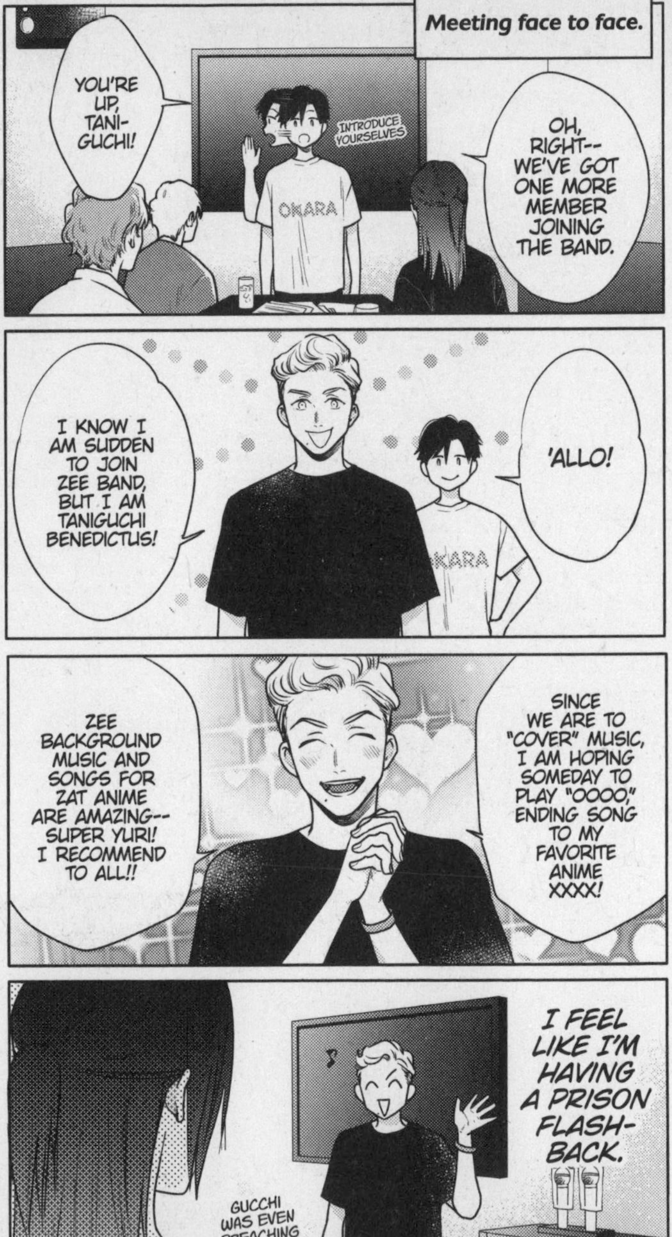
OH, RIGHT-- WE'VE GOT ONE MORE MEMBER JOINING THE BAND.
INTRODUCE YOURSELVES
YOU'RE UP, TANI-GUCHI!
'ALLO!
I KNOW I AM SUDDEN TO JOIN ZEE BAND, BUT I AM TANIGUCHI BENEDICTUS!
SINCE WE ARE TO "COVER" MUSIC, I AM HOPING SOMEDAY TO PLAY "OOOO," ENDING SONG TO MY FAVORITE ANIME XXXX!
ZEE BACKGROUND MUSIC AND SONGS FOR ZAT ANIME ARE AMAZING-- SUPER YURI! I RECOMMEND TO ALL!!
I FEEL LIKE I'M HAVING A PRISON FLASH-BACK.
GUCCHI WAS EVEN PREACHING ABOUT YURI, TOO...

## SECONDHAND INFO

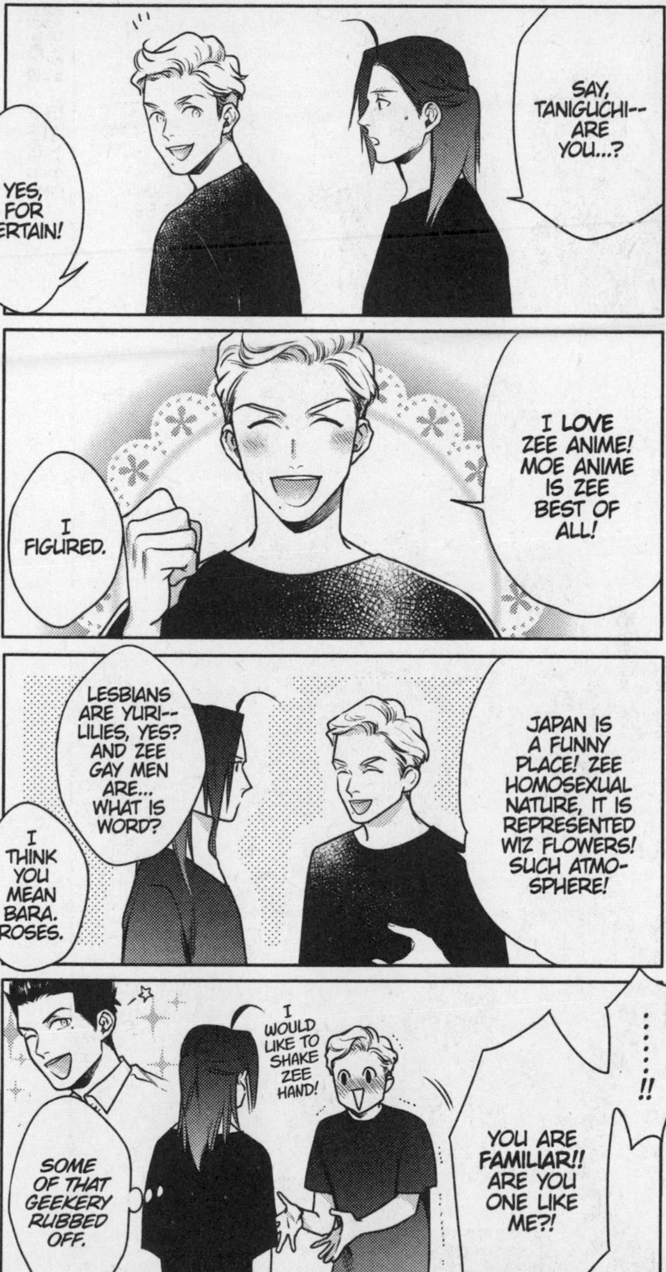
SAY, TANIGUCHI-- ARE YOU...?
YES, FOR CERTAIN!
I LOVE ZEE ANIME! MOE ANIME IS ZEE BEST OF ALL!
I FIGURED.
JAPAN IS A FUNNY PLACE! ZEE HOMOSEXUAL NATURE, IT IS REPRESENTED WIZ FLOWERS! SUCH ATMO-SPHERE!
LESBIANS ARE YURI-- LILIES, YES? AND ZEE GAY MEN ARE... WHAT IS WORD?
I THINK YOU MEAN BARA. ROSES.
......!!
YOU ARE FAMILIAR!! ARE YOU ONE LIKE ME?!
I WOULD LIKE TO SHAKE ZEE HAND!
SOME OF THAT GEEKERY RUBBED OFF.

JUST SMILE

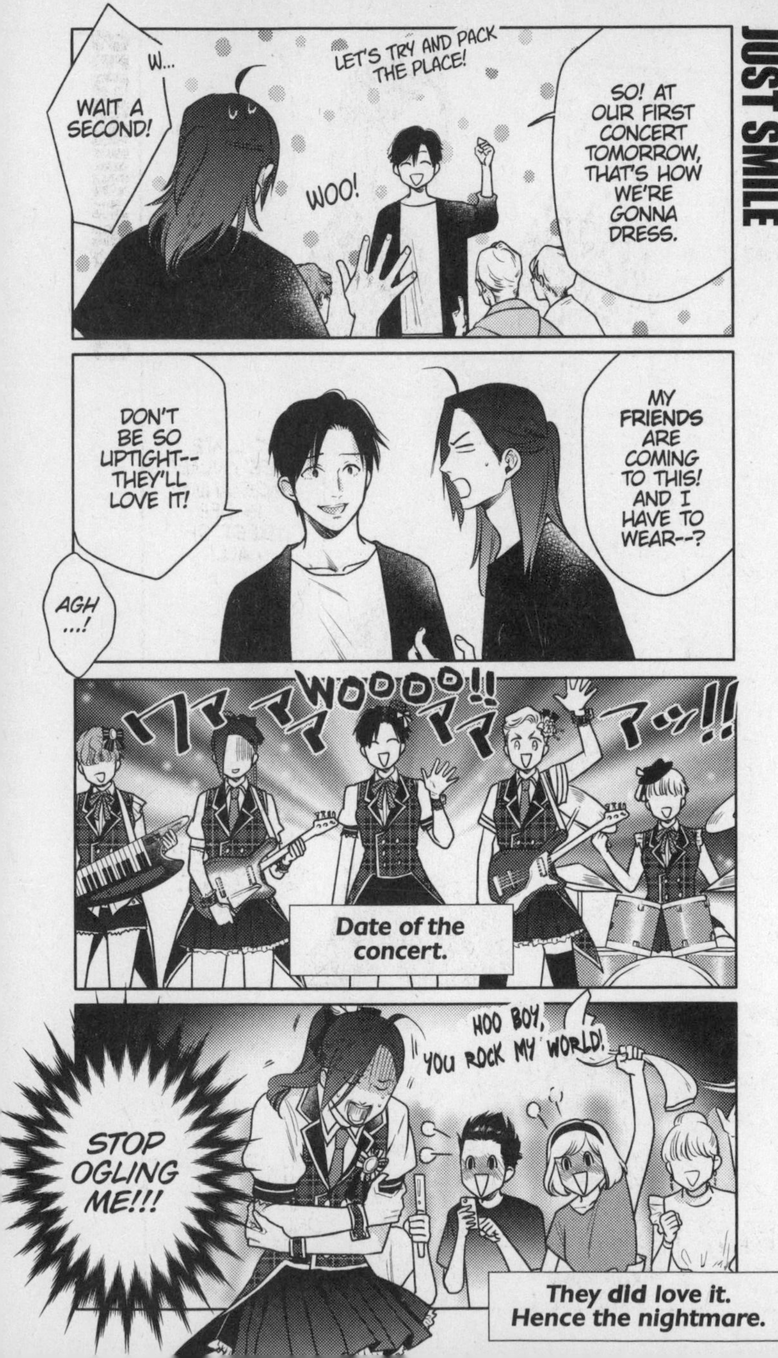
SO! AT OUR FIRST CONCERT TOMORROW, THAT'S HOW WE'RE GONNA DRESS.
LET'S TRY AND PACK THE PLACE!
WOO!
W...
WAIT A SECOND!
MY FRIENDS ARE COMING TO THIS! AND I HAVE TO WEAR--?
DON'T BE SO UPTIGHT-- THEY'LL LOVE IT!
AGH ...!
WOOOO!!
Date of the concert.
HOO BOY, YOU ROCK MY WORLD!
STOP OGLING ME!!!
They did love it. Hence the nightmare.

# AN EXCITING AFTER-SCHOOL DATE

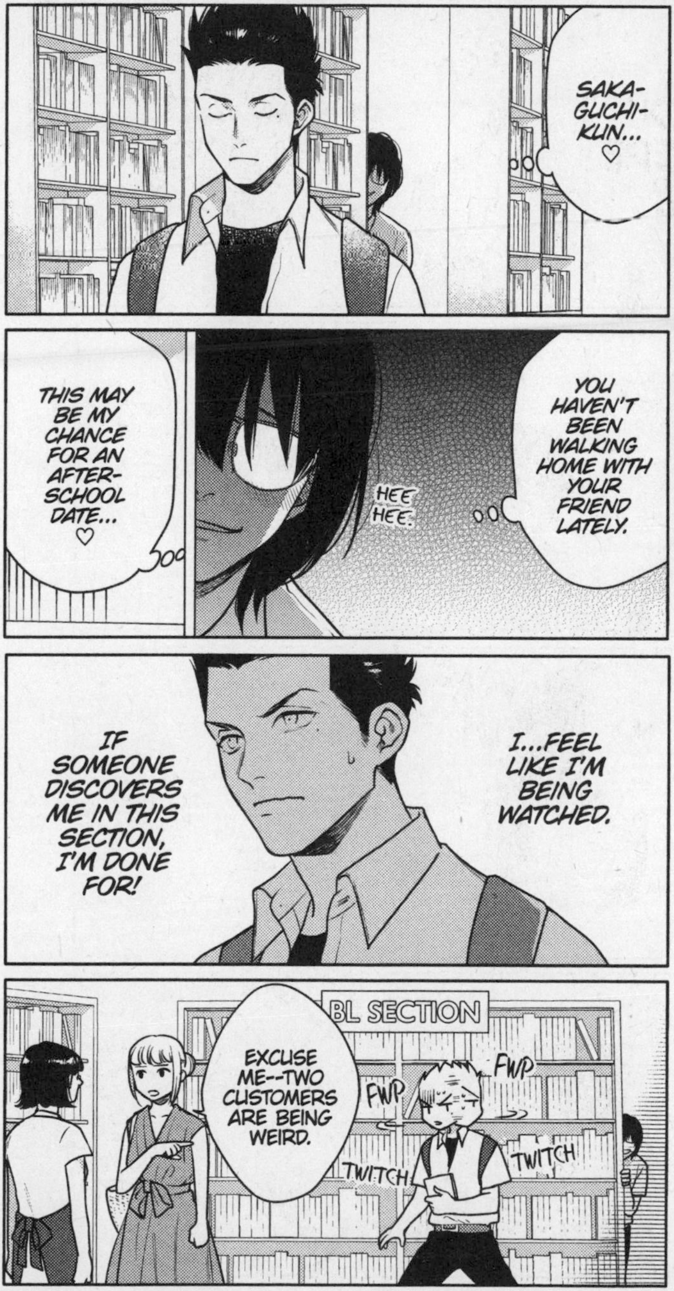

SAKA-GUCHI-KUN... ♡
YOU HAVEN'T BEEN WALKING HOME WITH YOUR FRIEND LATELY.
HEE HEE.
THIS MAY BE MY CHANCE FOR AN AFTER-SCHOOL DATE... ♡
I...FEEL LIKE I'M BEING WATCHED.
IF SOMEONE DISCOVERS ME IN THIS SECTION, I'M DONE FOR!
BL SECTION
FWP
FWP
EXCUSE ME--TWO CUSTOMERS ARE BEING WEIRD.
TWITCH
TWITCH

# I'LL NEVER LET GO

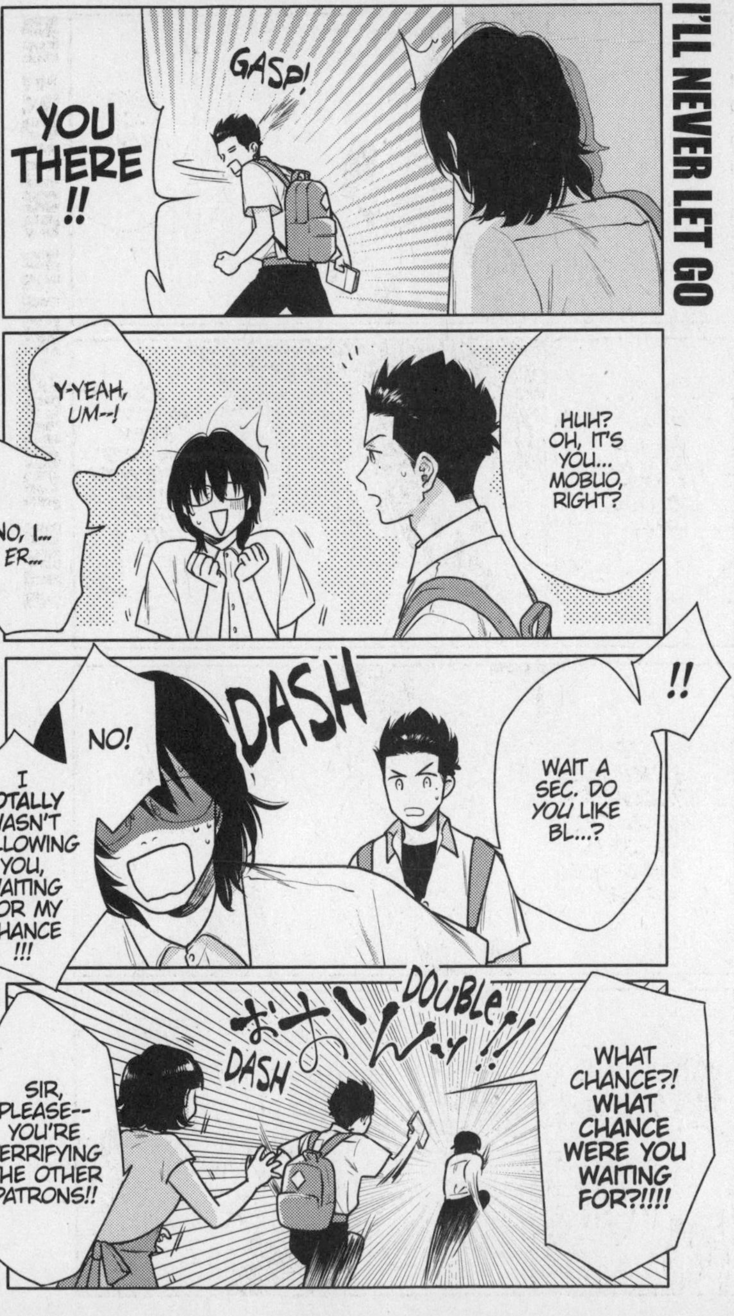
GASP!
YOU THERE!!
HUH? OH, IT'S YOU... MOBUO, RIGHT?
Y-YEAH, UM--!
NO, I... ER...
!!
WAIT A SEC. DO YOU LIKE BL...?
DASH
NO! I TOTALLY WASN'T FOLLOWING YOU, WAITING FOR MY CHANCE!!!
WHAT CHANCE?! WHAT CHANCE WERE YOU WAITING FOR?!!!!
DOUBLE DASH
SIR, PLEASE-- YOU'RE TERRIFYING THE OTHER PATRONS!!

# EGOCENTRIC

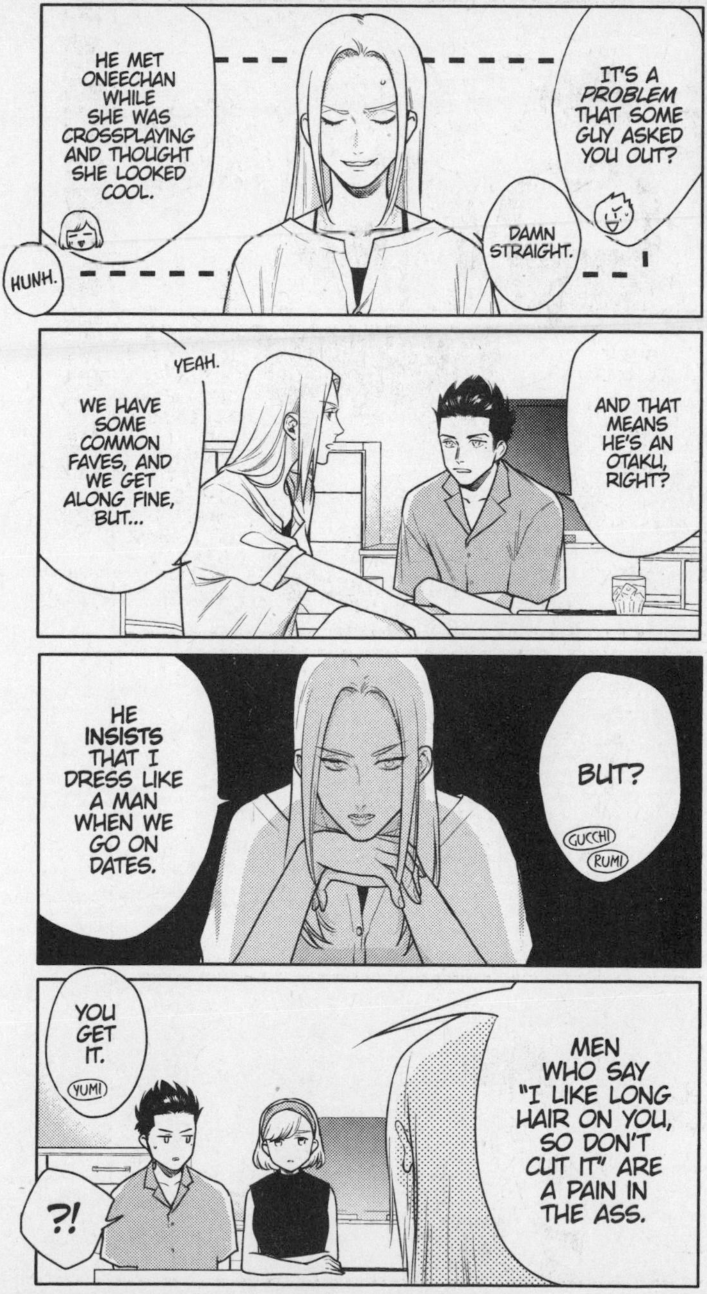
IT'S A *PROBLEM* THAT SOME GUY ASKED YOU OUT?
DAMN STRAIGHT.
HE MET ONEECHAN WHILE SHE WAS CROSSPLAYING AND THOUGHT SHE LOOKED COOL.
HUNH.
AND THAT MEANS HE'S AN OTAKU, RIGHT?
YEAH.
WE HAVE SOME COMMON FAVES, AND WE GET ALONG FINE, BUT...
BUT?
GUCCHI
RUMI
HE INSISTS THAT I DRESS LIKE A MAN WHEN WE GO ON DATES.
MEN WHO SAY "I LIKE LONG HAIR ON YOU, SO DON'T CUT IT" ARE A PAIN IN THE ASS.
YOU GET IT.
YUMI
?!

# A NEW TALENT IS DISCOVERED

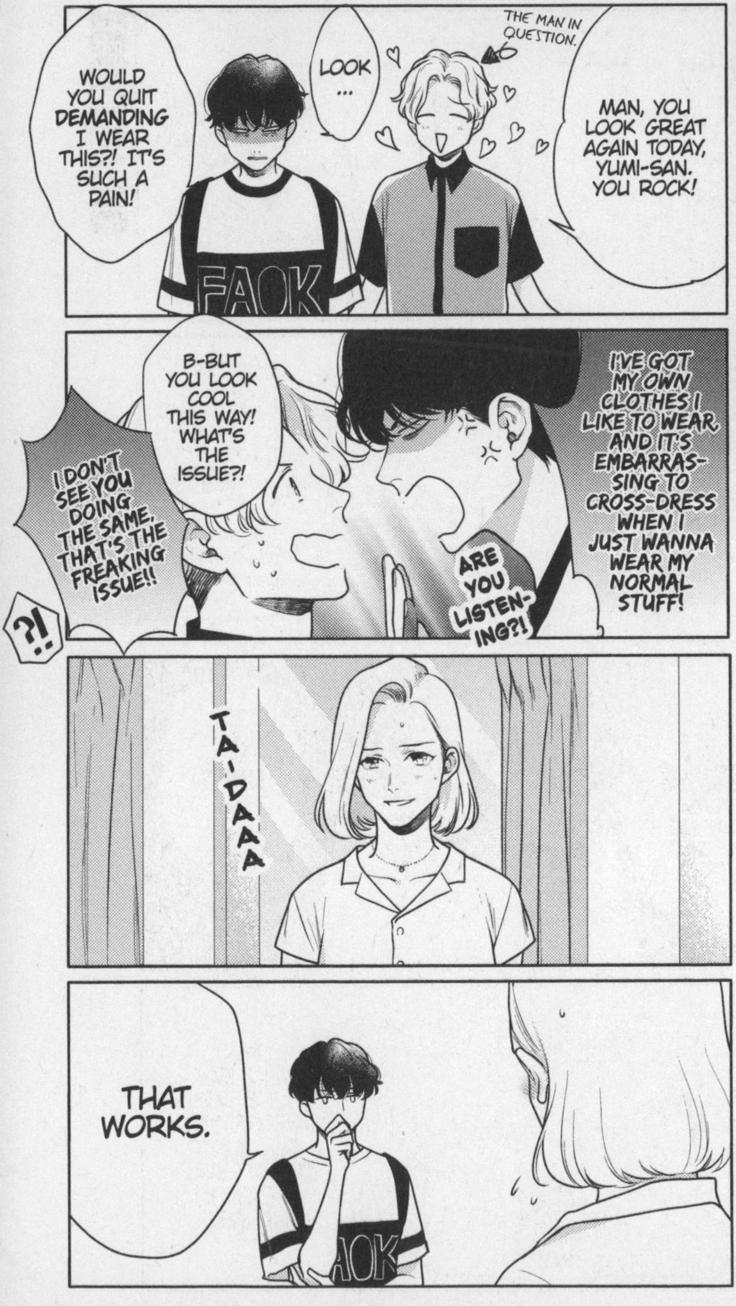
THE MAN IN QUESTION.
MAN, YOU LOOK GREAT AGAIN TODAY, YUMI-SAN. YOU ROCK!
LOOK ...
WOULD YOU QUIT DEMANDING I WEAR THIS?! IT'S SUCH A PAIN!
FAOK
I'VE GOT MY OWN CLOTHES I LIKE TO WEAR AND IT'S EMBARRAS-SING TO CROSS-DRESS WHEN I JUST WANNA WEAR MY NORMAL STUFF!
ARE YOU LISTEN-ING?!
B-BUT YOU LOOK COOL THIS WAY! WHAT'S THE ISSUE?!
I DON'T SEE YOU DOING THE SAME. THAT'S THE FREAKING ISSUE!!
?!
TA-DAAAA
THAT WORKS.

# WHAT THE HELL!?

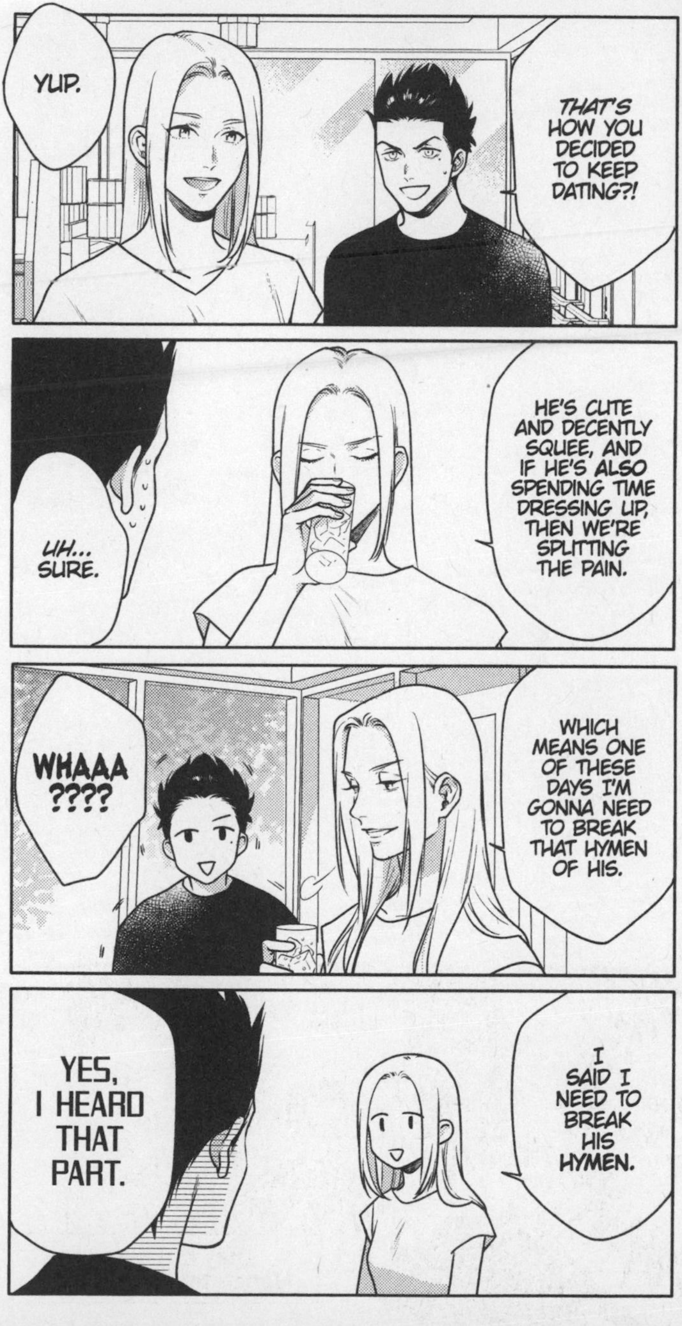
THAT'S HOW YOU DECIDED TO KEEP DATING?!
YUP.
HE'S CUTE AND DECENTLY SQUEE, AND IF HE'S ALSO SPENDING TIME DRESSING UP, THEN WE'RE SPLITTING THE PAIN.
UH... SURE.
WHICH MEANS ONE OF THESE DAYS I'M GONNA NEED TO BREAK THAT HYMEN OF HIS.
WHAAA ????
I SAID I NEED TO BREAK HIS HYMEN.
YES, I HEARD THAT PART.

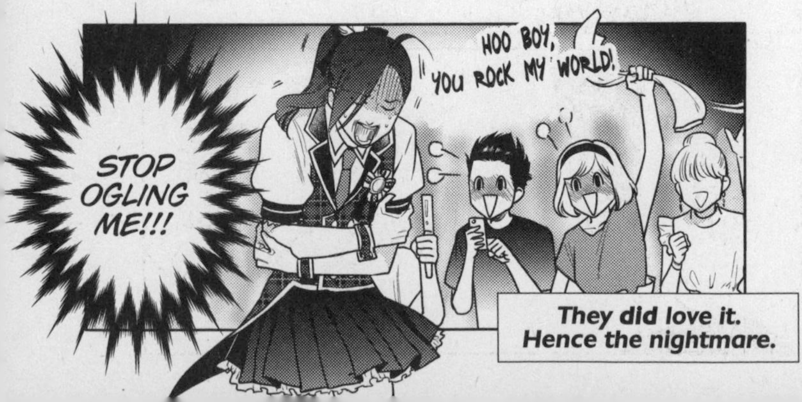
HOO BOY, YOU ROCK MY WORLD!
STOP OGLING ME!!!
They did love it. Hence the nightmare.

K

F S

# FINAL CHAPTER: Plan for the Future

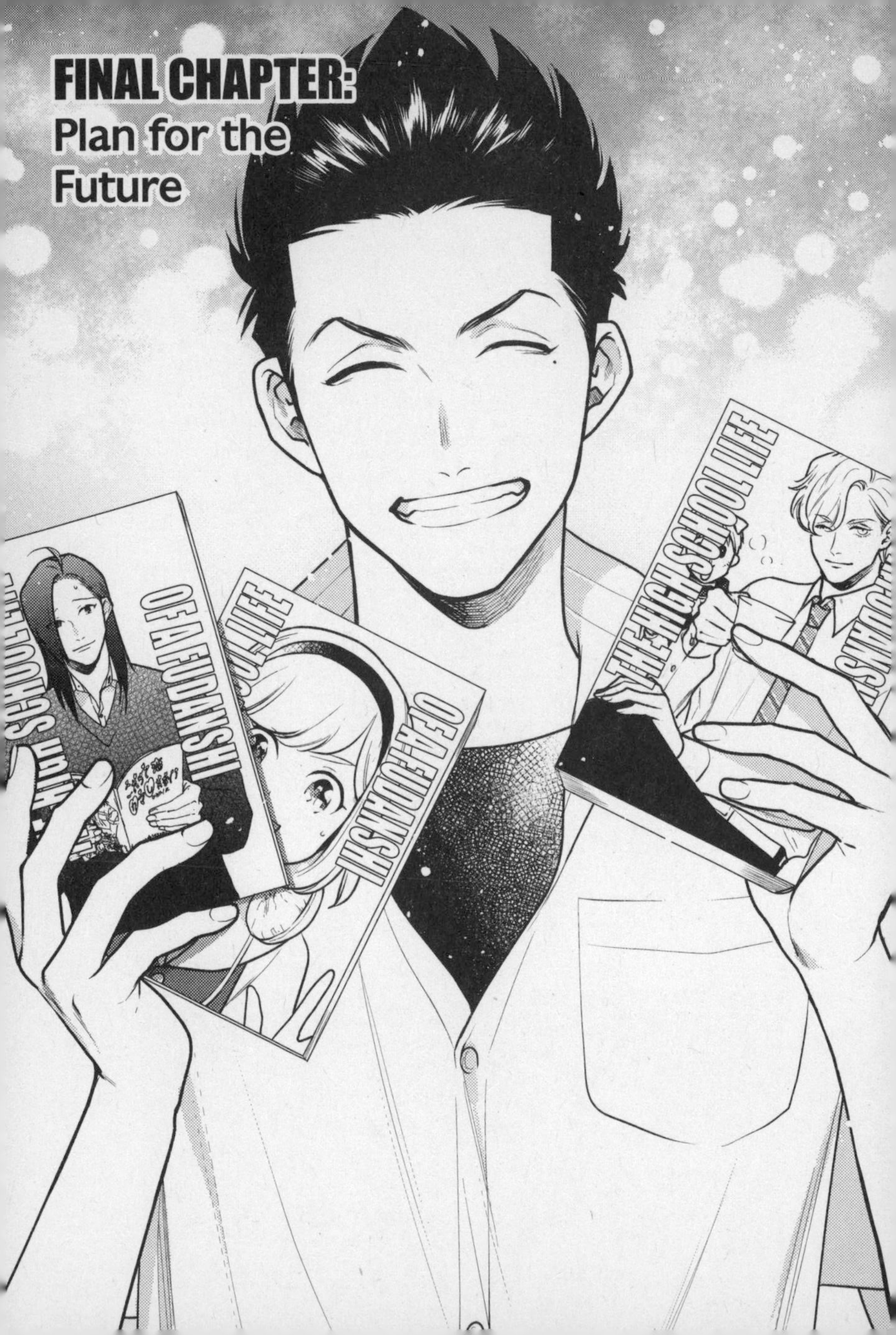
OF A FUDANSHI
OF A FUDANSHI
THE HIGH SCHOOL LIFE

# YOU CAN TELL?

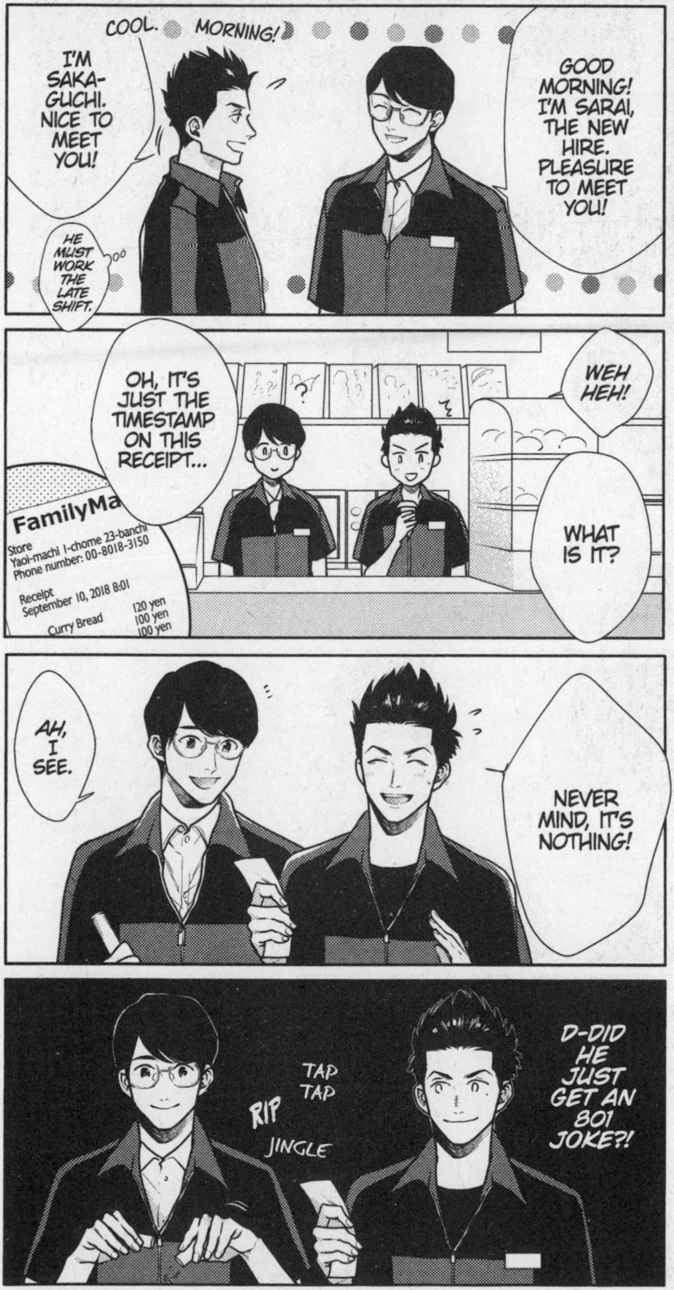
GOOD MORNING! I'M SARAI, THE NEW HIRE. PLEASURE TO MEET YOU!
MORNING!
COOL.
I'M SAKA-GUCHI. NICE TO MEET YOU!
HE MUST WORK THE LATE SHIFT.
WEH HEH!
WHAT IS IT?
OH, IT'S JUST THE TIMESTAMP ON THIS RECEIPT...
FamilyMa
Store
Yaoi-machi 1-chome 23-banchi
Phone number: 00-8018-3150
Receipt
September 10, 2018 8:01
Curry Bread
120 yen
100 yen
100 yen
NEVER MIND, IT'S NOTHING!
AH, I SEE.
D-DID HE JUST GET AN 801 JOKE?!
TAP TAP
RIP
JINGLE

# CHAMPING AT THE BIT

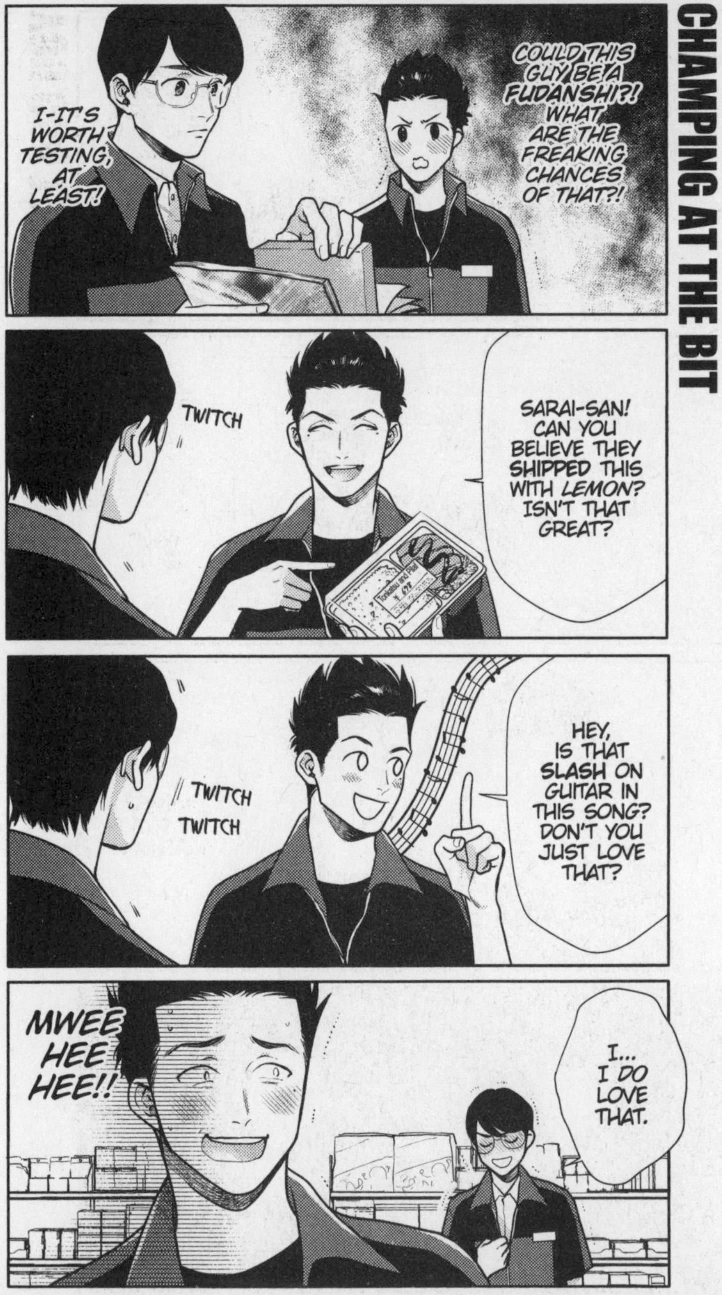
COULD THIS GUY BE A FUDANSHI?! WHAT ARE THE FREAKING CHANCES OF THAT?!
I-IT'S WORTH TESTING, AT LEAST!
SARAI-SAN! CAN YOU BELIEVE THEY SHIPPED THIS WITH *LEMON*? ISN'T THAT GREAT?
TWITCH
HEY, IS THAT SLASH ON GUITAR IN THIS SONG? DON'T YOU JUST LOVE THAT?
TWITCH
TWITCH
I... I *DO* LOVE THAT.
MWEE HEE HEE!!

## OR BOOKS, PERHAPS

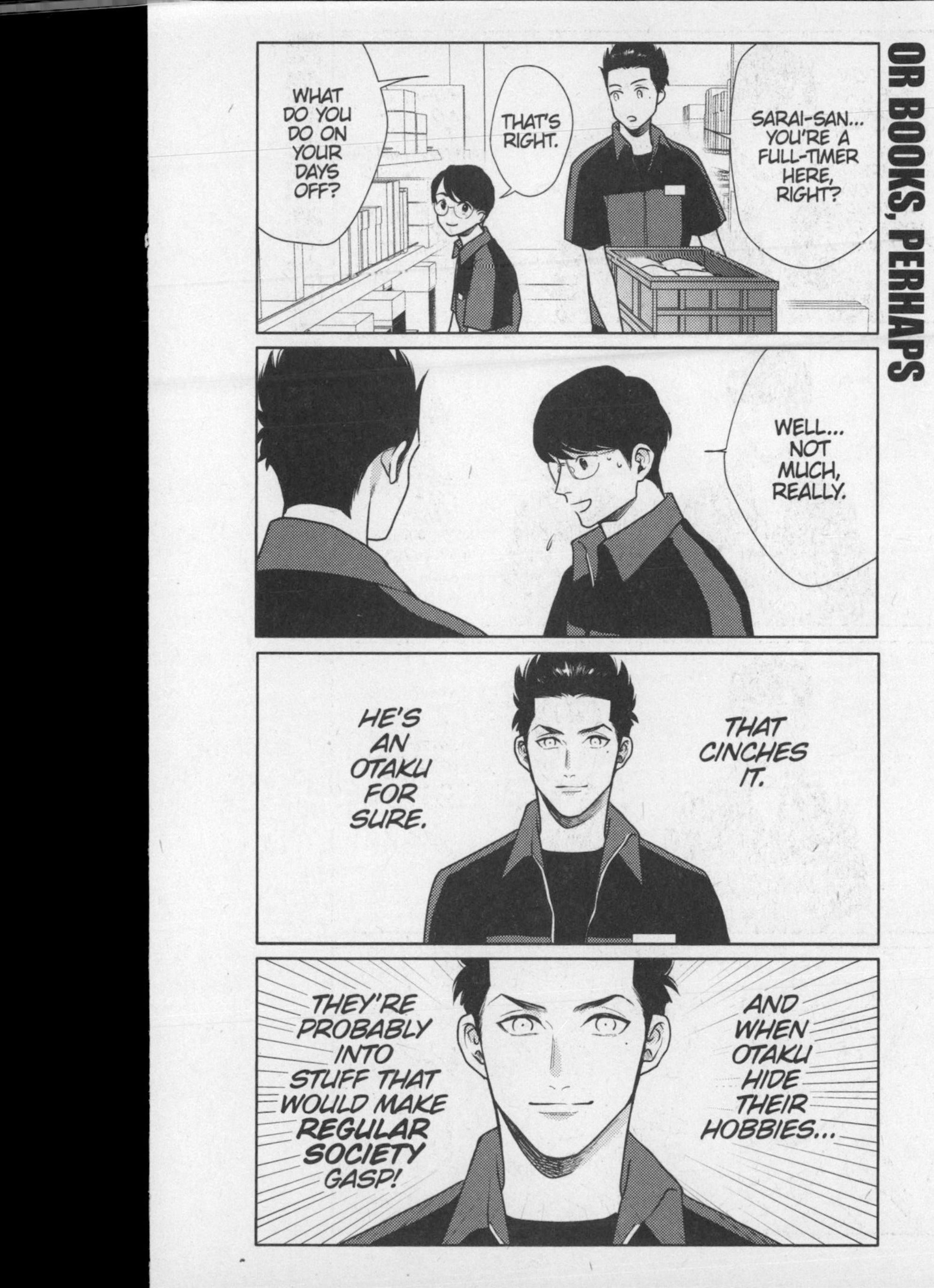
SARAI-SAN... YOU'RE A FULL-TIMER HERE, RIGHT?
THAT'S RIGHT.
WHAT DO YOU DO ON YOUR DAYS OFF?
WELL... NOT MUCH, REALLY.
THAT CINCHES IT.
HE'S AN OTAKU FOR SURE.
AND WHEN OTAKU HIDE THEIR HOBBIES...
THEY'RE PROBABLY INTO STUFF THAT WOULD MAKE REGULAR SOCIETY GASP!

AUGH, I KNOW IT-- I JUST KNOW THAT SARAI-SAN'S INTO BL! I WANNA TALK TO HIM ABOUT IT SO BAD...!
STARE...
HUFF!
HUFF!
BUT ON THE OFF CHANCE THAT I'M WRONG, I'LL EMBARRASS US BOTH AND OUT MYSELF AS A FUDANSHI! IT'S SO RISKY!
BUT I STILL... I STILL JUST WANNA TALK TO HIM! TO SHARE OPINIONS!
I HAVE TO MUSTER ALL MY COURAGE AND ASK...!
BLUSH
AH...!
GASP!
BA DUMP
......!!

MASTER DETECTIVE NISHIHARA

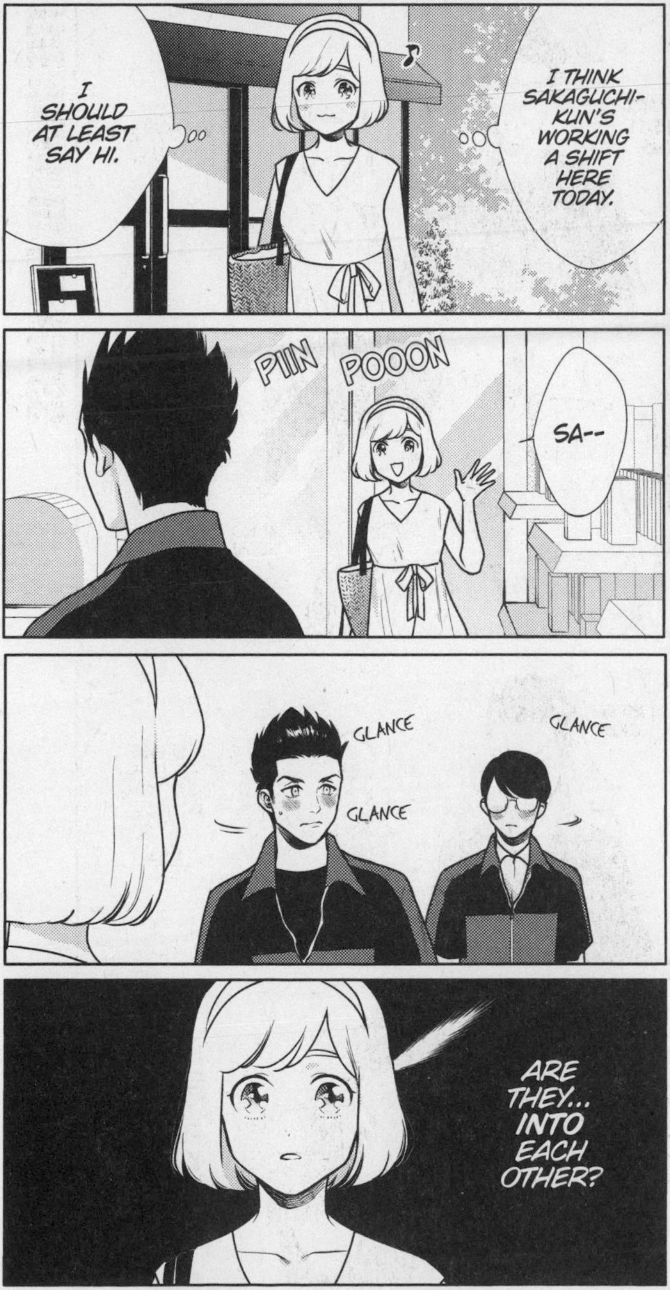
I THINK SAKAGUCHI-KUN'S WORKING A SHIFT HERE TODAY.
I SHOULD AT LEAST SAY HI.
SA--
PIIN POOON
GLANCE
GLANCE
GLANCE
ARE THEY... INTO EACH OTHER?

# THE BASHFUL PRINCESS

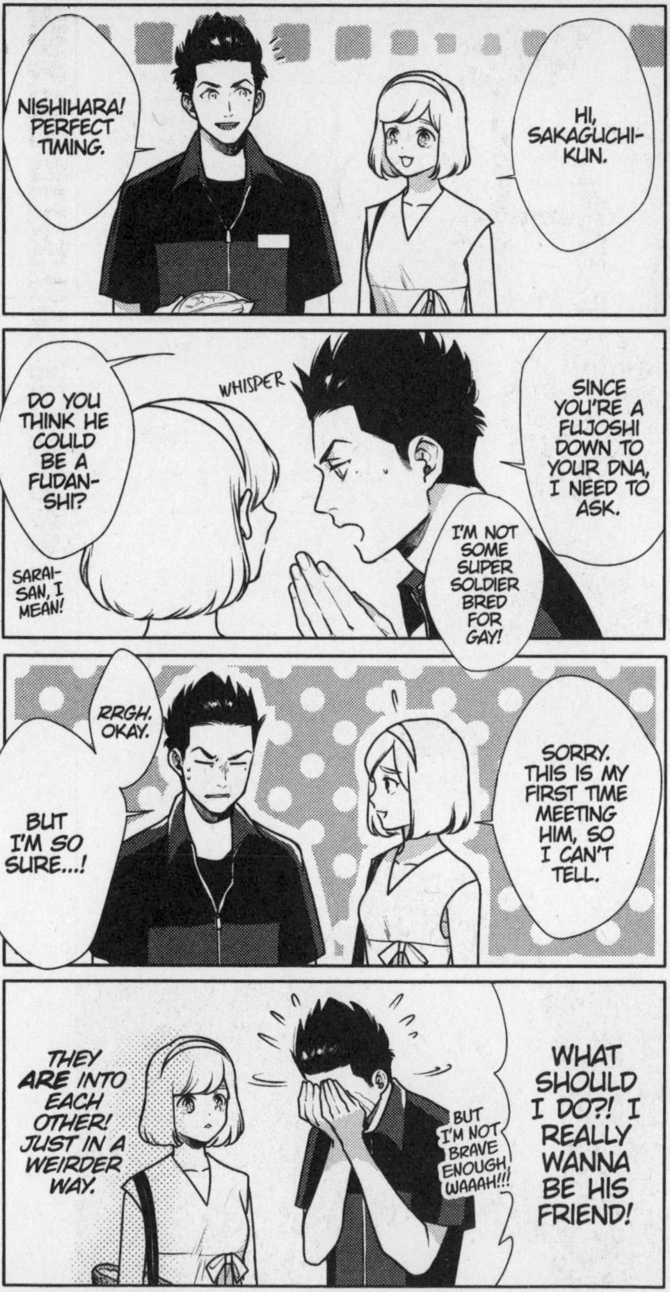
HI, SAKAGUCHI-KUN.
NISHIHARA! PERFECT TIMING.
SINCE YOU'RE A FUJOSHI DOWN TO YOUR DNA, I NEED TO ASK.
I'M NOT SOME SUPER SOLDIER BRED FOR GAY!
WHISPER
DO YOU THINK HE COULD BE A FUDAN-SHI?
SARAI-SAN, I MEAN!
SORRY. THIS IS MY FIRST TIME MEETING HIM, SO I CAN'T TELL.
RRGH. OKAY.
BUT I'M SO SURE...!
WHAT SHOULD I DO?! I REALLY WANNA BE HIS FRIEND!
BUT I'M NOT BRAVE ENOUGH, WAAAH!!!
THEY ARE INTO EACH OTHER! JUST IN A WEIRDER WAY.

# POKER FACE, ALWAYS

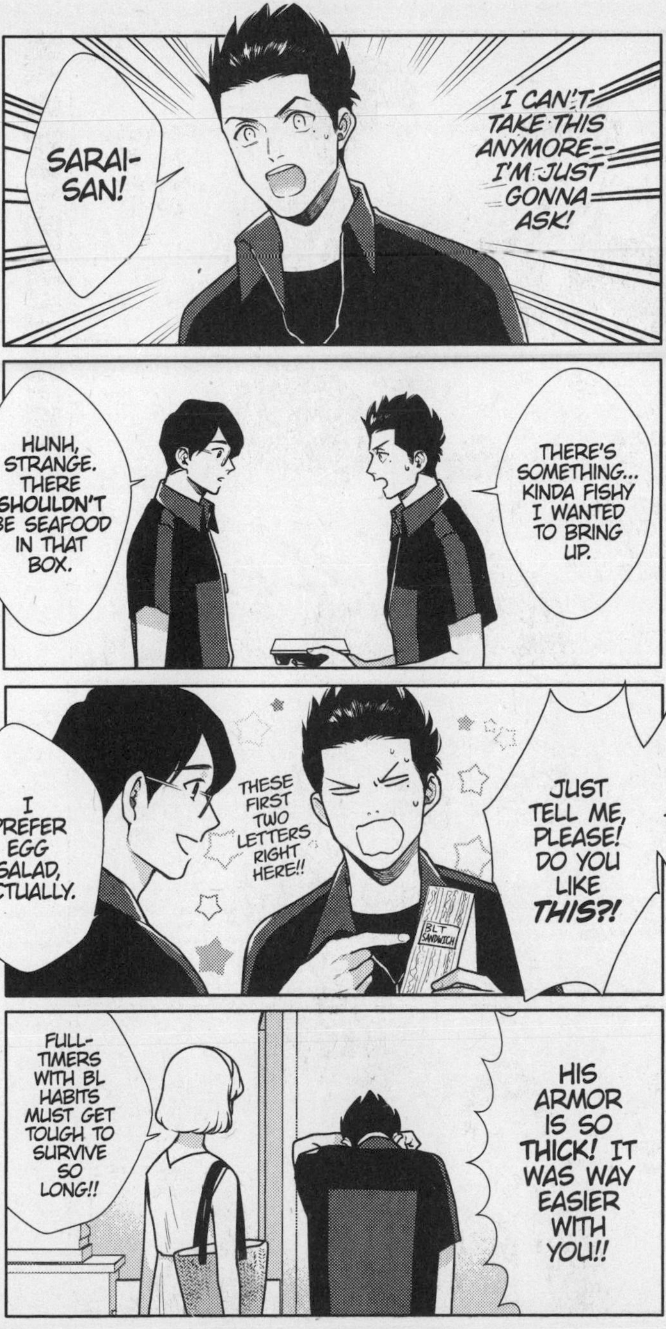
I CAN'T TAKE THIS ANYMORE-- I'M JUST GONNA ASK!
SARAI-SAN!
THERE'S SOMETHING... KINDA FISHY I WANTED TO BRING UP.
HUNH, STRANGE. THERE SHOULDN'T BE SEAFOOD IN THAT BOX.
NOT THE BENTO BOX-- I WAS TOSSING THAT!!
JUST TELL ME, PLEASE! DO YOU LIKE *THIS?!*
THESE FIRST TWO LETTERS RIGHT HERE!!
BLT SANDWICH
I PREFER EGG SALAD, ACTUALLY.
HIS ARMOR IS SO THICK! IT WAS WAY EASIER WITH YOU!!
FULL-TIMERS WITH BL HABITS MUST GET TOUGH TO SURVIVE SO LONG!!

# MY OWN PRIVATE SPACE

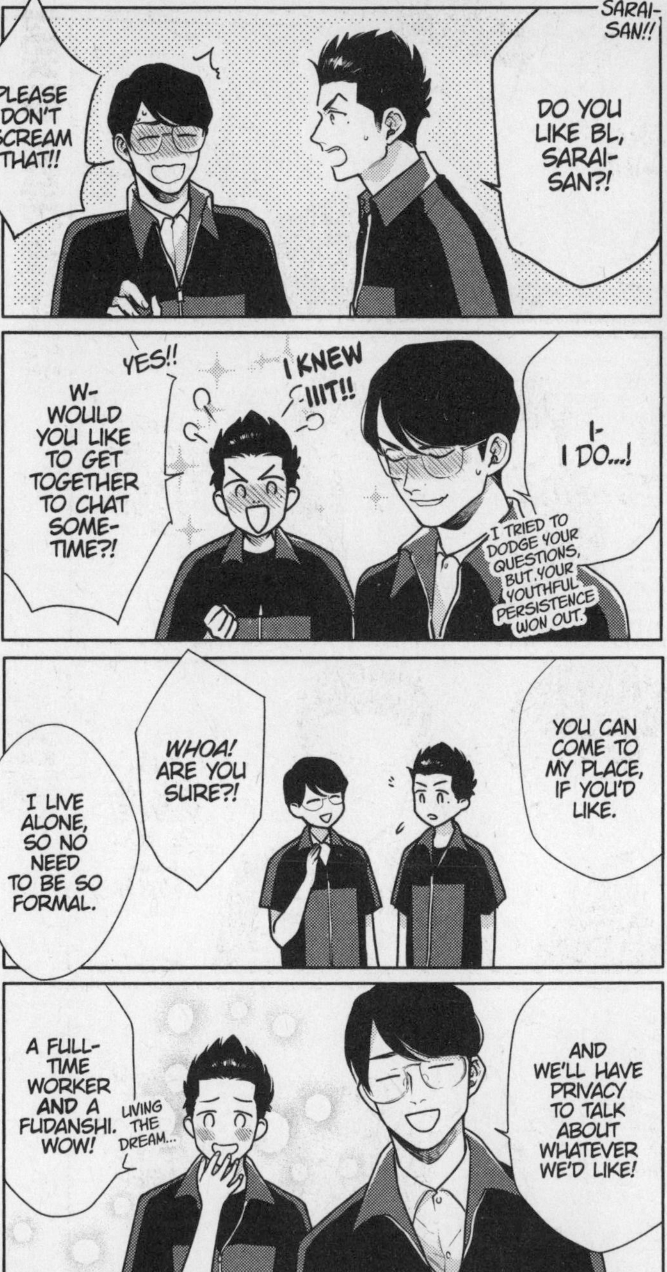

SARAI-SAN!!
DO YOU LIKE BL, SARAI-SAN?!
PLEASE DON'T SCREAM THAT!!
I- I DO...!
I TRIED TO DODGE YOUR QUESTIONS, BUT YOUR YOUTHFUL PERSISTENCE WON OUT.
I KNEW IIIT!!
YES!!
W- WOULD YOU LIKE TO GET TOGETHER TO CHAT SOMETIME?!
YOU CAN COME TO MY PLACE, IF YOU'D LIKE.
WHOA! ARE YOU SURE?!
I LIVE ALONE, SO NO NEED TO BE SO FORMAL.
AND WE'LL HAVE PRIVACY TO TALK ABOUT WHATEVER WE'D LIKE!
LIVING THE DREAM...
A FULL-TIME WORKER AND A FUDANSHI. WOW!

# I WON'T ABANDON YOU

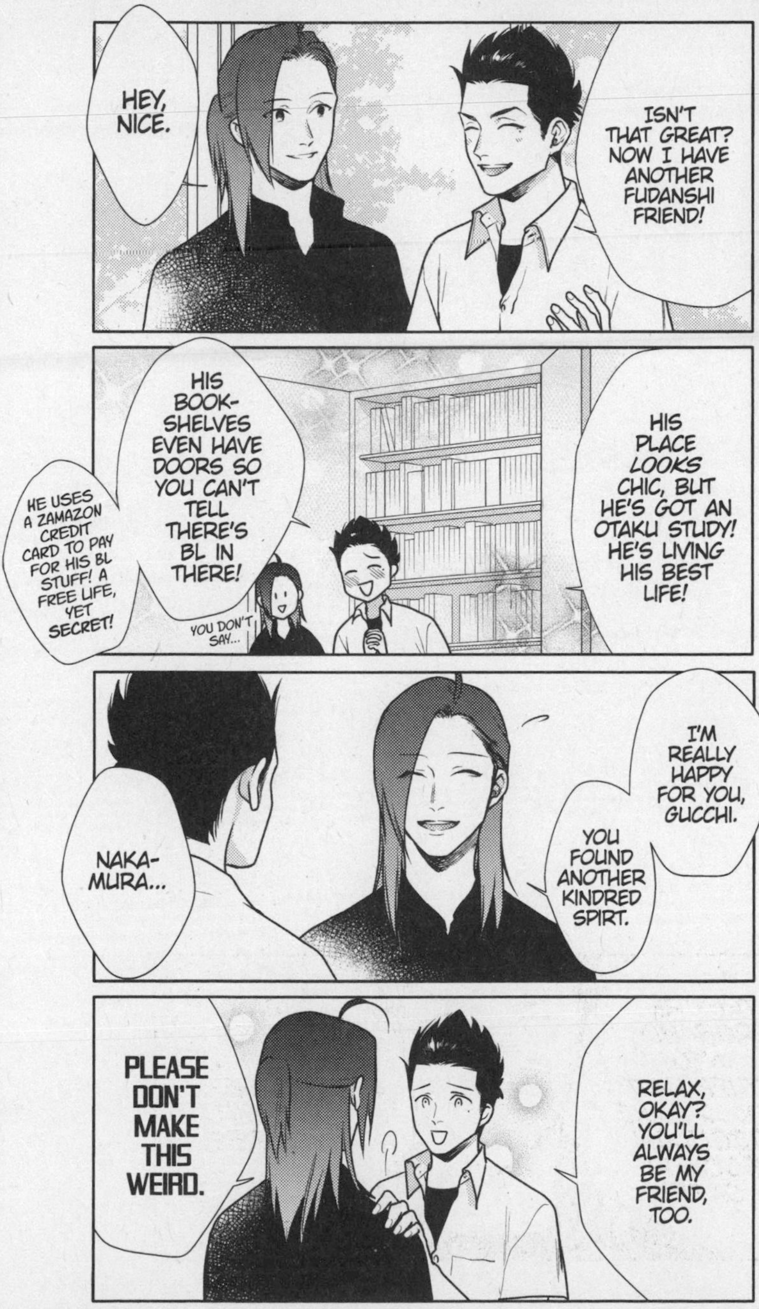
ISN'T THAT GREAT? NOW I HAVE ANOTHER FUDANSHI FRIEND!
HEY, NICE.
HIS PLACE *LOOKS* CHIC, BUT HE'S GOT AN OTAKU STUDY! HE'S LIVING HIS BEST LIFE!
HIS BOOK-SHELVES EVEN HAVE DOORS SO YOU CAN'T TELL THERE'S BL IN THERE!
YOU DON'T SAY...
HE USES A ZAMAZON CREDIT CARD TO PAY FOR HIS BL STUFF! A FREE LIFE, YET SECRET!
I'M REALLY HAPPY FOR YOU, GUCCHI.
YOU FOUND ANOTHER KINDRED SPIRT.
NAKA-MURA...
RELAX, OKAY? YOU'LL ALWAYS BE MY FRIEND, TOO.
PLEASE DON'T MAKE THIS WEIRD.

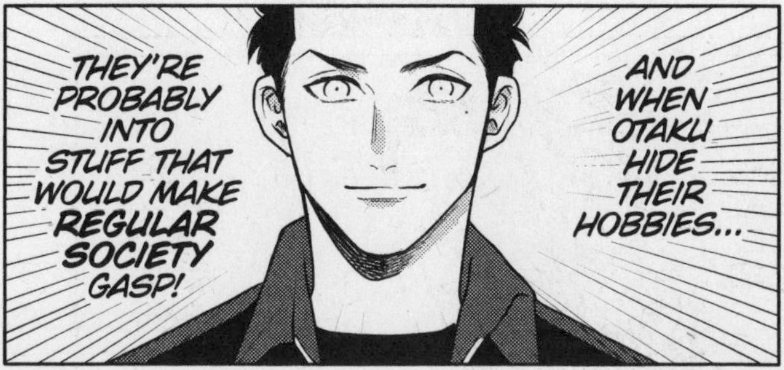
AND WHEN OTAKU HIDE THEIR HOBBIES...
THEY'RE PROBABLY INTO STUFF THAT WOULD MAKE REGULAR SOCIETY GASP!

K

F S

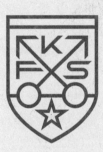

**SPECIAL**

# Volume-Exclusive Manga

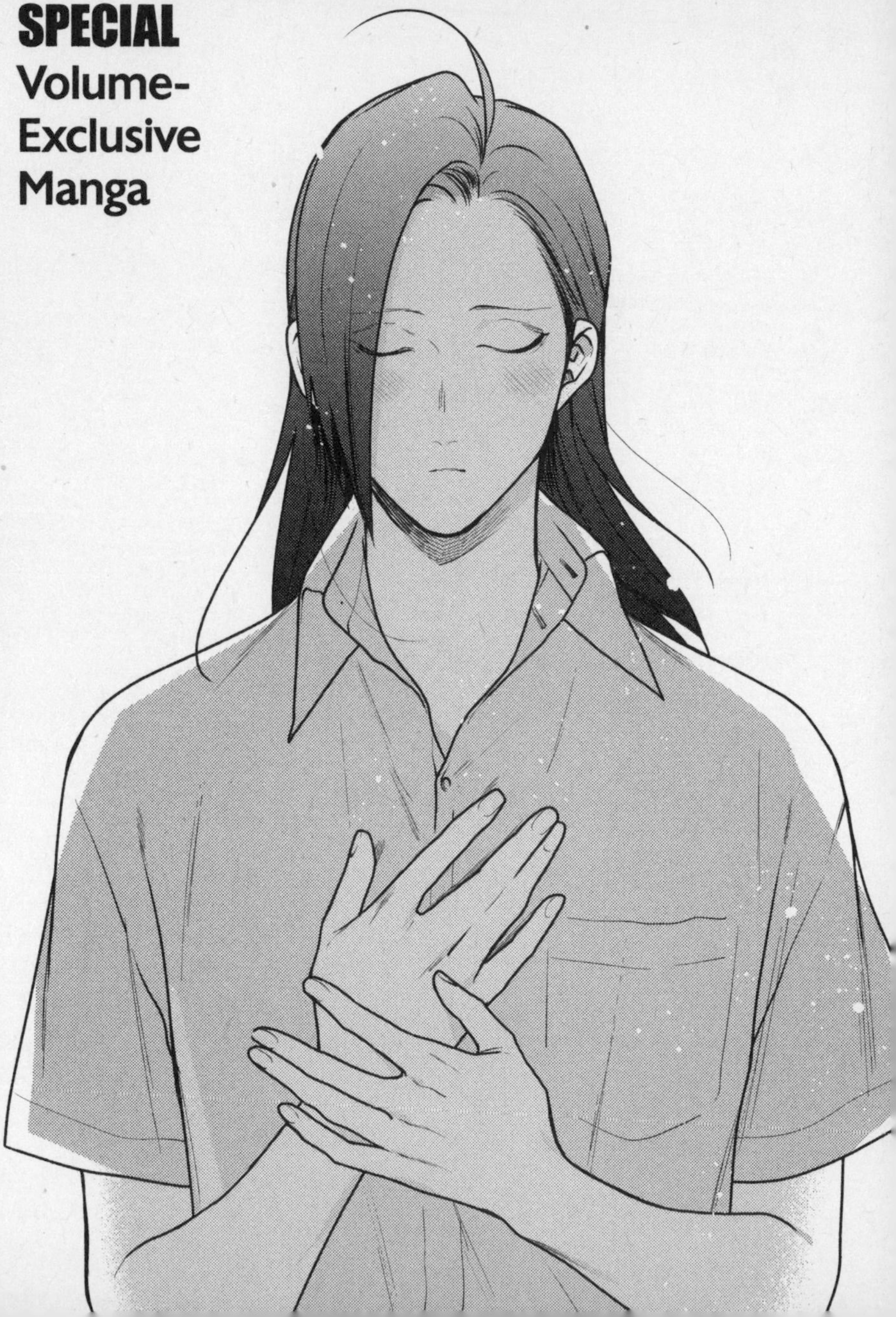

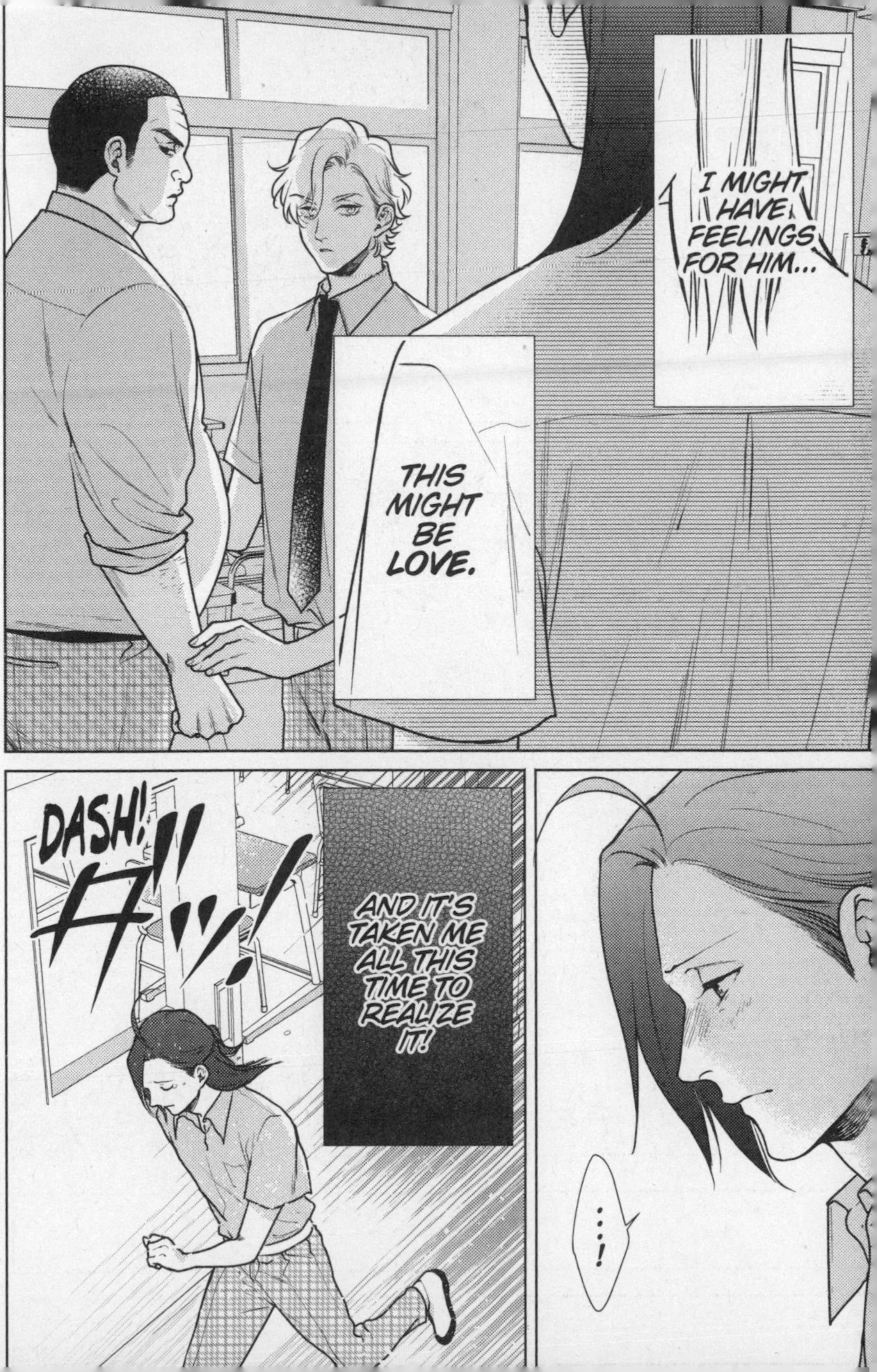
I MIGHT HAVE FEELINGS FOR HIM...
THIS MIGHT BE LOVE.
...!
AND IT'S TAKEN ME ALL THIS TIME TO REALIZE IT!
DASH!
ダッ!!

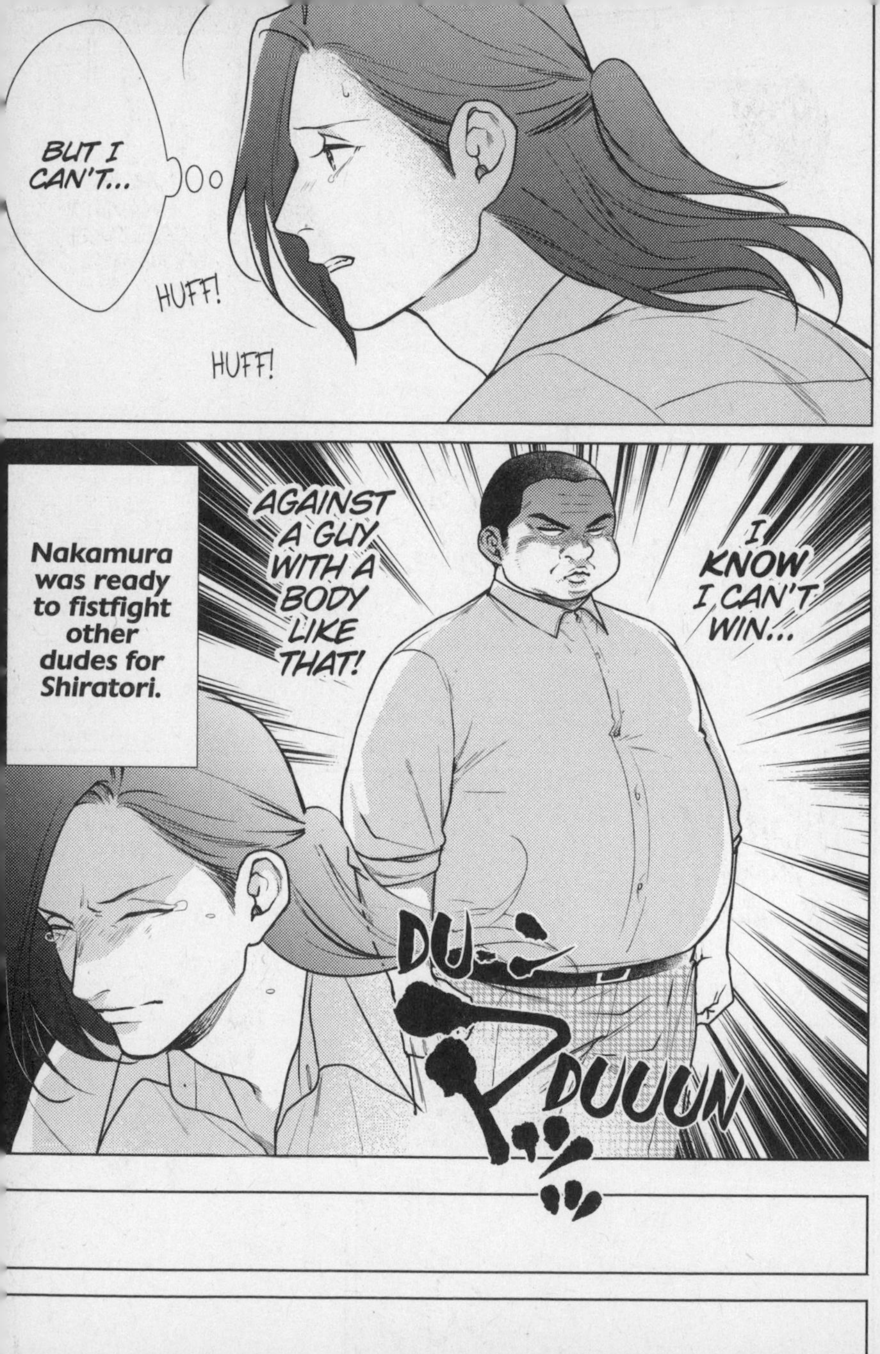
BUT I CAN'T...
HUFF!
HUFF!
I KNOW I CAN'T WIN...
AGAINST A GUY WITH A BODY LIKE THAT!
Nakamura was ready to fistfight other dudes for Shiratori.
DU-
DUUUN

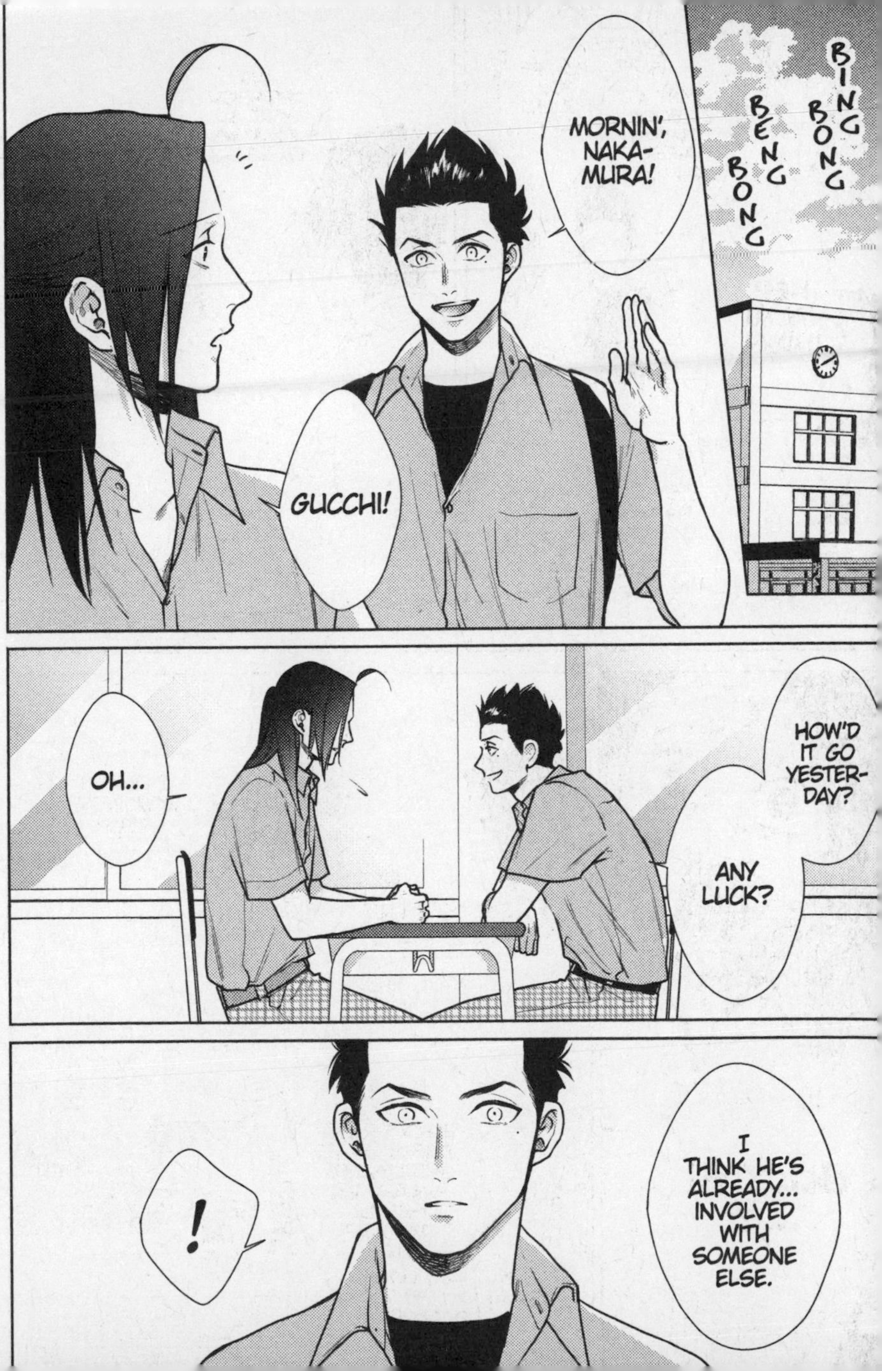
BING BONG
BENG BONG
MORNIN', NAKA-MURA!
GUCCHI!
HOW'D IT GO YESTER-DAY?
ANY LUCK?
OH...
I THINK HE'S ALREADY... INVOLVED WITH SOMEONE ELSE.
!

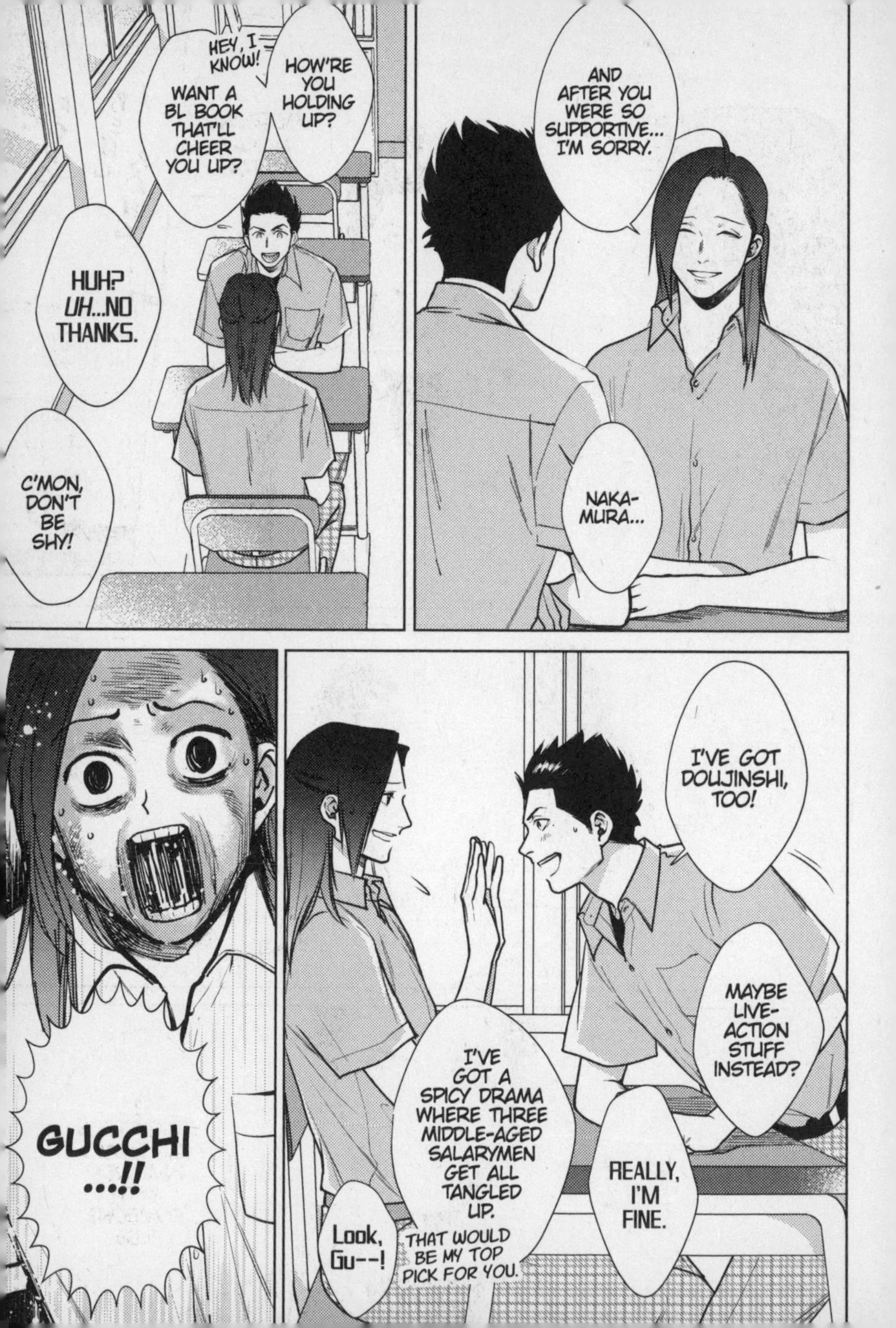
AND AFTER YOU WERE SO SUPPORTIVE... I'M SORRY.
NAKA-MURA...
HOW'RE YOU HOLDING UP?
HEY, I KNOW!
WANT A BL BOOK THAT'LL CHEER YOU UP?
HUH? UH...NO THANKS.
C'MON, DON'T BE SHY!
I'VE GOT DOUJINSHI, TOO!
MAYBE LIVE-ACTION STUFF INSTEAD?
I'VE GOT A SPICY DRAMA WHERE THREE MIDDLE-AGED SALARYMEN GET ALL TANGLED UP.
REALLY, I'M FINE.
THAT WOULD BE MY TOP PICK FOR YOU.
Look, Gu--!
GUCCHI ...!!

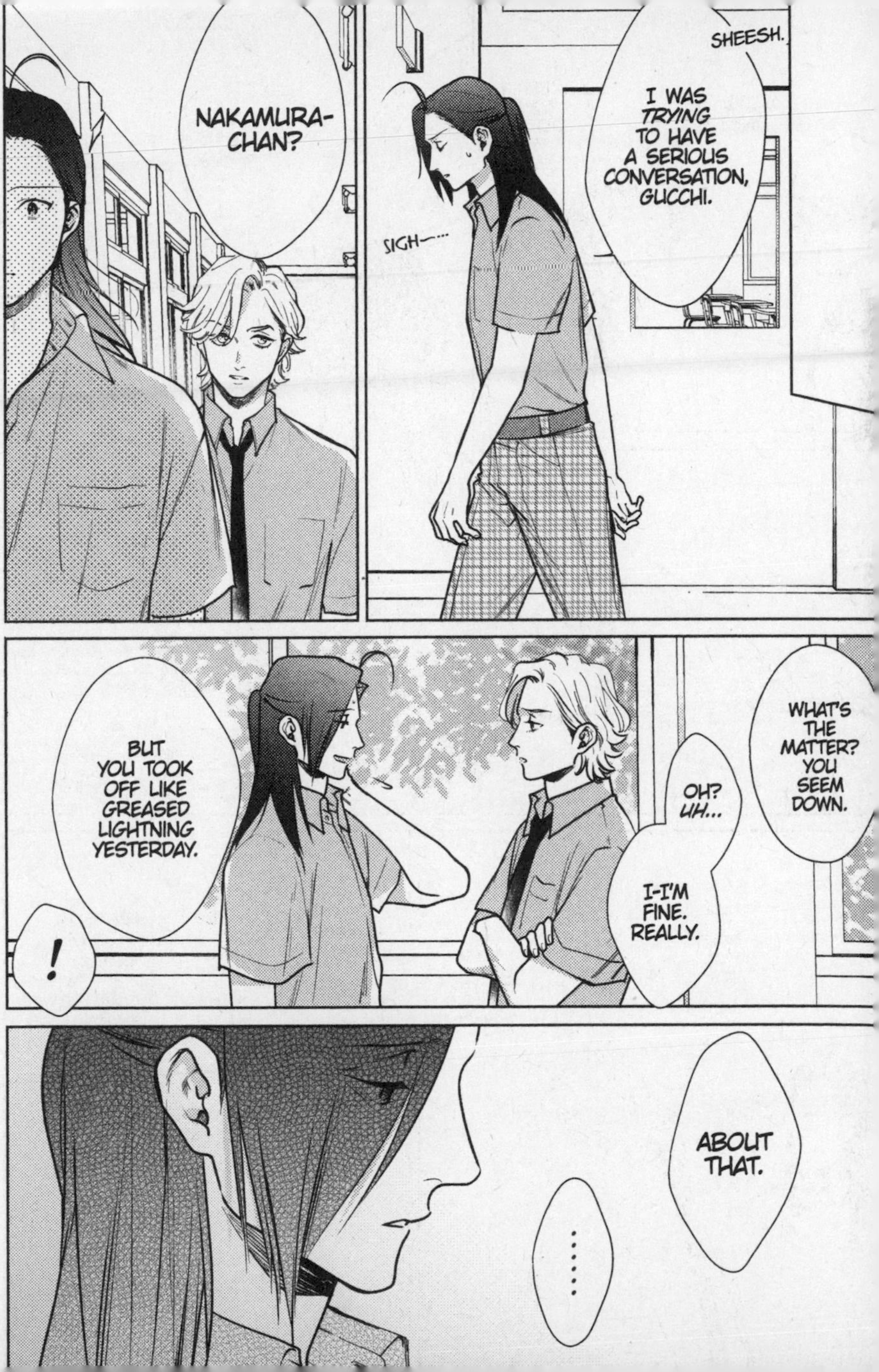
SHEESH.
I WAS *TRYING* TO HAVE A SERIOUS CONVERSATION, GUCCHI.
SIGH—...
NAKAMURA-CHAN?
WHAT'S THE MATTER? YOU SEEM DOWN.
OH? UH...
I-I'M FINE. REALLY.
BUT YOU TOOK OFF LIKE GREASED LIGHTNING YESTERDAY.
!
ABOUT THAT.
......

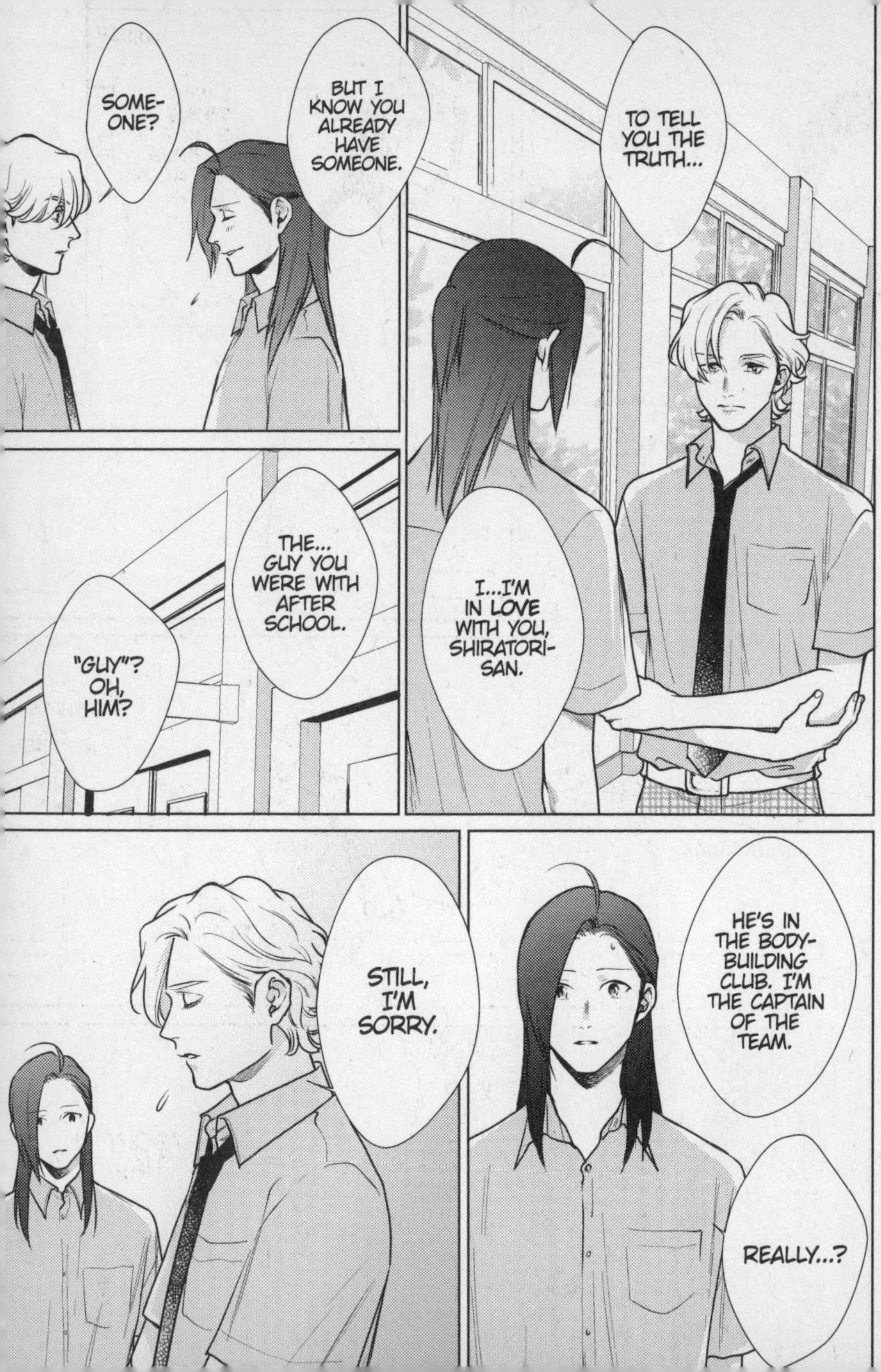
TO TELL YOU THE TRUTH...
I...I'M IN LOVE WITH YOU, SHIRATORI-SAN.
BUT I KNOW YOU ALREADY HAVE SOMEONE.
SOME-ONE?
THE... GUY YOU WERE WITH AFTER SCHOOL.
"GUY"? OH, HIM?
HE'S IN THE BODY-BUILDING CLUB. I'M THE CAPTAIN OF THE TEAM.
REALLY...?
STILL, I'M SORRY.

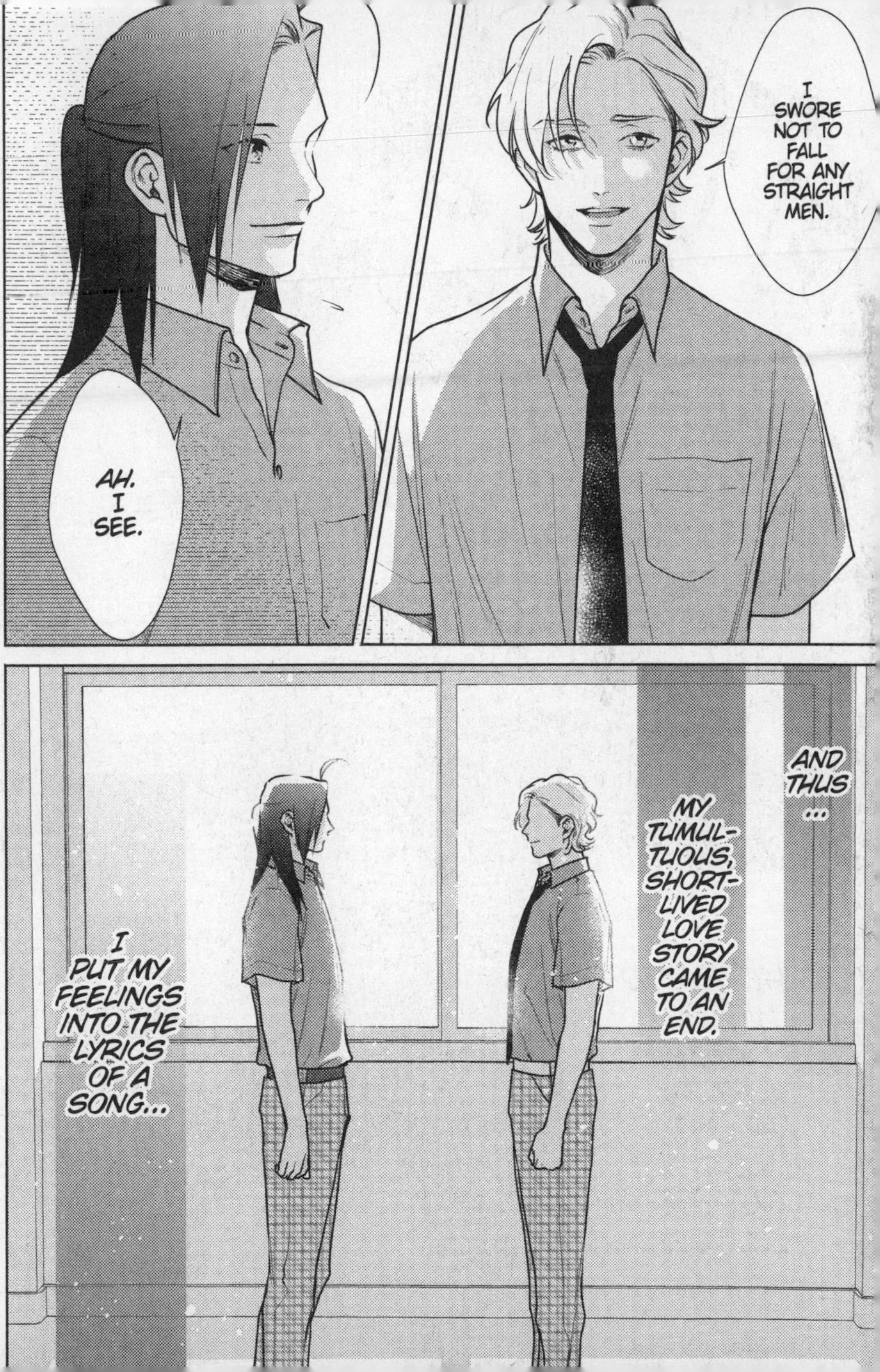
I SWORE NOT TO FALL FOR ANY STRAIGHT MEN.
AH. I SEE.
AND THUS...
MY TUMULTUOUS, SHORT-LIVED LOVE STORY CAME TO AN END.
I PUT MY FEELINGS INTO THE LYRICS OF A SONG...

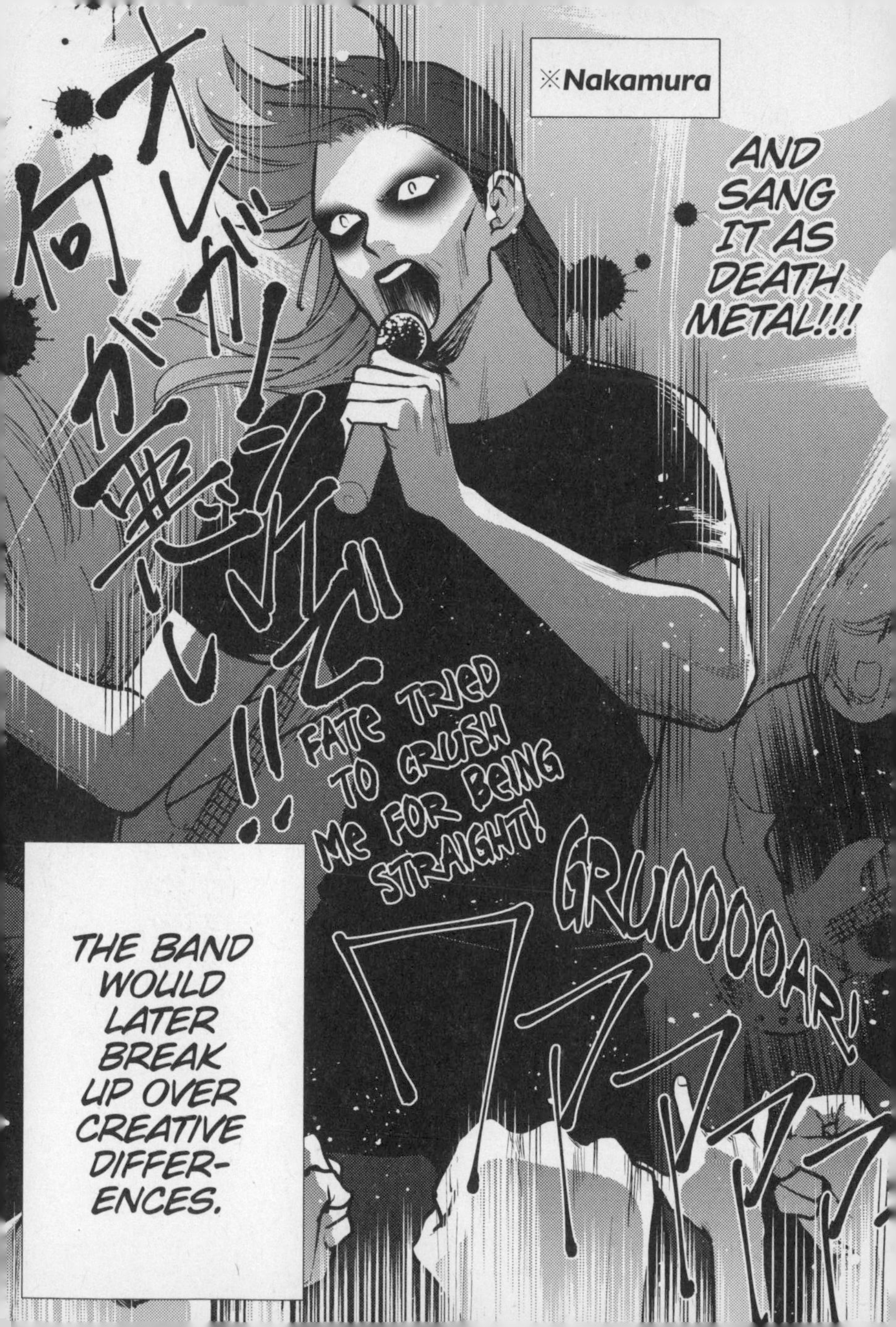
※Nakamura
AND SANG IT AS DEATH METAL!!!
FATE TRIED TO CRUSH ME FOR BEING STRAIGHT!
GRUOOOOOAR!
THE BAND WOULD LATER BREAK UP OVER CREATIVE DIFFER-ENCES.

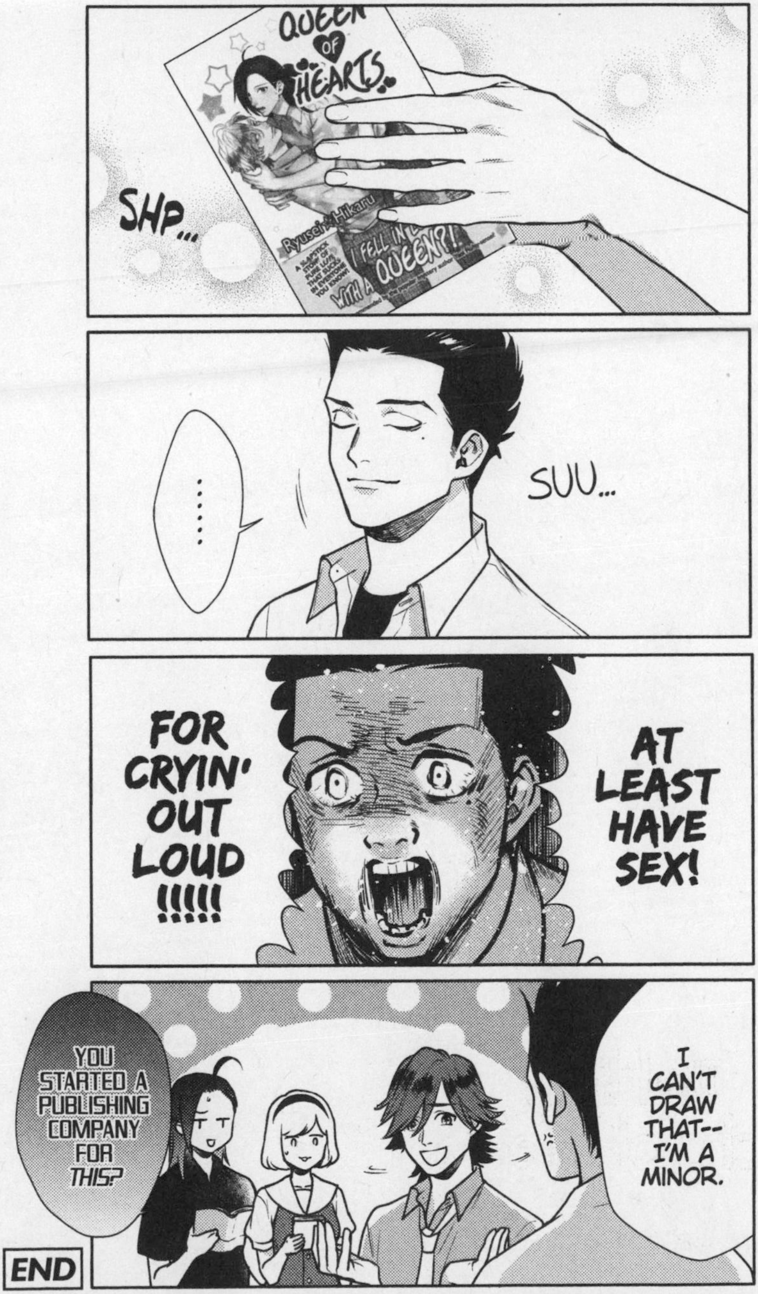
QUEEN OF HEARTS
Ryusei♥Hikaru
SHP...
SUU...
......
AT LEAST HAVE SEX!
FOR CRYIN' OUT LOUD!!!!!
I CAN'T DRAW THAT-- I'M A MINOR.
YOU STARTED A PUBLISHING COMPANY FOR *THIS?*
END

The High School Life of a FUDANSHI

K

F S

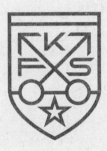

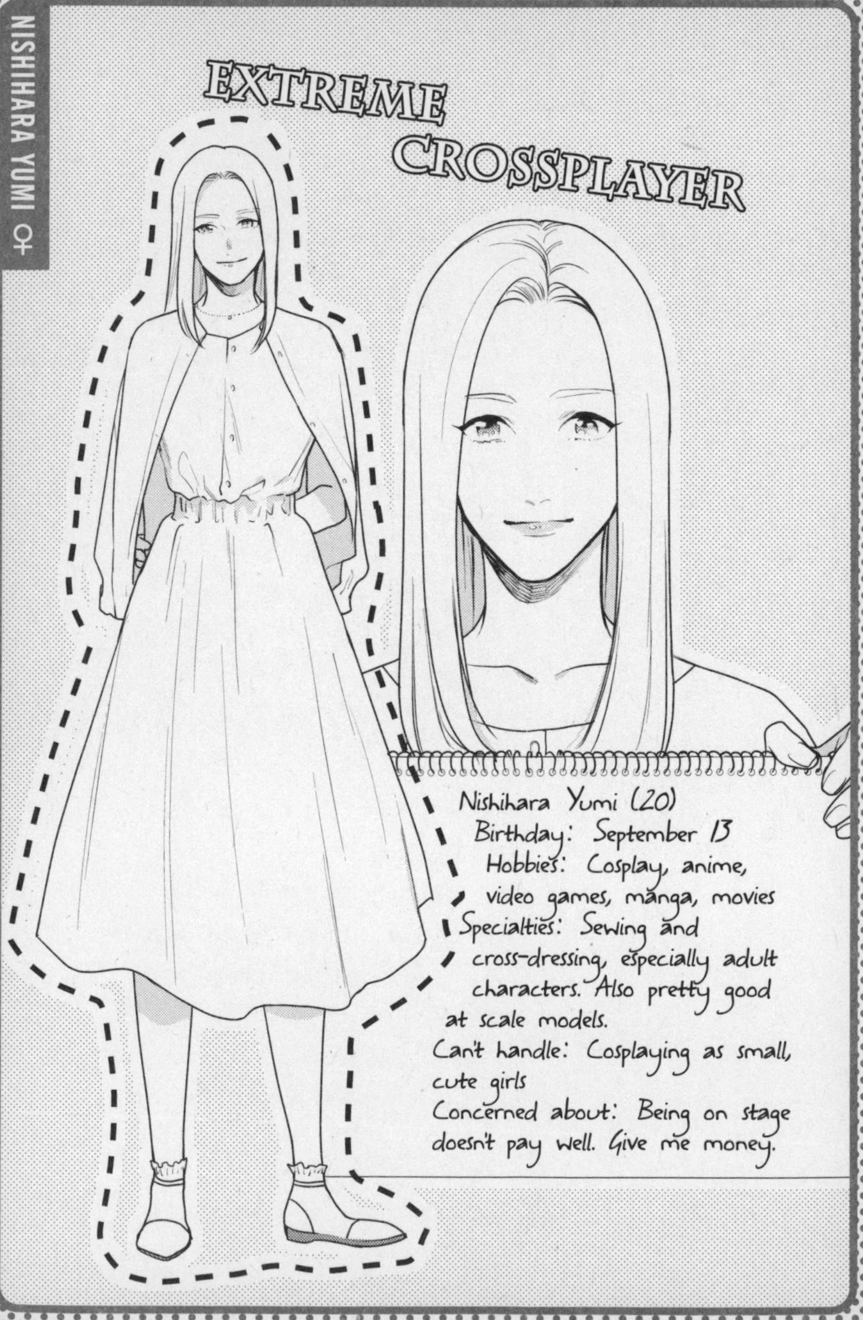
NISHIHARA YUMI ♀
EXTREME CROSSPLAYER
Nishihara Yumi (20)
Birthday: September 13
Hobbies: Cosplay, anime, video games, manga, movies
Specialties: Sewing and cross-dressing, especially adult characters. Also pretty good at scale models.
Can't handle: Cosplaying as small, cute girls
Concerned about: Being on stage doesn't pay well. Give me money.

KINJO SHOHACHI ♂

# THE TOTALLY PROFESSIONAL TEACHER

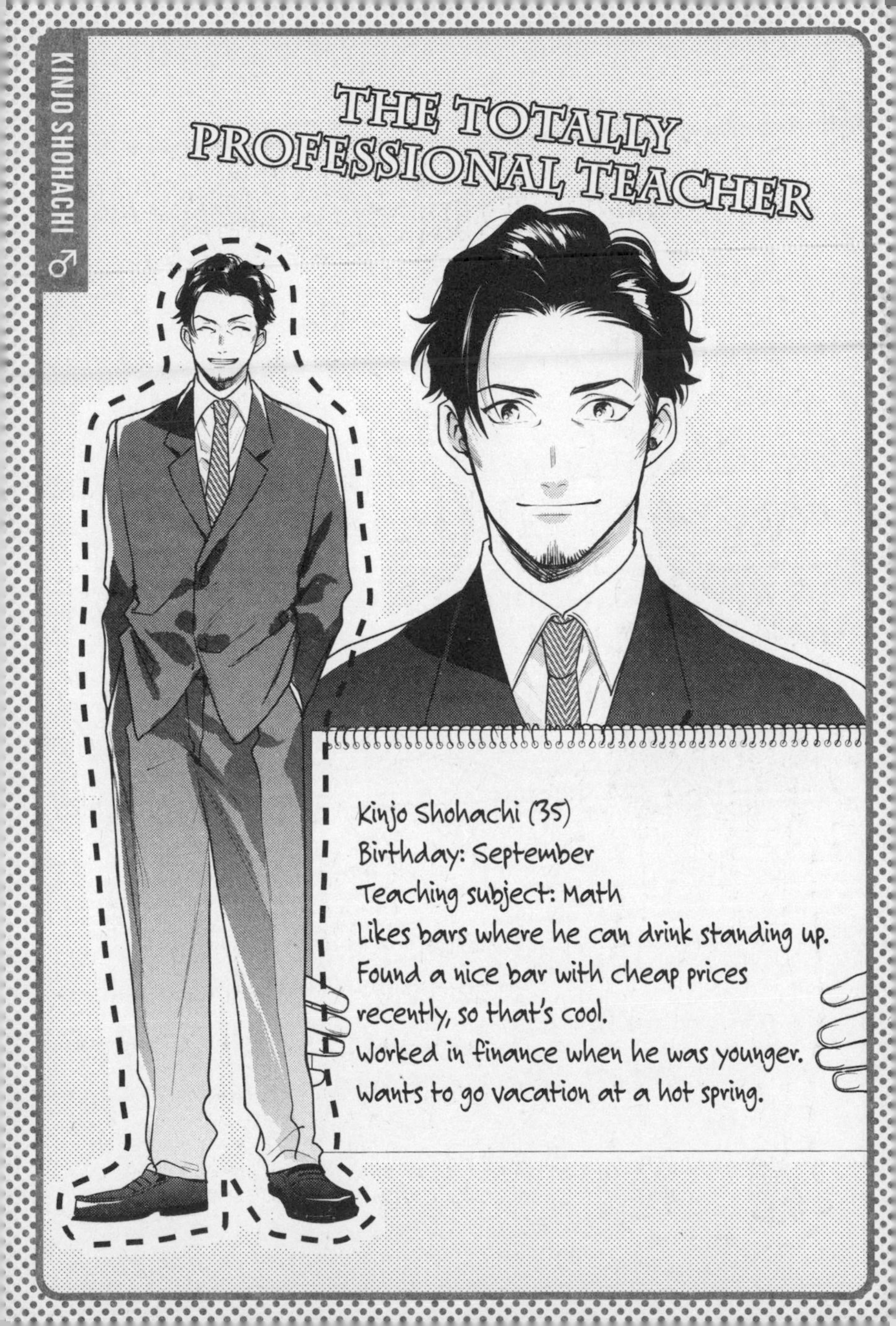

Kinjo Shohachi (35)
Birthday: September
Teaching subject: Math
Likes bars where he can drink standing up.
Found a nice bar with cheap prices recently, so that's cool.
Worked in finance when he was younger.
Wants to go vacation at a hot spring.

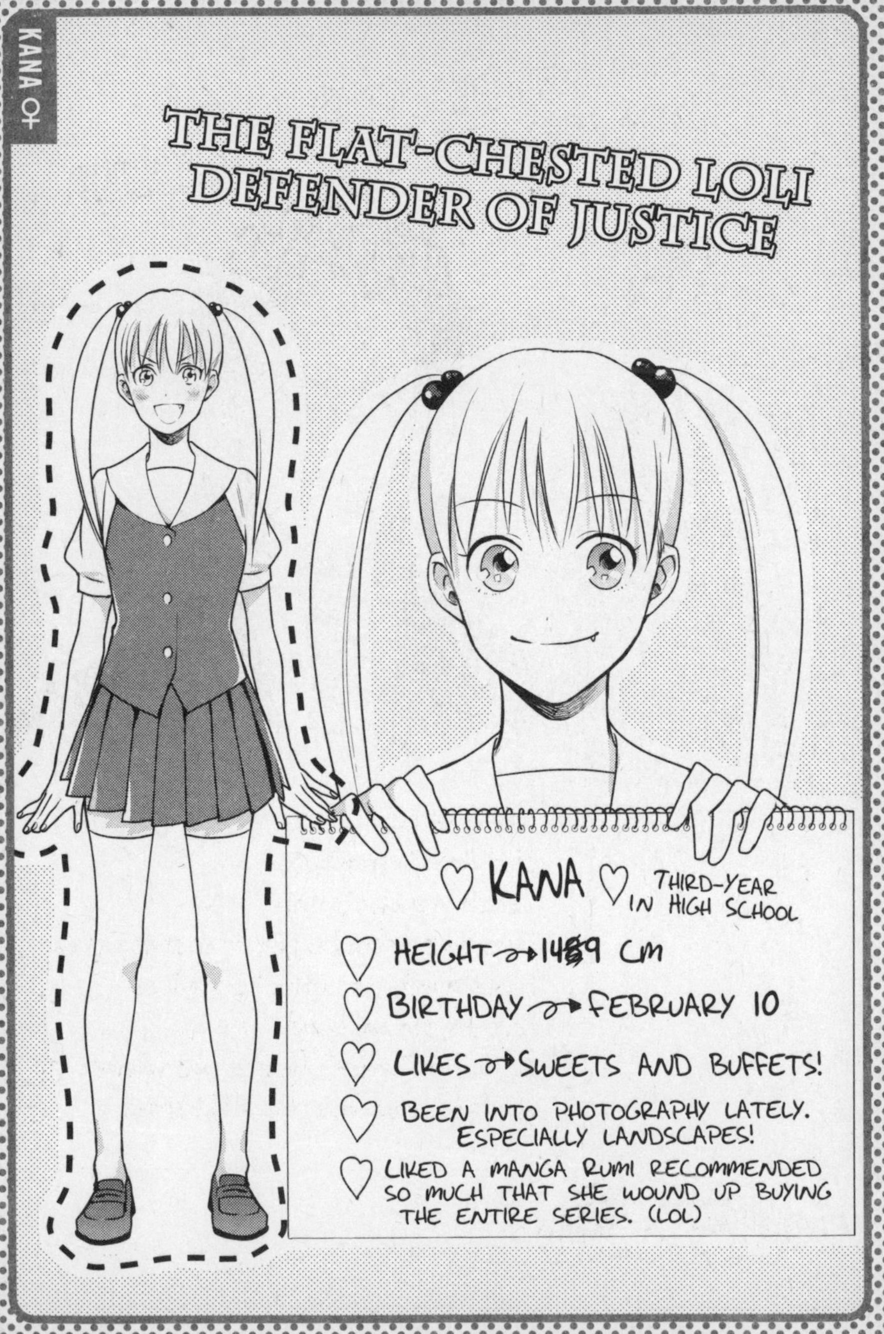
KANA ♀
THE FLAT-CHESTED LOLI DEFENDER OF JUSTICE
♡ KANA ♡ THIRD-YEAR IN HIGH SCHOOL
♡ HEIGHT → 14~~8~~9 CM
♡ BIRTHDAY → FEBRUARY 10
♡ LIKES → SWEETS AND BUFFETS!
♡ BEEN INTO PHOTOGRAPHY LATELY. ESPECIALLY LANDSCAPES!
♡ LIKED A MANGA RUMI RECOMMENDED SO MUCH THAT SHE WOUND UP BUYING THE ENTIRE SERIES. (LOL)

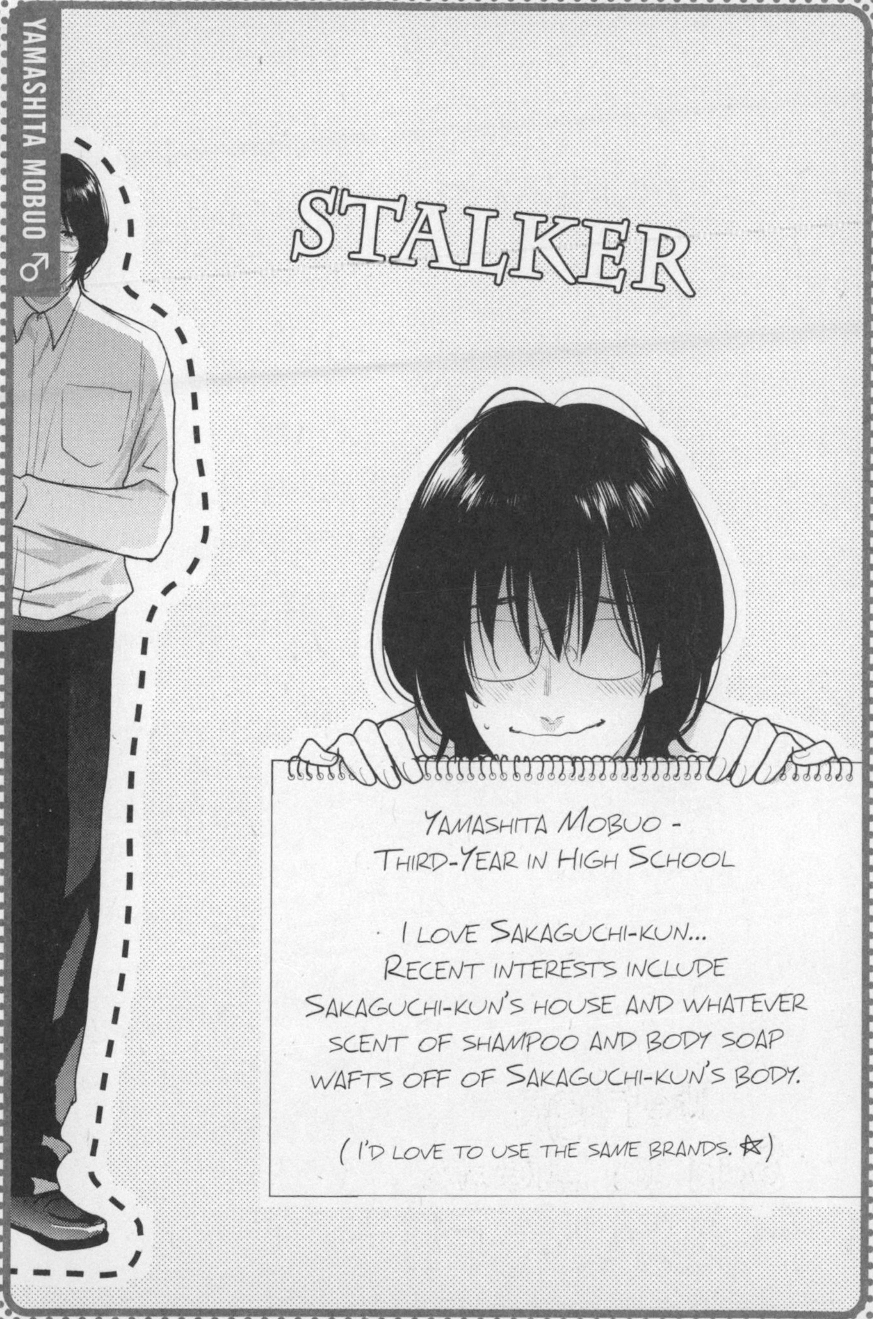
YAMASHITA MOBUO ♂
STALKER
YAMASHITA MOBUO -
THIRD-YEAR IN HIGH SCHOOL
· I LOVE SAKAGUCHI-KUN...
RECENT INTERESTS INCLUDE
SAKAGUCHI-KUN'S HOUSE AND WHATEVER
SCENT OF SHAMPOO AND BODY SOAP
WAFTS OFF OF SAKAGUCHI-KUN'S BODY.
(I'D LOVE TO USE THE SAME BRANDS. ☆)

The High School Life of a FUDANSHI

KFS

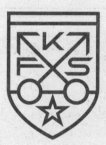

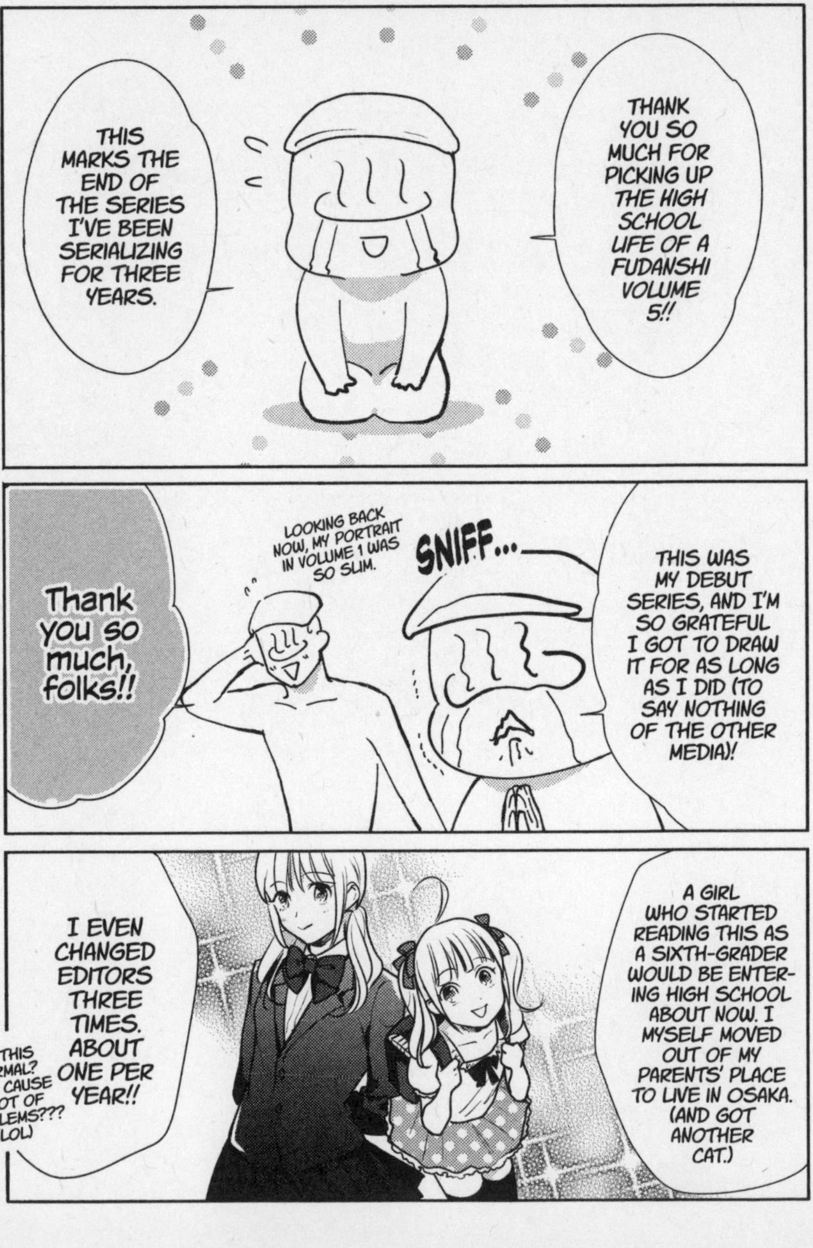
THANK YOU SO MUCH FOR PICKING UP THE HIGH SCHOOL LIFE OF A FUDANSHI VOLUME 5!!
THIS MARKS THE END OF THE SERIES I'VE BEEN SERIALIZING FOR THREE YEARS.
THIS WAS MY DEBUT SERIES, AND I'M SO GRATEFUL I GOT TO DRAW IT FOR AS LONG AS I DID (TO SAY NOTHING OF THE OTHER MEDIA)!
SNIFF...
LOOKING BACK NOW, MY PORTRAIT IN VOLUME 1 WAS SO SLIM.
Thank you so much, folks!!
A GIRL WHO STARTED READING THIS AS A SIXTH-GRADER WOULD BE ENTERING HIGH SCHOOL ABOUT NOW. I MYSELF MOVED OUT OF MY PARENTS' PLACE TO LIVE IN OSAKA. (AND GOT ANOTHER CAT.)
I EVEN CHANGED EDITORS THREE TIMES. ABOUT ONE PER YEAR!!
IS THIS NORMAL? DO I CAUSE A LOT OF PROBLEMS??? (LOL)

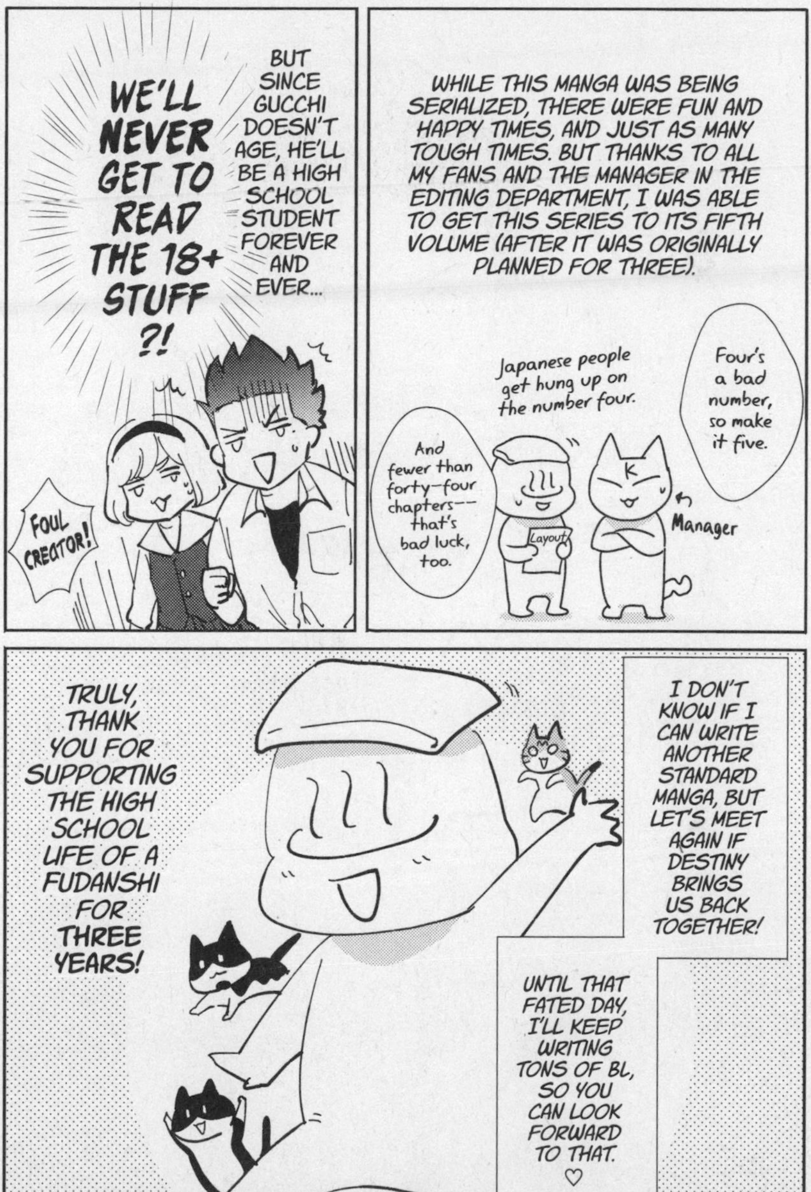

WHILE THIS MANGA WAS BEING SERIALIZED, THERE WERE FUN AND HAPPY TIMES, AND JUST AS MANY TOUGH TIMES. BUT THANKS TO ALL MY FANS AND THE MANAGER IN THE EDITING DEPARTMENT, I WAS ABLE TO GET THIS SERIES TO ITS FIFTH VOLUME (AFTER IT WAS ORIGINALLY PLANNED FOR THREE).
Four's a bad number, so make it five.
Japanese people get hung up on the number four.
Manager
And fewer than forty-four chapters--that's bad luck, too.
Layout
BUT SINCE GUCCHI DOESN'T AGE, HE'LL BE A HIGH SCHOOL STUDENT FOREVER AND EVER...
WE'LL NEVER GET TO READ THE 18+ STUFF ?!
FOUL CREATOR!
I DON'T KNOW IF I CAN WRITE ANOTHER STANDARD MANGA, BUT LET'S MEET AGAIN IF DESTINY BRINGS US BACK TOGETHER!
TRULY, THANK YOU FOR SUPPORTING THE HIGH SCHOOL LIFE OF A FUDANSHI FOR THREE YEARS!
UNTIL THAT FATED DAY, I'LL KEEP WRITING TONS OF BL, SO YOU CAN LOOK FORWARD TO THAT. ♡

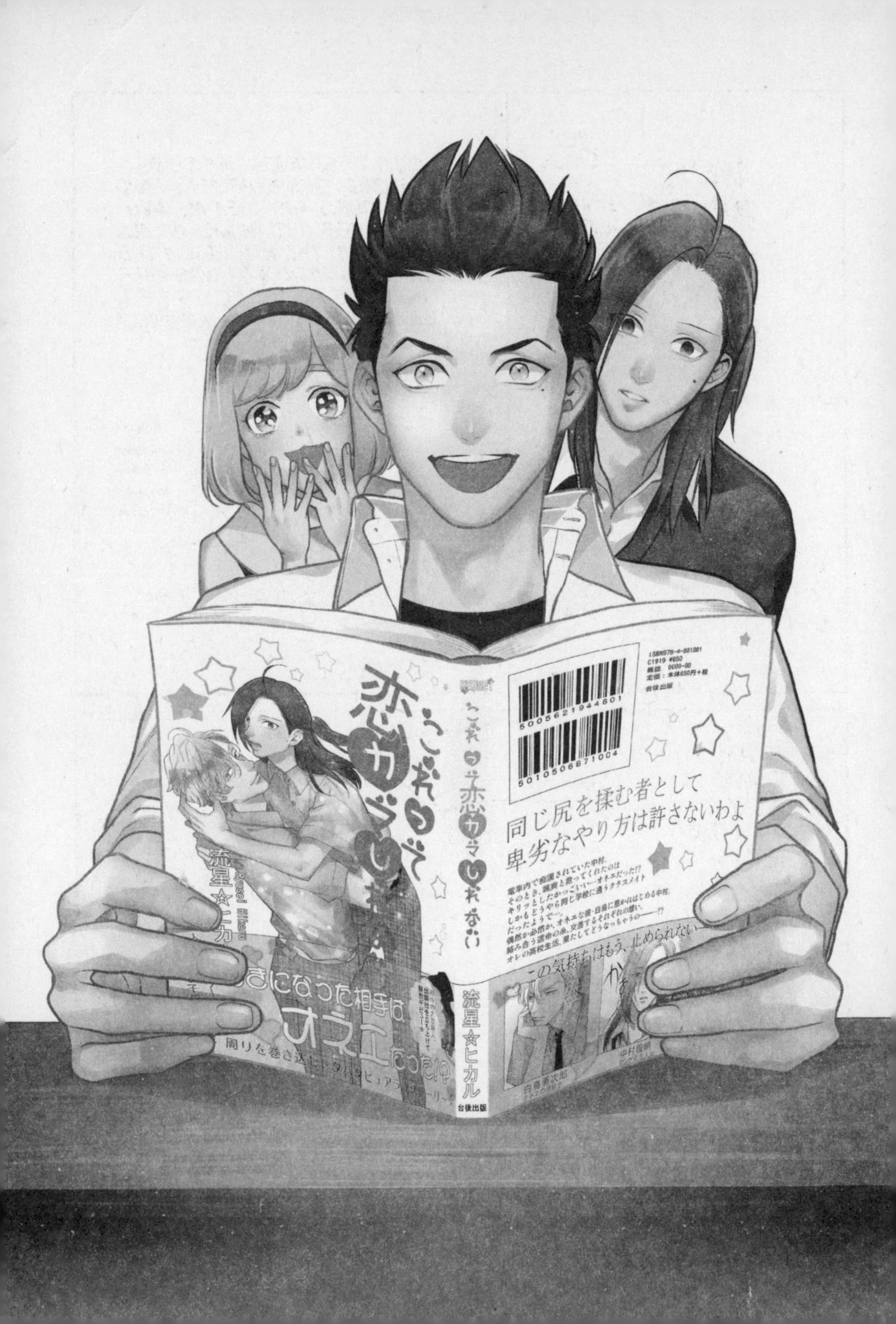
これって恋かもしれない
流星☆ヒカル
台依出版
同じ尻を揉む者として
卑劣なやり方は許さないわよ
この気持ちはもう、止められない
流星☆ヒカル
台依出版

# HIGH SCHOOL LIFE

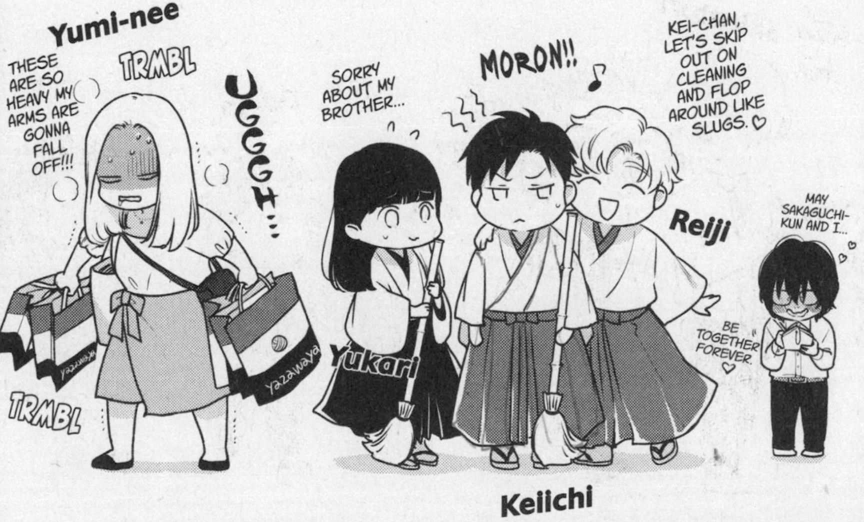

MAY SAKAGUCHI-KUN AND I...
BE TOGETHER FOREVER. ♡
Reiji
KEI-CHAN, LET'S SKIP OUT ON CLEANING AND FLOP AROUND LIKE SLUGS. ♡
MORON!!
Keiichi
SORRY ABOUT MY BROTHER...
Yukari
UGGGH...
TRMBL
Yumi-nee
THESE ARE SO HEAVY MY ARMS ARE GONNA FALL OFF!!!
yazawaya
yazawaya
TRMBL


THANK YOU SO MUCH!!

# OF A FUDANSHI

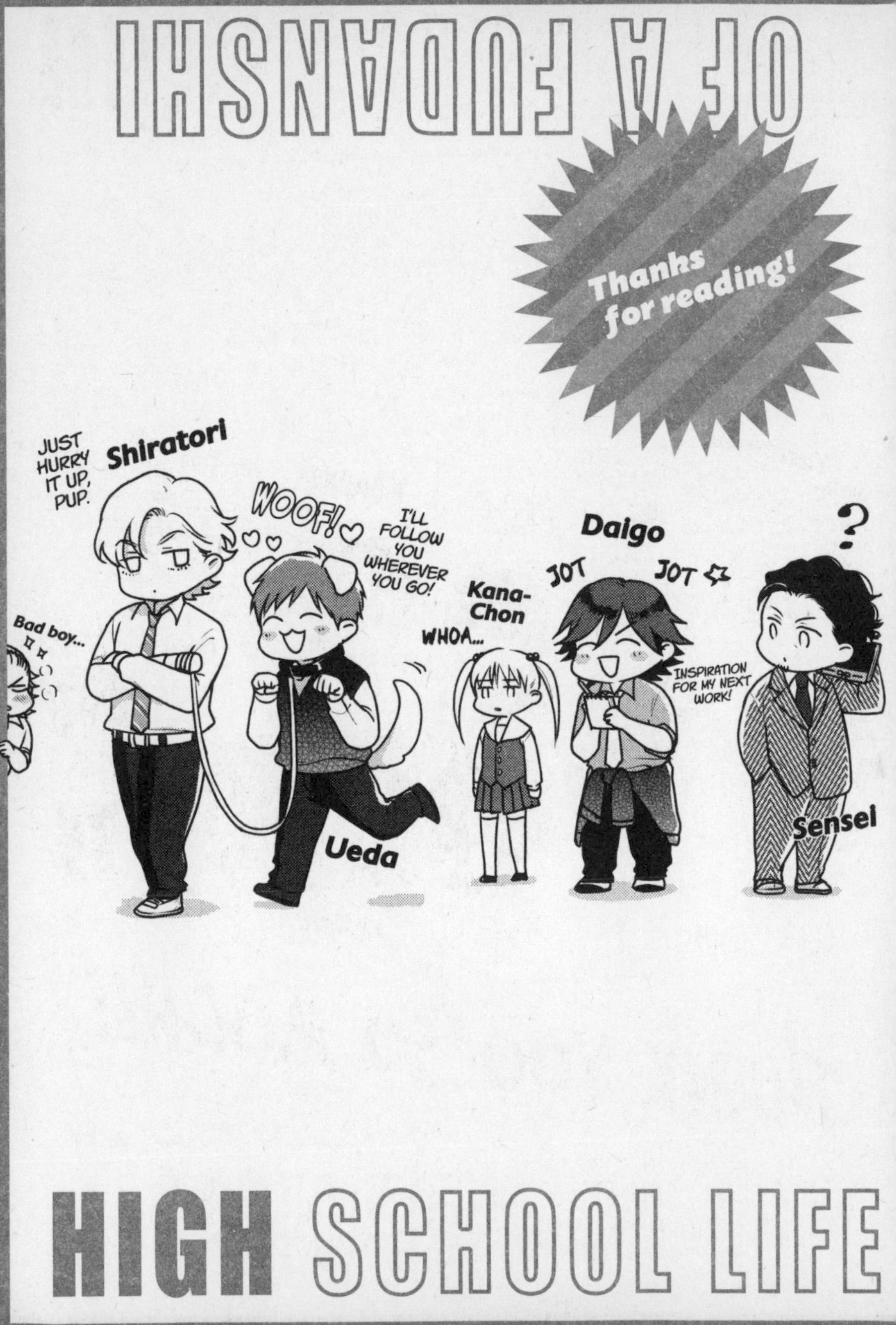
OF A FUDANSHI
Thanks for reading!
?
Sensei
Daigo
JOT JOT
INSPIRATION FOR MY NEXT WORK!
Kana-Chon
WHOA...
I'LL FOLLOW YOU WHEREVER YOU GO!
WOOF!
Ueda
Shiratori
JUST HURRY IT UP, PUP.
Bad boy...
HIGH SCHOOL LIFE

The High
School Life of a
FUDANSHI